Israel: An Uncommon Guide

Israel: An Uncommon Guide

by Joan Comay

Maps by Rafael D. Palacios

Random House   New York

First Printing

Copyright © 1962, 1966, by Joan Comay
Copyright © 1969 by Random House, Inc.

All rights reserved under International and Pan-American Copyright Conventions. Published in the United States by Random House, Inc., New York, and simultaneously in Canada by Random House of Canada Limited, Toronto.

Library of Congress Catalog Card Number: 69-16461

Manufactured in the United States of America
by H. Wolff Book Manufacturing Company

Photographs courtesy of Israel Information Services

FOREWORD

It is not easy to capture the mood of a developing country. But Joan Comay has done it in this book. It is a well-written account of Israel and its people, whose roots go back to Biblical antiquity.

The beauty of a timeless landscape, the dramatic highlights of a history which molded this cradle of civilization, the dynamic quality of a new state turning desert into garden and welding heterogeneous immigrant groups into a sturdy nation are clearly presented in this book. It helps greatly to an understanding of Israel.

No words can serve as a substitute for a personal visit. But the tourist who reaches Israel after reading Joan Comay's book will find his visit vastly enriched.

David Ben-Gurion

CONTENTS

FOREWORD by DAVID BEN-GURION   vii

INTRODUCTION: WHY ISRAEL?   xv

PART ONE: PROFILE of a NATION

1. *THE LAST FOUR THOUSAND YEARS*   3

   The Patriarchs—The Exodus—The Period of the Judges—The Kingdoms—The Prophetic Spirit—The Babylonian Captivity—The Second Temple—The Maccabees—The Roman Occupation—The Coming of Christianity—The Arabs—The Crusaders—Turkish Rule—The Zionist Movement—The Period of the Mandate—The Birth of the State—The Sinai Campaign—The Six-Day War

2. *THE HUMAN LANDSCAPE*   29

   The Jews: The Ingathering—Some Pieces in the Mosaic
   The Israel Arabs: The Bedouin—The Druses—The Circassians
   The New Territories

3. *RUNNING THE STATE*   53

   The President—The Knesset—The Legal System—

• ix

CONTENTS

Religion—The Armed Services—The Police—The Foreign Service—The Jewish Agency

4. *"OUR DAILY BREAD"*   63

Elements of Economic Growth—Aid to Developing Countries—The Histadrut—Cooperative Farming

PART TWO: FROM DAN to EILAT

5. *JERUSALEM, THE GOLDEN*   77

The Turbulent History
The Old City: The Western Wall—The Church of
   The Holy Sepulcher—The Stations of the Cross
   —Haram-esh-Sharif—Church of St. Anne—A
   Walk through the Old City
Outside the Old City: Mount Zion—Mount Scopus
   —Mount of Olives—The Garden of Gethsemane
   —Valley of Kidron—The Rockefeller Museum
   —The Tombs of the Kings—Herod's Family
   Tomb—Tombs of the Sanhedrin—The Jewish
   Agency—Hechal Shlomo—The Khan—International Cultural Center for Youth—Ramat
   Rachel—The Knesset—The Hebrew University
   —The Israel Museum—The Wizo Baby
   Home and Child Care Centre—Mount
   Herzl—Hadassah-Hebrew University
   Medical Center—Ein Karem

6. JUDEA AND SAMARIA 134

Bethlehem: The Church of the Nativity
Hebron: The Cave of Machpelah (Tomb of the
   Patriarchs)
Jericho: Hisham's Palace—Qumran—Ford of
   Bethabara
Nablus: The Samaritans—Sebastia—Jenin

7. THE SHEFELAH 152

From Jerusalem to Tel Aviv: The Latrun Highway—
   The Hartuv Highway—Ramla—Lod
The Rehovot Area: Rishon-le-Zion—Ness Ziona—
   Rehovot—The Weizmann Institute
The Coast: Ashdod—Ashkelon
The Gaza Strip
The Lachish-Adullam Area: Kiryat Gat

8. THE NEGEV AND THE SINAI DESERT 175

The Open Frontier
Beersheba
Beersheba to Sdom: The Dead Sea—Sdom—Arad—
   Masada—Ein Gedi—Qumran
Beersheba to Eilat: Shivta—Sde Boker—Avdat—
   Yotvata—Be'er Ora—Timna
Eilat
The Sinai Desert: El Arish—The Monastery of
   St. Catherine

• xi

CONTENTS

9. TEL AVIV—JAFFA 212

Tel Aviv: History—The Esplanade—Music and
   Theater—Street Scenes—Yarkon River—The
   University—The Ha'aretz Museum
Jaffa: History—Night Spots

10. THE SHARON PLAIN 233

The Old Main Road
The Coastal Road: Herzliya—Natanya
Hadera to Haifa: Hadera—Caesarea—Zichron
   Ya'akov—Tantura—Atlit—Ein Hod

11. HAIFA 250

The City: The Lower Town—Hadar ha-Carmel—
   The Bahai Shrine—The Haifa Bay Area
Mount Carmel: Har ha-Carmel—The Elijah Story
   —Technion City—Carmelite Monastery—Druse
   Villages

12. THE GALILEE 264

Western Galilee: Acre—Nahariya—Rosh ha-Nikra
   —Montfort
The Galilee Highlands: Meiron—Safad—Nazareth—
   Kafr Kanna
The Emek: Megiddo—Beit She'arim—Mount Tabor
   —Beit Shan Valley—Belvoir—Beit Shan

CONTENTS

The Sea of Galilee: Capernaum—Tabgha—Korazim
—Tiberias—Degania
The Huleh Valley
The Golan Heights

13. *INFORMATION PLEASE*   313

The Climate—Measurements and Miscellany—
Where to Stay—What to Wear—Language—Some
Israel Dishes—The Calendar— Some Suggested
Tours—Summary of Historical Events

Index   327

LIST OF MAPS

Israel	front endpaper
Israel and Her Neighbors	back endpaper
Division of Canaan among Hebrew Tribes	5
Palestine in the Time of Jesus	9
Jerusalem	86
The Old City of Jerusalem	97
Judea and Samaria	137
The Shefelah	155
The Negev	177
City of Tel Aviv–Jaffa	215
The Sharon Plain	235
City of Haifa	253
Northern Israel	266

INTRODUCTION
WHY ISRAEL?

Israel this year will welcome over three hundred thousand tourists. They will come from the United States, Canada, South America, Britain, South Africa, France, Holland, Belgium and Scandinavia. Whether their stay is one day on a luxury cruise or a whole month of sightseeing, they will leave with a feeling of regret for places unvisited and sights unexplored.

Yet, not considering the vast empty Sinai Desert, Israel is a small land. In most maps of the Middle East, the name "Israel" sticks out into the Mediterranean. The country is 260 miles long, tapering down to a point six miles across. Lying in the eastern curve of the Mediterranean, its land borders are sealed off by four hostile Arab neighbors: the United Arab Republic (Egypt), Syria, Jordan and Lebanon. It is hard to discover exactly why this little struggling cut-off State moves and excites its visitors and keeps this single country sharply etched in the traveler's mind, when a score of other countries blur and fade. It cannot be physical beauty: Israel boasts no snow-clad peaks or roaring cataracts, no imposing Parthenon, pyramids, or palaces, no Colosseum or towering Inca temples; nor the sophisticated

INTRODUCTION: WHY ISRAEL?

pleasures of European capitals; nor the exotic splendors of the East. Yet this ancient landscape, with its small sculptured hills and its winding valleys, was the setting for the most familiar story on earth, and is today witnessing a new and dramatic chapter in the same story.

Here the most casual visitor can rub shoulders with the Biblical past—can stare at the little harbor from which Jonah set sail, the cave where Samson hid from the Philistines, the precipice on Mount Carmel down which Elijah hurled the false prophets of Baal, the battlefields of Armageddon. He can go up to Jerusalem, which was an old Jebusite city three thousand years ago at the time King David made it the capital of his Hebrew Kingdom. He can walk through the scenes of Christ's boyhood in Nazareth or round the shore of the jewel-like Sea of Galilee where He preached.

He can almost hear rustling in the evening breeze the old stirring prophecies in which Isaiah and Jeremiah and Amos foretold a better world, where men would love by God's law, and the lion would lie down with the lamb. In Israel the past echoes vividly through the present, and even the very language of the Scriptures, after so many centuries, comes off the lips of the children at play in the streets.

And yet, this is a land where the present matters more than the past, and the future even more than the present. Two decades ago, modern Israel was born on a battlefield. It has since been rapidly shaping itself out of the remnants of sixty lands; it has made an advanced economy out of what used to be a backward provincial Turkish economy and has fashioned new patterns for co-operative living and work, which representatives from the emerging States of Asia and Africa have come to study and adapt.

What the visitor encounters from the first day he arrives

INTRODUCTION: WHY ISRAEL?

is the lingering voices of the Biblical past and the exciting shapes of the future, blended uniquely in a sunny, friendly and busy land.

J.C.

Part One

Profile of a Nation

CHAPTER 1

The Last Four Thousand Years

In 2000 B.C., nobody would have picked the Hebrews as the nation most likely to survive.

To the northeast of them in the river basin of the Tigris and the Euphrates, to the south of them in the fertile valley of the Nile, to the west across the sea, powerful empires rose and fell, building their colossal pyramids and temples, marching their armies and stamping arrogant hooves upon the faces of their subject peoples.

In Canaan, that strip of land between the desert and the sea, the peoples were constantly trampled underfoot by imperial powers, and they enjoyed independence only in the brief periods when one wave of conquest had receded and another had not yet taken its place. But against the big battalions, against the fearsome idols of bronze and stone, the little Hebrew hill-nation brought its secret weapon: a single and invisible God.

PROFILE OF A NATION

It had something more—a superb gift for telling its own story. By word of mouth, from father to son, the Hebrews related the deeds of their kings and warriors, the wisdom of their prophets and sages, until this matchless tribal diary was set down for all mankind in the Books of the Old Testament. In the end the pen was mightier than the sword; the idea outlived the empires. Abraham, Moses and Isaiah loom more majestically through the mists of time than Rameses or Nebuchadnezzar; Ruth the Moabite girl is more familiar to us than the great, glittering queens of Babylon and Thebes who have passed on to dusty oblivion.

It is with a thousand years of rising and falling empires as background that the Bible unfolds the Hebrew story, starting with that time-blurred patriarchal figure, Father Abraham. He is described in the Book of Genesis as coming from the city of Ur of the Chaldees (now Iraq). With his wife Sarah, his nephew Lot, his kinsmen and servants and his flocks and herds, he trekked slowly across the desert to the land which the Lord had promised to him and his descendants. In Canaan he found a number of small cities, most of them walled and fortified, and each ruled by its own "king." Abraham's advent was typical of the recurrent eruptions of nomadic tribes into settled and fertile areas—the eternal struggle between "the desert and the sown." (Several centuries after Abraham, the Hebrews under Joshua would again come out of the eastern desert and cross the fords of the Jordan River into Canaan.)

Abraham begat Isaac who begat Jacob, later renamed Israel (Prince of God). Jacob had twelve sons, from whom the Tribes of Israel were descended. When one of the sons, Joseph, became an important man at the Egyptian court, Jacob and the whole family settled there. Later the Pha-

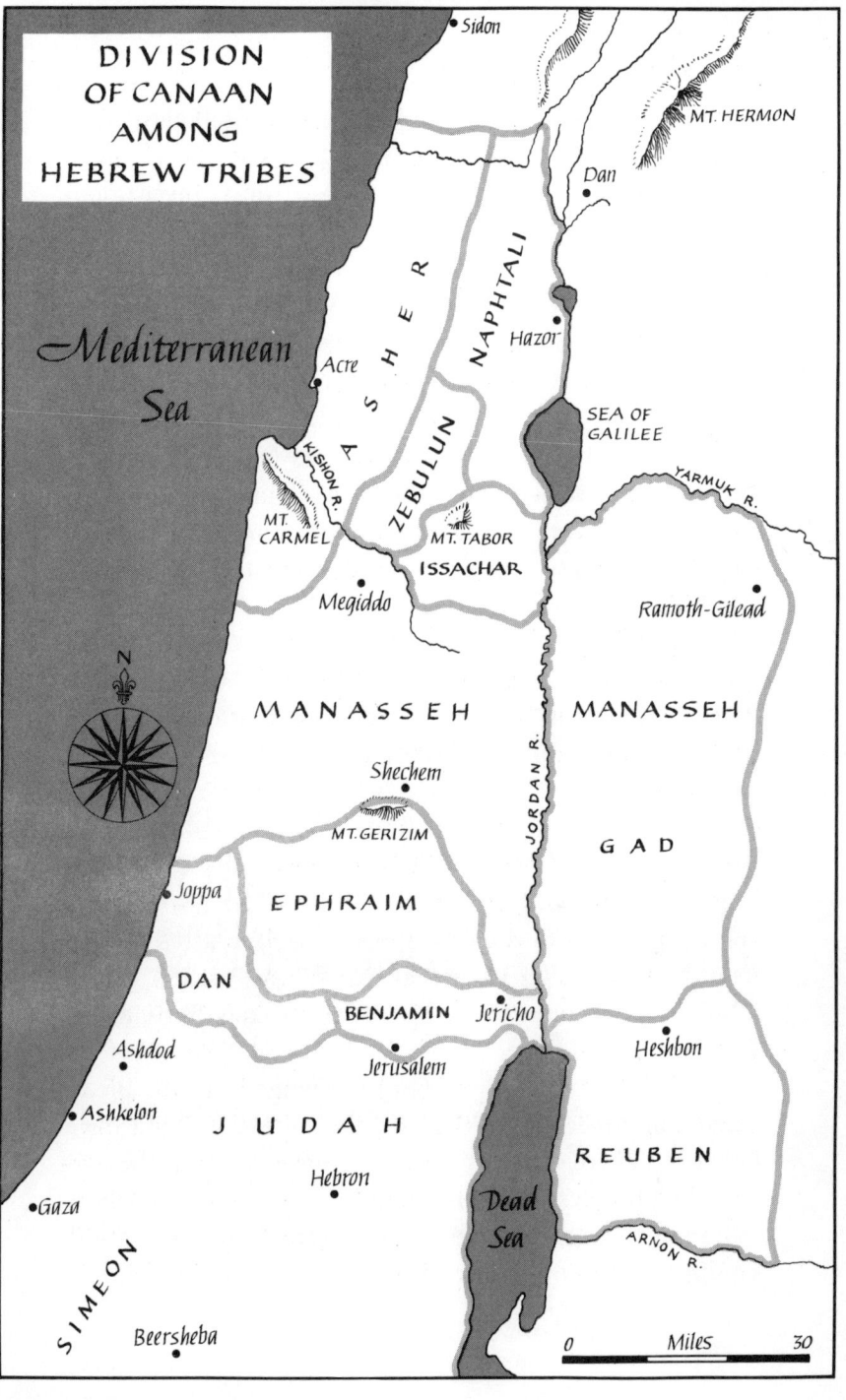

roahs turned their descendants into slaves, until they were delivered by Moses. Each year at Passover, Jews gather round the ceremonial supper table and relate once more how the Children of Israel escaped out of bondage and set out on the weary forty-year migration to the Promised Land. This took place about the thirteenth century B.C.

Moses towers as the greatest figure in the history of the Jews because he was both liberator and lawgiver. The most solemn episode in the long Jewish saga is that in which Moses is depicted as coming down from Mount Sinai bearing the stone tablets with the Ten Commandments engraved upon them. From that time onwards the Rule of Law was to govern the lives of all, from the king to the humblest bondsman.

Moses died before the Israelites at last entered the Promised Land. Under the command of Joshua, they crossed the River Jordan near Jericho and triumphed after a series of battles against local Canaanite kings. The land was divided among the Twelve Tribes, which took their names from Jacob's sons Reuben, Simeon, Judah, Dan, Naphtali, Gad, Asher, Issachar, Zebulun and Benjamin, and Joseph's two sons Manasseh and Ephraim. The Tribe of Levi, which provided priests for all the others, was not given a territory of its own. When later history speaks of "the lost ten tribes" all of them are meant except the two flanking Jerusalem—Judah and Benjamin.

The Book of Judges pictures the change from the life of wandering herdsmen to that of tillers of the soil and town dwellers. There was a constant struggle against the surrounding peoples, and from time to time the Tribes had to band together for self-defense. When the Canaanite troops, equipped with horsedrawn chariots, massed in the Valley of

Jezreel, the Israelites, led by the prophetess Deborah, defeated them in infantry charges.

When a new wave of nomads, the camel-riding Midianites, invaded the country from the desert, they were routed by Gideon, who led his commando groups in a night attack, skillfully using the tactics of surprise, noise and lighted torches to create panic.

The Israelites' most serious enemies, however, were the Philistines, a skilled people believed to be of Greek origin who occupied the southern coastal area. The exploits of the Hebrew strong man, Samson, were against these Philistines, and it was the temple of their god Dagon, in Gaza, that he pulled down after he had been captured and blinded. Goliath, whom the young David killed with a stone from his sling, was also a Philistine champion.

The Israelites were not strong enough to survive long as a number of scattered tribes, so they agreed that Saul should be king of all the tribes. When Saul fell in battle against the Philistines, David was anointed as the new ruler. His reign lasted for forty years, from about 1000 B.C. He built up a large kingdom which took in nearly all of Canaan, together with what is now Syria and Jordan. He captured the city of Jerusalem and made it his capital.

David was succeeded by his son, the wise and brilliant King Solomon, who promoted the wealth and strength of the kingdom. He erected many fine buildings, including the Temple and the royal palace in Jerusalem. Solomon also opened a sea route to Africa through the Gulf of Aqaba and the Red Sea, as the Israelis have now done once more at the port of Eilat.

After Solomon's death, rival factions split the country into the Kingdom of Israel in the north and the Kingdom

PROFILE OF A NATION

of Judah in the south, whose capital remained in Jerusalem. These two shrunken and rival states could not survive against new dangers. The Northern Kingdom was wiped out by the Assyrians in 722 B.C. Most of the inhabitants were taken away as captives, and history has since referred to them as "the lost ten tribes." Over a century later—in 587 B.C.—the Southern Kingdom, Judah, came to an end when Jerusalem was destroyed by a Babylonian army under King Nebuchadnezzar. Again, thousands of the Judeans were carried off into exile where, as told in Psalm 137, "By the rivers of Babylon, there we sat down, yea, we wept, when we remembered Zion." *

During the period of the two kingdoms there arose a succession of prophets who scolded the rulers and the people for disobeying the Lord and foretold the troubles that would befall them. Some of these prophets came from a simple country background, like Amos the herdsman and Hosea the farmer. Others, like Isaiah and Jeremiah, were statesmen and diplomats. Their talent for expressing their thoughts places the prophetic books of the Bible among the best literature ever written.

In the United Nations building in New York, on a stone wall opposite the entrance, is the first disarmament proposal, uttered by a Hebrew prophet almost three thousand years ago:

> And they shall beat their swords into ploughshares, and their spears into pruninghooks: nation shall not lift up sword against nation, neither shall they learn war any more.
>
> —Isaiah 2: 4

---

* Zion was a Jebusite stronghold in Jerusalem, captured by David; the word has since been used as a spiritual symbol.

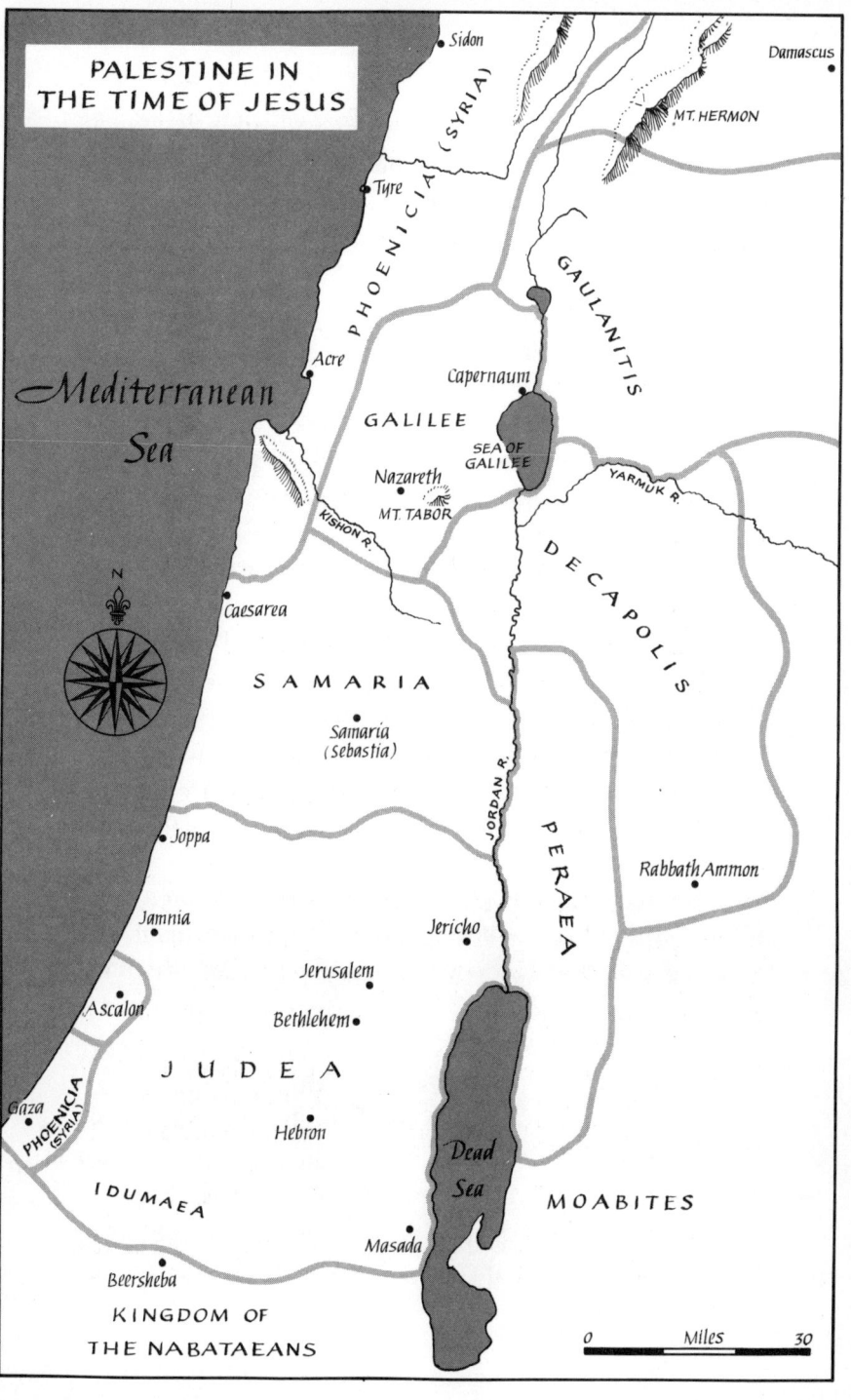

PROFILE OF A NATION

In the sixth century B.C. the Persian King Cyrus, who had conquered Babylon, allowed some of the Jewish exiles to return and start rebuilding Jerusalem and the Temple, as is recorded in the Books of Ezra and Nehemiah. But the land did not remain at peace for long.

Alexander the Great, who had been a provincial governor at sixteen and an army general at eighteen, had become ruler of the world while still in his twenties. After his early death, in 323 B.C., the area which included Judea was taken over by one of his generals, whose successors tried to stamp out the Jewish religion and impose Greek ways, until the Jews successfully revolted under Judas Maccabaeus and his brothers. This event is celebrated by the Jews each year during the festival of Channukah.

Then came a new power from the west, the Romans. In 63 B.C. they captured the country, which remained part of the Roman Empire for several centuries.

The Jews stubbornly kept alive their thirst for freedom. A rebellion broke out in A.D. 66 which was ended only after the Roman legions under Titus had sacked Jerusalem and destroyed the second Temple, in A.D. 70. Thousands of Jews were massacred and the survivors were led in chains through the streets of Rome, an event that was carved on Titus' arch of triumph still standing in Rome today. One small group of rebels held out for three years on the imposing rock fortress of Masada, near the Dead Sea, until they finally killed themselves rather than surrender. Sixty years later there was another revolt under the Jewish hero Simon Bar Kochba (Son of a Star), but this uprising was crushed and Jerusalem was leveled and rebuilt as a Roman city. It was renamed Aelia Capitolina as part of the policy of the suppression of the Jews. During the Roman period the country became known as Palestine, a name which originally had referred to the coastal area occupied by the Philistines.

It was after the Romans had become masters of the country that a young Jew called Jesus, from the small Galilean town of Nazareth, started to preach to the humble villagers and fisherfolk round the beautiful Sea of Galilee. Illustrating His message with simple parables and performing miracles, He gathered to Himself a group of disciples and gained a small following. During the celebration of the feast of Passover in Jerusalem, He was arrested by the Roman authorities, tried by the Procurator, Pontius Pilate, and put to death by crucifixion (then the usual form of Roman execution). These events caused little stir at the time, and for a while the followers of Jesus remained an obscure Jewish sect.

The first known record of His life and teachings was in the Gospels of Matthew, Mark, Luke and John, written probably between forty and seventy years after His death. The new Christian faith spread rapidly through the eastern part of the Roman Empire, promoted by the journeys of an energetic convert, Saul of Tarsus, who later became known as Saint Paul. In A.D. 325, under the Emperor Constantine, Christianity became the official religion of the Empire.

Palestine remained a neglected and unimportant corner of the Roman Empire until the seventh century, when it was again invaded from the desert, this time by Moslems, the followers of the Prophet Mohammed. They came surging out of Arabia and established a vast Moslem Empire stretching from Spain in the west to what is now Indonesia in the Far East. To regain the Holy Land from the "infidels," the Christian rulers of Europe launched a series of

Crusades. In 1099, Jerusalem was taken by the Christian armies and the Crusader Kingdom was set up. The Crusaders' hold on most of the country was broken by the Saracen (Arab) leader Saladin, but the stronghold city of Acre was recaptured by an army under Richard the Lion-Heart, King of England, only to be lost again in 1291, the end of the Crusader period. Some of the ruined castles of the Crusaders can still be seen in Israel today.

After Arab rule came Turkish rule, and the Christian world did not regain Palestine again until 1917, when a British army under General Allenby swept up from the south, defeated the Turks and entered Jerusalem.

Throughout the ages the Jews never gave up the yearning for their ancient homeland. From time to time in the Middle Ages, a self-styled Messiah would cause a flurry of excitement among the Jewish masses in Europe and start some of them moving behind him towards the distant Holy Land.

In the eighteenth century, an age of enlightenment seemed to dawn, which held out to the harried Jews also that promise of "liberty, equality and fraternity" which had inspired the French Revolution. This emancipation was reflected in the Haskalah movement and in the efforts of Moses Mendelssohn and his successors to draw Jewish intellectual and social life into the general European stream. But the vast Jewry of Russia and Poland, living in the Pale of Settlement, came to realize in the nineteenth century that their own release from the confinement of the ghetto was a mirage. Some started to believe that the key to their future lay in recreating their own nation-state, just as other submerged national groups in Europe aspired to do. Small societies sprang up called *Hovevei Zion* (Lovers of Zion), and at the end of the century several groups of colonists found their way to Palestine and started the first Jewish farming villages, such as Rishon-le-Zion (First in Zion), Petah Tikvah (Gateway of Hope) and Zichron Ya'akov (Memory of Jacob). The settlers called themselves Bilu, from the Hebrew initials of the Biblical phrase *Beit Ya'acov lechu venelecha*—"O House of Jacob, come ye and let us go." Without experience or capital, these colonists of the First Aliyah (wave of immigration) could hardly have survived the grim conditions but for the interest of the Baron Edmond de Rothschild, who not only supported the villages financially, but helped to create an economic base for them by introducing winemaking and other enterprises. By 1900 these slow beginnings had produced seventeen Jewish villages in Palestine.

In 1896, the stirrings of Zionism among the Eastern European Jews were converted into a dramatic international movement by Dr. Theodor Herzl, a handsome black-bearded Viennese playwright and journalist. The previous year he had covered the Dreyfus trial as the Paris representative of a leading European liberal newspaper, the *Neue Freie Presse*, and had been shocked at the ugly wave of anti-Semitism released by the trial. Quite unaware of earlier works, such as that by Pinsker, he wrote a pamphlet called *Der Judenstaat* (The Jewish State) that advocated a national solution for the Jewish problem. This solution was not at first related to any specific territory, but he soon became persuaded that the answer to the problem was statehood in Palestine. He called a congress at Basel in 1897 and established the World Zionist Organization, which was to give birth to the State of Israel fifty years later (as Herzl himself predicted in his diaries).

Driven by a compulsive sense of destiny, Herzl spent his few remaining years in a frustrated plea for a settlement charter for Palestine similar to that of the British East India Company or the Hudson's Bay Company in Canada. He enlisted the sympathies of influential members of the British Government, particularly the Colonial Secretary, Joseph Chamberlain. The response in London was two offers for an interim area of settlement—one in the El Arish area of the Sinai Peninsula, which was blocked by Lord Cromer of Egypt; and the other, an empty tract of land in Uganda (now in Kenya), which was fiercely rejected by the Russian Zionists and produced a bitter split in the Zionist Movement. Herzl died soon after in 1904, at the early age of forty-four.

With the hope of a political breakthrough fading out, the Zionist movement turned to fostering practical settlement work in Palestine. A new brand of *chalutz* (pioneer) appeared—the young, idealistic men and women of the Second Aliyah (wave of immigration) bent on self-help and manual labor. They evolved a type of collective settlement, the *kibbutz* (the first of which was founded at Degania in 1909), fought hunger and malaria while they carved farmsteads out of stony hills and swampy valleys; and, in order to protect themselves against marauding Arabs, set up posses of *shomrim* (armed watchmen) who were the forerunners of the Haganah, the defense army during the British Mandate.

In 1909, a group of residents of Jaffa moved to the sandhills farther north and established a little suburb which later grew into the all-Jewish city of Tel Aviv.

When World War I broke out in 1914, and Turkey became the ally of Germany, there was already in Palestine a well-established Jewish community of 80,000 souls.

During the war the Zionist movement was kept alive in Britain, and Dr. Chaim Weizmann, a Russian-born chemist teaching at Manchester University, became its leader. Helped by influential gentile friends and by Dr. Weizmann's own important research in connection with munitions, the Zionist idea reached the level of the War Cabinet. On November 2, 1917, the following letter was addressed by the Foreign Secretary, Lord Balfour, to Lord Rothschild as the leader of Anglo-Jewry:

> Dear Lord Rothschild:
>
> I have much pleasure in conveying to you on behalf of His Majesty's Government, the following declaration of sympathy with Jewish Zionist aspirations, which has been submitted to and approved by the Cabinet:
>
> "His Majesty's Government views with favour the establishment in Palestine of a national home for the Jewish people, and will use their best endeavours to facilitate the achievement of this object, it being clearly understood that nothing shall be done which may prejudice the civil and religious rights of existing non-Jewish communities in Palestine, or the rights and political status enjoyed by Jews in any other country."
>
> I should be grateful if you would bring this Declaration to the knowledge of the Zionist Federation.
>
> Yours sincerely,
> Arthur James Balfour

The historic Balfour Declaration was endorsed by Britain's allies France and Italy and by the American President, Woodrow Wilson. Written into the League of Nations Mandate for Palestine, the Declaration supplied the politi-

PROFILE OF A NATION

cal and legal basis for Jewish efforts to redeem the ancient homeland—it was the equivalent of that charter for which Herzl had so vainly struggled.

As General Allenby entered Jerusalem on foot, out of respect for the Holy City, in December, 1917, 400 years of Turkish rule came to an end and thirty years of British rule began. For the first time since the Crusades, the Holy Land was in Christian hands. France acquired the League of Nations mandates over Syria and Lebanon, and Britain over Iraq and Palestine. The Palestine Mandate included Trans-Jordan, but in 1922 the latter was excluded from the provisions relating to the Jewish National Home.

At the beginning, the Arab leaders who had led the revolt against the Turks were not opposed to a Zionist state in Palestine. Their chief spokesman at the Peace Conference at Versailles was the Emir Faisal (later King of Iraq), who had Lawrence of Arabia as his adviser. In 1919, Faisal signed an agreement with Dr. Weizmann approving of Jewish immigration and land settlement in Palestine, provided that an Arab state was set up in the surrounding territories. In a letter dated March 3, 1919, to an American Jewish leader, Justice Felix Frankfurter, Faisal stated:

> We Arabs . . . look with the deepest sympathy on the Zionist Movement. Our deputation here in Paris is fully acquainted with the proposals submitted yesterday by the Zionist Organization to the Peace Conference, and we regard them as moderate and proper. We will do our best, insofar as we are concerned, to help them through; we will wish the Jews a most hearty welcome home.

But among the Arabs of Palestine itself a more militant and anti-Zionist nationalism was beginning to emerge. In

1921 and 1929 there were ugly anti-Jewish riots, and from then on Britain sought to disengage itself from the commitment to "facilitate" the Jewish National Home. In 1936 an Arab rebellion started, led by the Mufti of Jerusalem. A Royal Commission under the chairmanship of Lord Peel proposed a partition scheme and the setting up of independent Jewish and Arab states. But in the Munich appeasement era Britain had lost the will to implement such a bold compromise—especially as German and Italian influence was growing in the Arab world. In 1939, the British government issued the White Paper, described at the time as a "Palestine Munich." By its terms the whole country would become an independent Arab state within ten years, with the Jewish minority not to exceed 30 percent of the population and with further Jewish immigration and land acquisition rigidly limited.

Shortly after, however, the question of Palestine's future was pushed aside by the outbreak of World War II. In David Ben-Gurion's famous dictum, the Jews of Palestine resolved to "fight the War as if there were no White Paper and the White Paper as if there were no War." While the Arabs held aloof, the Jews flung themselves fully into the struggle against Hitler's Germany. Refused at first the right to join the fighting forces, they recruited a large number of transport and supply units which rendered yeoman service in the East African and Western Desert campaigns. Later the ban on combatant duty was revoked and the Jewish brigade group took part in the liberation of Europe.

Jewish hopes ran high in 1945 with the defeat of Germany and the return to power in Britain of a Labour government with a strong pro-Zionist plank in its platform.

PROFILE OF A NATION

The horror of the Holocaust (the Nazi massacre of six million European Jews) could no longer be concealed, nor could the plight of the homeless remnants in the displaced persons' camps be ignored. In the Attlee Cabinet, Foreign Secretary Ernest Bevin took over from the Colonial Office the direct handling of the Palestine problem. It soon became evident that his advisers had persuaded him to maintain a policy subordinated to Britain's relations with the Arab world. The bitter resistance of the Jews to what they regarded as a fresh "sellout" found expression in many ways: an appeal to world opinion, particularly in the United States; *Aliyah Bet*, the "illegal" immigration of Jewish survivors of the Nazi concentration camps; the breakdown of cooperation between the British and Jewish authorities in Palestine; a more activist policy by the Haganah, the Jewish underground defense militia; and the exploits of two independent terrorist groups, the Irgun Zvai Leumi and the Stern Gang.

In an effort to turn the rising tide of American criticism, the British Government arranged for a joint Anglo-American Committee of Enquiry to go to Palestine early in 1946. Its crucial recommendation was for the immediate grant of immigration certificates to 100,000 Jewish displaced persons then in German camps, a proposal endorsed by President Truman but angrily rejected by the Attlee Government, which prepared to crush Jewish resistance by military force in accordance with proposals put before it by Field Marshal Montgomery.

On "black Saturday," June 30, 1946, the British Army arrested and imprisoned a number of Palestine Jewish leaders, occupied the Jewish Agency building in Jerusalem and rounded up some 3,000 members of kibbutzim which were

THE LAST FOUR THOUSAND YEARS

thought to be key Haganah centers. This show of force failed to produce submission and persuaded the Jews that there was nothing left to hope for from Britain. At the Zionist Congress in Basel in December, 1946, Dr. Weizmann, regarded as a moderate, resigned his position as President of the movement. At that time informal talks were still being held in London with the Cabinet; these had produced a plan for the establishment of Jewish and Arab cantons. When this plan petered out, Mr. Bevin admitted failure to solve the problem and it was referred to the United Nations.

In April, 1947, the United Nations General Assembly called the first special session in its history and appointed the United Nations Special Committee on Palestine (UNSCOP), made up of representatives of eleven small powers not directly involved in the conflict. UNSCOP was unanimous in concluding that the Mandate should be terminated and independence granted to both Jews and Arabs. The UNSCOP majority, reverting to the approach of the Peel Report ten years earlier, drew up a partition plan under which there would be independent Jewish and Arab states and an international enclave of Jerusalem, all combined in an economic union. The minority preferred a federal scheme, but it was clear that the conflict between the two nationalisms had gone beyond immediate cooperation in a single state.

In the fall, the General Assembly again debated the issue for nearly three months and on November 29, 1947, by 33 votes to 13, with 11 abstentions, it endorsed the proposal of partition with economic union. The Arab representative threatened that the proposal would be opposed by force; Britain refused to implement any solution which did not

• 19

have the agreement of both sides and declared that its Mandate would end on May 14, 1948.

On the day the Partition Resolution was approved in New York, the first Arab attack was made in Jerusalem and fighting spread through the country. The Haganah, in sharp local engagements, gained physical control of much of the area allotted to the Jewish State. Later, Jewish Jerusalem was cut off and started eking out its existence with the last meager reserves of food and water. The Arab population began to stream out of Jewish-controlled areas into Arab areas and the surrounding countries, driven by panic and by the commands of their leaders, who wanted them out of the way. The armies of the Arab states were massing on the borders in order to move in as soon as the Mandate ended and "drive the Jews into the sea." It was under these circumstances that on the afternoon of May 14, 1948, a group of thirty-seven Jewish leaders gathered in a small museum in Tel Aviv and signed the Proclamation of Independence of the State of Israel—1,878 years after the Roman legions had destroyed the Second Temple in Jerusalem.

At the United Nations, where its discussions had been left far in the rear of events, the General Assembly went home after appointing as mediator Count Folke Bernadotte of Sweden, who was murdered by Jewish terrorists the following September. The Security Council was left to cope with the Palestine War.

The odds seemed heavily against the survival of the State of Israel, since the Jews were far outnumbered and had no weapons heavier than rifles, Bren guns and homemade mortars, and no planes other than a few Piper Cubs and Auster trainers. Matters took their course in Palestine and if the

Jewish defenders had been overrun, the State of Israel would never have seen out its first month.

Ben-Gurion, who had assumed personal command of operations, boldly decided to fight on in every Jewish village and every urban quarter. These last-ditch stands were made with fierce tenacity and most of the isolated settlements in the path of the advancing Arab armies remained unconquered, though the buildings were smashed by gunfire and the settlers, fighting from their foxholes, had to repulse tank attacks with homemade Molotov cocktails.

Of some 300 agricultural villages, only 4 were lost (12 others were temporarily abandoned and later recovered), while the Jewish quarter of the Old City of Jerusalem was cut off and overrun by the Jordan Arab Legion. In four weeks of fighting, the Arab advance had been halted in the suburbs of Jerusalem, at a point 20 miles south of Tel Aviv, 10 miles inland from the coast between Tel Aviv and Haifa, and in the north, at the very wire fences of the Galilee border settlements at Ein Gev and Degania. The siege of Jerusalem had been lifted by the opening of a "Burma Road" which linked the city to the coast and ensured a supply line for the beleaguered population.

A month's truce was then arranged, but when it ended the Arabs refused to extend it. In the next ten days of fighting the Jewish forces took the offensive, captured Lod (Lydda) and Ramla in the center and Nazareth in the north, and broadened the corridor to Jerusalem. The Security Council hurriedly ordered a fresh truce.

In October, 1948, fighting flared up again. This time the Egyptian line in the south was broken, Beersheba was captured, the Negev settlements relieved, and the Galilee

PROFILE OF A NATION

swept clear of the so-called "Arab Liberation Army" of irregulars. In December–January, further defeats were inflicted in the south on the Egyptians, who by then had had enough of the Palestine War, and had become willing to negotiate an armistice agreement.

In the first half of 1949, separate armistice agreements were signed with Egypt, Jordan, Lebanon and Syria, marking out the demarcation lines. The agreements confirmed that the armistice was to be regarded as a transitional stage to an early peace settlement. In May, 1949, Israel was admitted to membership of the United Nations, and that summer a peace conference was convened at Lausanne by the Palestine Conciliation Commission, which had been set up by the United Nations and consisted of the United States, France and Turkey. The conference failed, largely because of the refusal of the Arab representatives to meet with the Israelis. By 1951, hopes of a quick political settlement had vanished.

There followed years of uneasy armistice, punctuated by constant infiltration and marauding from the Arab side and by occasional local actions by the Israel army. These border troubles might have been borne philosophically and the border might have settled down in due course but for the emergence of a new and formidable threat in the Nasser regime in Egypt.

Starting in September of 1955, large quantities of Soviet-bloc military equipment started flowing into Egypt. Israel managed to buy some tanks and planes, mainly from France. Late in 1956, Egypt entered into a military alliance with Syria and Jordan for a coordinated attack on Israel. Meantime, groups of armed guerrillas called *fedayeen* were being dispatched deep into Israel territory, murdering civilians, blowing up installations, mining the roads and gathering intelligence information preparatory to a more general onslaught. Finding itself in imminent danger, Israel struck into the Sinai Desert at the end of October, 1956, and in less than a week had wiped out the Egyptian invasion bases, reached the Suez Canal, occupied the Gaza Strip and mopped up the Egyptian position at the entrance to the Gulf of Aqaba, thus opening the Gulf to Israel navigation.

This swift and brilliant campaign coincided with the abortive Anglo-French expedition which entered Port Said but failed to occupy the Suez Canal zone before the attempt was abandoned under pressure from home and abroad. In spite of all the weight of the United Nations disapproval now concentrated upon it, the Government of Israel deferred the withdrawal of its troops until a United Nations Emergency Force had been stationed in the Gaza Strip on the Egyptian side of the Sinai border and at the Straits of Tiran, entrance to the Gulf of Aqaba, and until the United States and other maritime powers had publicly reaffirmed Israel's right of free passage through the gulf and the straits.

During the next decade there was no serious outbreak of fighting, but the conflict remained unresolved. Behind the fence of United Nations "peace-keeping," the Egyptian and Syrian armies were steadily developed by the Soviet Union, which supplied both modern weapons and training. At the beginning of 1964 an Arab "summit conference" in Cairo adopted a program to prepare for a future showdown with Israel. It included the setting up of the "Palestine Liberation Organization," with its own armed forces; placing the armies of Israel's Arab neighbors under a united command headed by an Egyptian commander-in-chief; diverting the tributaries of the Jordan River, thus cutting off a large part of Israel's vital water supply; and tightening the economic boycott. Tensions mounted over the El Fatah terrorist raids, promoted and organized by Syria, across the borders into Israel. From time to time Israel carried out a local militay action to deter the raids.

In 1967 the smoldering conflict erupted again into war. In May, Egyptian infantry divisions, armored formations and air force units moved in strength across the Suez Canal into the Sinai Desert and massed within striking distance of the frontier of Israel. Within a couple of weeks this military build-up amounted to some 90,000 men, 900 tanks, 350 planes and great concentrations of artillery.

On May 17, the Egyptian Government demanded the withdrawal of the U.N. Emergency Force and Secretary-General U Thant complied.

On May 22, Egypt announced the closing of the Straits of Tiran, the entrance to the 100-mile-long Gulf of Aqaba, at the head of which is Israel's southern port, Eilat. (The Gulf had been in use by Israel shipping for a decade, since the Sinai Campaign.) The United States, Britain and other maritime powers declared such a blockade illegal; consultations started in Western capitals about sending naval ships through to challenge it, but the plan was abortive.

On May 26, President Nasser of Egypt declared that the war "will be total and the objective will be to destroy Israel. We feel confident that we can win and are ready now for a war with Israel."

On May 30, King Hussein of Jordan flew to Cairo and dramatically signed a military pact with his former enemy, Nasser. An Egyptian general was sent to take command of Jordan's forces. By this time a wave of excitement was sweeping through the Arab world, and the mullahs in the mosques were preaching a *jihad* (Holy War).

Israel appeared to be alone and in grim danger. The reserves were fully mobilized, and a government of national unity was created under Premier Levi Eshkol, with General Moshe Dayan, the hero of the Sinai Campaign, as Minister of Defense.

Hostilities broke out on the morning of June 5. The Israel air force immediately carried out a dazzlingly successful strike against enemy airfields in Egypt and some in Jordan, Iraq and Syria. More than 400 Arab war planes were destroyed, mostly on the ground. Israel had achieved air supremacy over the battlefields—a vital factor in its victory.

In the Sinai Desert the Israel infantry and armored forces broke through Egyptian fortified positions and routed enemy tank concentrations. In forty-eight hours the shattered Egyptian army was streaming across the Suez Canal in complete disorder, leaving behind thousands of dead or captured troops and huge quantities of equipment. By Wednesday, when a U.N. Security Council cease-fire order took effect, Israel's forces were on the east bank of the Canal and in possession of the Gaza Strip and the whole Sinai Peninsula down to Sharm-el-Sheikh on the Straits of Tiran.

On the first day of the war, June 5, Jordan launched a heavy artillery bombardment of Jerusalem and areas in the coastal belt. Troops were hurriedly brought up to meet this threat. In fierce hand-to-hand fighting Jordanian positions were taken on the strategic high ground overlooking Jerusalem. On Wednesday the Old City fell, and the whole West Bank area was occupied as far as the Jordan River.

In the last phase of the fighting the belt of fortifications on the Golan Heights in the north was pierced, the Syrian army was rolled back towards Damascus and the town of Kuneitra was captured.

The war had started on Monday morning; by Saturday night it was over, after one of the swiftest and most shattering feats of arms in military history.

The Government of Israel made it clear that it regarded the armistice agreements of 1949 as having been swept away by Arab belligerence against Israel; and that there could be no return to the demarcation lines that existed on June 4. All the territory occupied during the fighting and contained within the cease-fire lines would remain under Israel's control until a final peace settlement was negotiated between Israel and its neighbors and secure frontiers were established and agreed upon.

The two parts of Jerusalem were reunited under a single municipality. The safety of the Holy Places and access to them were guaranteed; the government indicated that it was willing to give them special status under the control of the faiths to which they belonged.

At the United Nations the cease-fire was followed by continuous political debate for six months in the Security Council and in an emergency session of the General Assembly. Arab-Soviet attempts to place the blame for the hostilities on Israel were defeated, as were proposals for the unconditional withdrawal of the Israel forces. During this period, the uneasy calm after the war was broken from time to time by resumed small-scale terrorist attacks from the Jordanian-Syrian side and by artillery duels along the Suez Canal and the Jordan River. The most dramatic episode was the sinking of the Israel destroyer *Eilat* by Russian missiles supplied to the Egyptians, and Israel's artillery reply two days later, which set ablaze and largely destroyed the Egyptian oil refineries in the Suez area.

On November 22, the Security Council unanimously approved a compromise resolution sponsored by the United Kingdom. It requested the Secretary-General to appoint a special representative to contact the parties and promote agreement on a "just and lasting peace," including secure and recognized frontiers, withdrawal of forces, mutual respect for each other's statehood and security, freedom of navigation in the Suez Canal and the Gulf of Aqaba and a solution of the refugee problem. Ambassador Gunnar Jarring of Sweden was appointed as the Special Representative of the U.N. He set up his headquarters in Nicosia, Cyprus, and started his slow and demanding task. It had taken only six days to win the war, but it was obviously going to take a long time to win the peace.

Meanwhile a new and exciting dimension had been added to a visit to Israel. The Mandelbaum Gate had vanished, together with the barbed wire of no man's land, and the Old City of Jerusalem was now just a few minutes away from the center of the modern town. Bethlehem, Jericho, Nablus, Hebron and Gaza were no longer across enemy frontiers, but included in daily bus tours. On the Golan Heights one could drive through mile after mile of captured Syrian minefields and pillboxes and look down on the Israel villages below that had lain open to their gunfire. A plane excursion trip or a drive in a Land Rover took visitors across the battlefields in the Sinai Desert to the jagged purple mountains of southern Sinai and the startlingly blue

PROFILE OF A NATION

water of Sharm-el-Sheikh at the entrance to the Gulf of Aqaba.

Whatever the political future might be, Israel no longer felt tiny and hemmed-in. In greater numbers than ever before, visitors thronged to see the historic sites and the modern renaissance in the Land of the Bible.

CHAPTER 2

The Human Landscape

THE JEWS

The Ingathering

It is still too early to say what kind of new community will emerge from all the assorted Jewish tribes who have poured into the country. In order to understand the problems of integration in Israel, one must know something of the vastly different backgrounds from which its immigrants have come.

Over the centuries, Jewish life in the Diaspora developed in three main areas.

First, there were the Oriental communities that remained in the Arab Middle East and slowly spread farther eastward, even as far as India and China.

Second, there were those Jews who followed the westward march of Islam into North Africa and Spain and shared brilliantly in the developments in science and medicine, poetry and philosophy, of the Moorish civilization. After their expulsion from Spain in 1492, some of these *Sephardim* (Spaniards) settled in Holland and England, but most of them spread around the rim of the Mediterranean and into the Ottoman Empire, where large, thriving communities sprang up, especially in Constantinople and Salonika. They carried with them the Castilian tongue, which became the Ladino dialect. (It is written in Hebrew characters.)

Third, there were the Jews of medieval Germany, who were called *Ashkenazim* (Germans). In the fifteenth and sixteenth centuries, Jews from this group migrated in large numbers into Russia and Poland, where their trading and financial skills were in demand because of the lack of a local middle class. They lived in their own separate communities and spoke Middle German, which developed into the Yiddish dialect, written in Hebrew script.

As with the peoples among whom they lived, the numbers and the condition of the Jews in the Arab countries remained stagnant until the twentieth century. This was not so with the Ashkenazim. From the eighteenth century onwards their isolation in ghettos was breaking down in a changing Europe. New religious and intellectual movements sprang up among them—Chasidic mysticism, in revolt against arid learning; the *Haskalah* (Enlightenment) movement led by Moses Mendelssohn, drawing the Jews into the general stream of European culture; the Reform Synagogue of the German Jews; and the stirring of nationalism which produced the Zionist movement. These Jews shared in the population explosion of nineteenth-century

THE HUMAN LANDSCAPE

Europe; they multiplied sixfold in three generations and swelled the flood of migration crossing the seas to the New World—to the United States, Canada, Australia, South Africa, the Argentine and Brazil.

In the middle of the nineteenth century, three-quarters of the members of the small *Yishuv* (Palestine Jewish community) were Sephardic. The Ashkenazic element lived mainly in the Orthodox quarters of the four Jewish Holy Cities of medieval Palestine (Jerusalem, Safad, Tiberias and Hebron), living off the *halukkah* (alms) sent from Europe and maintaining Yiddish as their daily tongue. From the eighties onward, a new kind of Jew arrived on the scene —the early Zionist pioneers from Russia and Poland, eager to work on the land. Immigration from those countries grew, and when the State of Israel was established nearly 80 percent of its 650,000 Jews were of European origin. Their energy and their secular, nationalistic outlook had by then given an indelible Western image to the Yishuv.

Then in 1948, the State of Israel was proclaimed, and its gates were dramatically flung open. In the next decade nearly a million Jewish immigrants were taken in. But this great tidal wave was no longer predominantly European or Zionist. The Jewish masses of Eastern Europe who would have been the reservoir of population for the new Israel had mostly disappeared into Hitler's gas chambers; there were only a few hundred thousand of them left alive as potential immigrants. (This reckoning excludes nearly three million Jews in the Soviet Union who were not allowed to emigrate.) From the free and comfortable countries of the Western world, only small numbers came to settle in Israel. On the other hand, whole communities were transplanted from the Arab countries. When the first wave of *aliyah* had spent itself by 1951, the population had become visibly more Oriental. Today, the ratio is about fifty-fifty.

In the first few years of the State, Israel's leaders and officials were absorbed in coping with the immediate needs of mass immigration—transportation, food, homes, health and jobs. With the slackening of these first pressures, more thought has been given to the long-range aspects of building a nation. The Almighty had promised long ago that

> Behold, I will take the Children of Israel from among the heathen, whither they be gone, and will gather them on every side, and bring them into their own land . . . and they shall be no more two nations.
> —Ezekiel 37: 21–22

But that is easier said than done, for the question persists whether, after they have been gathered into their own land, the Children of Israel will remain "two nations." How can the gap between East and West be bridged in a way which will produce a "leveling up" instead of a "leveling down"? There are deep-rooted differences in ways and outlook between Jews from European countries and Jews from Moslem countries, and the synthesis between the two groups is slower and more complex than was thought at first.

The European Jew is a strong individualist and yet, paradoxically, an Organization Man. He moves easily in a world of ballot boxes, political parties, labor unions, youth movements, women's groups and social services. Through these collective instruments his restless, Western spirit is constantly trying to remold the society in which he lives. To the Oriental Jew, such social dynamism and its framework of institutions are baffling. He clings to a traditional way of life based on the twin pillars of religious piety and a patriarchal family unit. He has a fatalistic acceptance of authority —whether divine or human—tends to follow notables rather than political programs, is accustomed to the business methods of the bazaar (where a price ticket is the opening gambit for a bargaining session) and regards officials and policemen as hostile forces—which they were in his country of origin—to be placated with bribes and flattery.

There is nothing biological about such different traits. They are inbred, after centuries of Jewish minority life elsewhere, and the patterns mingle and change under the common impact of Israel. There are many agencies of integration in the national life which help to break down barriers. The children mingle—in the same kindergartens and classrooms, the youth movements and the army. Immigrants, whether Ashkenazim or Sephardim, find themselves projected side by side into occupations quite different from those they left behind; and whether they become cultivators in the new villages or factory hands in the new industries, the conditions are the same for all. In some instances the transition to modern social ideas is expressly brought about by law—for instance, by laws abolishing polygamy, declaring the equal status of women and a minimum age of sixteen for marriage, and banning child labor.

But declaring people equal in law does not automatically make them equal in fact. The progress of Israel's Oriental communities is slowed by poverty and large families. A special effort is being made in the school system in immigrant areas to close the gap. But for some time to come, it will still be mainly the Ashkenazim, with their driving energy and enterprise, who will dominate the running of the country.

Yet in spite of—or perhaps because of—the Western atmosphere of Israel, those looking for things that are distinctively "Israeli" are finding them more and more in the Oriental contributions to the life of the country—in the folk dances and songs, in the exquisite embroidery and silver work of Yemenite craftsmen, in the Arabic-tinged slang of the *sabras* (the native-born), and in the Middle Eastern dishes like hummus and tachina, felafel and shashlik, rather than the customary Eastern European Jewish dishes like gefilte fish and blintzes. The Hebrew of Israel, moreover, is spoken in the Sephardic way and not with the Ashkenazic accent which the Jews from Eastern Europe carried with them to the United States and other Western countries. In practice the Hebrew of the average sabra lies somewhere between the hard inflections of the Yiddish-speaking immigrants and the throaty lilt of the Arabic-speaking ones.

Like the adults in most countries, older Israelis endlessly ask themselves what kind of new generation they are producing and how it will stand up to the challenges that lie ahead. Anyone watching a school or a movie house emptying out in Israel will find it as difficult to spot a "typical" young Israeli as it is to find a "typical" Jew among his immigrant parents. But undoubtedly there are some common characteristics. Self-reliance, an independence of bearing, a rejection of the subtle compromises of Diaspora life—these are qualities natural in young Jews growing up in a Jewish country which they are building and defending themselves. Some people criticize them for being brash and lacking in humility, but maybe this is natural in a new state in which pioneering and defense go hand in hand. They cheerfully accept the nickname "sabra," which is the fruit of the cactus plant, prickly outside but sweet and wholesome inside.

THE HUMAN LANDSCAPE

Of course there are problem children, but on the whole Israel is as good a place for children to live in as any in the world, and the children are, in a way, the only privileged class in the country. For the visitor there is nothing more attractive, or more reassuring for the future, than to see groups of healthy, relaxed and suntanned children in the schools and kibbutzim, singing through the fields and over the hills on a *tiyul* (excursion) in the spring or summer, dancing the hora in the streets and public squares on some national festival, or swinging by smartly in the Independence Day parade.

Some Pieces in the Mosaic

Israel, too, has its Establishment—the Zionist *chaverim* (comrades) who came from Eastern Europe in the Second Aliyah before World War I, or in the twenties, and who built up the kibbutzim, the Histadrut (the labor federation), the labor parties and the Haganah. More than any other single element, it is this group which paved the way for the state and is still its backbone. But the ranks of these oldtimers are thinning, and the leadership is beginning to pass into the hands of a rising *sabra* generation.

There is another group of Eastern European Jews whose geographical origins are the same as those of the socialist chaverim but whose outlook and purposes are utterly different. This is the quite unmistakable group of the Orthodox Jews who inhabit quarters like Mea Shearim in Jerusalem and parts of Bnei Brak and Safad. Such quarters are the remaining strongholds of a way of life based on the Torah and the Talmud and shaped in the Russian Pale of Settlement more than a hundred years ago. And every now and then some specific question of religious observance flares into public controversy: the marriage regulations for the Bene Israel community from India, a non-Kosher kitchen on a luxury liner, public transport on the Sabbath, or autopsies in hospitals.

The antithesis of the *aduk*, or fiercely Orthodox Yiddish-speaking Jew, is the emancipated and worldly Jew from Germany, Austria or Czechoslovakia. Numbers of Jews left Germany in the few years of grace from 1933 onwards, and more than 70,000 of them reached Palestine before the White Paper of 1939 slammed that door in their faces. This *Aliyah Chadasha* (new immigration) had a strong impact on the life of the Palestine community built up by those same *Ostjuden* (Eastern European Jews) whom the German Jews had tended to regard as unfortunate poor relations.

The German Jews integrated in due course, their children grew up as sabras and, having come in before the establishment of the state and the period of mass immigration, they have today the standing of oldtimers. What is more, there is general acknowledgment of the great value of the solid middle-class virtues brought to Israel by these orderly, industrious, polite and intellectual settlers.

The most romantic single episode of *Kibbutz Galuyot* (Ingathering of the Exiles) was that known as Operation Magic Carpet—the airborne evacuation of more than 50,000 Yemenite Jews to Israel in 1949 by eight-hour non-stop flights in chartered American Skymasters from Aden, at the tip of the Arabian Peninsula and at the entrance to the Red Sea—a distance of 1,760 miles. No fewer than 30,000 Yemenites were transported in the five-month period from July to November, 1949. The Jewish community of

THE HUMAN LANDSCAPE

Yemen had existed since Biblical times. The country had remained isolated and barbaric, and its Jews poor, malnourished and subject to various humiliating restrictions.

It shows the astonishing tenacity of the Jewish spirit that during many centuries of such wretched conditions these "forgotten men" never faltered in their religious faith, nor did they give up a belief in the ultimate return to Zion. The boys were educated in the *Cheder* (religious school), where they studied the Scriptures in the original Hebrew as well as in Aramaic and Arabic translations; and since there was never more than one book to a class, they could read it just as easily upside down or sideways as right side up. Amidst the squalor around them they remained clean and industrious and kept alive a strange love of beauty that was expressed in their delicate handiwork and in their poetry, songs and folk dances.

Groups of Yemenite Jews had already found their way to Palestine after 1882 and had settled down as artisans and farm laborers. After World War II, a few started trekking from Yemen on foot across the desert to Aden, the British-held post on the Red Sea. With the establishment of Israel the trickle became a flood; and the air-shuttle service was organized to bring them to Israel. They had never seen a plane before and simply related their journey to the Biblical promise that the Lord would bring them to Israel on "eagles' wings" (Exodus 19:4). Among all the immigrant groups, these *Taymanim* (Hebrew: Yemenites) came out of the most primitive conditions, having never known beds, chairs or toilets, electric light or piped water, a railroad or a bus. Yet they, too, have made a rapid adjustment to the modern state, and thousands of them have been successfully settled on the land.

PROFILE OF A NATION

By common consent, the Yemenites are Israel's most appealing community. Their appearance is quite distinctive—they are slender, small and fine-boned, with the dark faces of the men invariably framed in the traditional long curls (*payot*) and the young girls sometimes startlingly beautiful, with delicate features and big liquid eyes. A Yemenite woman decked out for some festivity is a gay sight in all her finery—a striped blouse and tight black trousers under a long outer coat, and a silver-embroidered cowl over her head. Yemenite embroidery and Yemenite songs are becoming accepted as characteristic of Israel.

The Jewish community of Iraq goes back twenty-six centuries to the Babylonian Captivity. In modern times the Baghdadi Jewish traders penetrated eastward into India and China and produced such famous dynasties of merchant princes as the Ezras, the Gabbais, the Sassoons and the Kadoories. The great mass of the Iraqi Jews, however, remained in lower-middle-class urban occupations. Many of the educated young men went into white-collar jobs as minor officials and clerks in government departments, the customs office, post and telegraph offices, banks and business houses. A good proportion of these jobs in Israel are today filled by these same Iraqis. As Arab nationalism grew in the twentieth century the Iraqi Jews became increasingly insecure, and some of them started toward Palestine. With the establishment of Israel and the return of the Iraqi troops from their inglorious Palestine campaign, resentment turned against the local Jews. In 1950–51, repressive measures were taken against them; they were pressed to leave the country, while their property and possessions were confiscated. Here again, as with the Yemenite Jews just before

THE HUMAN LANDSCAPE

them, an airborne exodus on a mass scale had to be improvised. Within a matter of months 120,000 Iraqis were brought to Israel by what was called Operation Ali Baba.

Also stretching back into early Biblical times was the Jewish community of Iran (Persia). It was the Persian ruler Cyrus the Great who allowed some of his Babylonian Jewish subjects to return to Jerusalem to rebuild the Temple in the days of Ezra and Nehemiah, twenty-five centuries ago. By the twentieth century there was a small upper crust of wealthy Persian Jews, but the bulk of them lived in extreme poverty and backwardness—as humble peddlers in the rural towns and remote areas, as sweated labor in the big carpet- and silk-weaving concerns (they worked long hours for less than fifty cents a day), or even as beggars. Although they were not under the same political pressures as their brethren in nearby Arab countries, it is not surprising that with the advent of Israel many thousands of Persian Jews gathered from all over the country in the Jewish Agency camps at Teheran. From there they were evacuated to Israel by plane or were taken overland through Turkey and on to Haifa by boat.

One interesting group among the Persian immigrants were the thousand-odd souls who formed the Jewish community of the town of Meshed. In 1839 some of this community were massacred and the rest forcibly converted to Islam. Ever since then the Meshed Jews had led a double life like that of the Marranos in medieval Spain: outwardly Moslems, they secretly kept up the practice of the Jewish faith. These people have felt a special sense of liberation on becoming citizens of Israel.

• • •

PROFILE OF A NATION

In Jerusalem you can still wander through the old quarters of the Bukharan, Kurdish, Georgian and Armenian Jews who hailed from the little-known Jewish mountain tribes of the Caucasus and Central Asia. They must have settled in those parts in the days of the ancient Persian Empire. Even in modern times the Jews of Iran, Afghanistan and Bukhara spoke Persian dialects which they wrote in Hebrew script (as Yiddish and Ladino are written), while the Jews of Kurdistan still used the Aramaic spoken in Palestine at the time of Jesus. These *Kurdim* have a special reputation in Israel, not shared with the other Oriental groups, of being tough, hardy mountain folk. In Israel they naturally took the jobs needing physical strength, becoming, for example, farm laborers or *sabalim* (porters) who lug heavy furniture up and down the stairways in apartment buildings.

After 1948 the *aliyah* increased rapidly from the *Maghreb* (West), which is, in both Arabic and Hebrew, the name for the region which includes Libya, Tunisia, Algeria and Morocco. These North African Jews have never been a homogeneous community but a mixture of different groups: the Arabic-speaking Jews dating from the period of Moselm rule; the descendants of the Sephardim who settled in the coastal towns after the expulsion from Spain, who still speak a Spanish dialect; and more recent European elements, particularly merchants from France. Of these groups it is mostly the poorer classes who have come to Israel.

In the wake of the Moslem advance along the North African coast and across the Straits of Gibraltar into Spain, important centers of Jewish life and scholarship arose in Fez, Marrakech, Kairouan and other cities. There were brilliant and influential Jews among the courtiers, financiers

THE HUMAN LANDSCAPE

and diplomats of the Moroccan rulers and other North African potentates; and Jewish influence was so strong among some of the local Berber tribes that the members became converts to Judaism. But for most of the period of Moslem, and later Turkish, rule, life in the crowded *mellahs* (ghettos) of North Africa remained one of poverty and discrimination.

With the coming of French rule in most of North Africa such restrictions were lifted and the lot of the Jews, as a French-protected minority, improved. In recent years the sweep of Arab nationalism through North Africa has led to the independence of Libya (1951), Morocco (1956), Tunisia (1956) and Algeria (1962). Each in turn joined the Arab League. In 1948 there were more than 500,000 Jews in these four countries; and since then some 200,000 have settled in Israel. With the independence of Algeria, most of its non-Arab French citizens, including some 120,000 Jews, streamed across the Mediterranean into metropolitan France. It is hardly surprising that the remaining Jews in these North African lands feel themselves increasingly insecure and under pressure; no doubt many more will seek to emigrate.

The stream of immigration from North Africa has exposed some forgotten corners of Jewish life. There are, for instance, the cave dwellers of the Tigrinna concession in the Libyan hills, who had lived for centuries in underground dwellings; and the several thousand inhabitants of the two Jewish villages of the Island of Djerba off the Tunisian coast. This was the legendary island of the lotus-eaters in the story of Ulysses, and Jewish life seems to have remained intact since those ancient times.

Spanish, like French, is a language now frequently heard

• 41

PROFILE OF A NATION

in Israel. The dwindling Ladino-speaking Sephardic community was strongly reinforced in 1948–49 by the immigration of 90,000 persons from the predominantly Sephardic communities in the nearby Balkan countries—Bulgaria, Turkey, Greece and Yugoslavia—the area of the Ottoman Empire in which Jewish life flourished in the sixteenth and seventeenth centuries. Since 1949 there has been an increasing number of settlers from the Latin American countries, which contain about three-quarters of a million Jews, over half of them in the Argentine. There are a number of kibbutzim which are made up mainly of young Latin Americans, and business and investment interests are also growing rapidly.

The *Anglo-Saxim*, the settlers who have come from the English-speaking countries, are relatively few: there are altogether over 50,000 from Britain, South Africa, the United States, Canada and Australia. The importance of this group is qualitative, since they bring with them energy and ideas, professional and technical skills, investment capital and up-to-date methods—assets lacked by immigrants from backward areas. Their presence is also an essential living link with the free Jewish communities which supply so much of the material and moral support Israel needs.

The authorities recognize that some concessions must be made regarding customs duties, currency, housing and military service in order to attract more *Anglo-Saxim* immigrants. Even so, some go back where they came from for a variety of reasons—careers, family pressures, personal frustrations—but most of them settle down to cheerful and useful lives. They are Israelis simply because they want to be

THE HUMAN LANDSCAPE

Israelis, and they too are a distinctive strand in that "Joseph's coat of many colors" which is Israel today.

THE ISRAEL ARABS

Moving around Israel, as it existed before the June, 1967 war, the traveler soon becomes aware that one Israeli out of ten is an Arab. The road to Jerusalem passes the big and prosperous Arab village of Abu Ghosh, and on the highway to Haifa is the Arab village of Fureidis. In Haifa and Acre, in Jaffa, in Lydda (Lod) and Ramla, there are distinctive Arab quarters, where the menfolk, wearing *kheffiyahs*, sit in the hot summer evenings outside the cafés, drinking little cups of black Turkish coffee and playing *shesh-besh* (a kind of checkers) while Arab music blares from the radio inside. Although there is a Jewish suburb on the ridge above it, Nazareth remains an Arab city, with some 27,000 inhabitants.

The whole of the Galilee highlands is dotted with the cubelike stone houses of Arab villages blending into the hill slopes covered by ancient olive groves. Here rural Arab life seems to have kept intact its slow, ancestral patterns, outwardly little touched by Israel's convulsive birth and its bustling modern tempo. Down south, in the Negev, the feeling of timeless tradition is even stronger as one passes an encampment of low black Bedouin tents, with its herds of camels and goats seeking vegetation in the bleak landscape.

A third of the 300,000 Israel Arabs are townsfolk in Nazareth and the mixed cities; the rest, not counting the Bedouin tribes, live in more than a hundred villages. There are three main Arab areas in Israel. More than half the total

PROFILE OF A NATION

number of Arabs live in the Galilee, about 45,000 in the central Little Triangle area, and some 15,000 in the Negev. The majority are Moslems, but there are nearly 50,000 Christians and 23,000 Druses, who form a separate sect. The Christians are divided among a variety of denominations, the main ones being Greek Catholic, Greek Orthodox and Roman Catholic.

In spite of the surface impression that life has changed little for the Arab minority, these people have been going through a period of far-reaching adjustment. The improvements in their standards of life in two decades have been very impressive. They have been given complete political rights, with the vote in Knesset elections being exercised by both men and women—even the veiled wives of the primitive Bedouin tribes in the south. Arabs have also run as candidates for office on behalf of various parties, and there have been a number of Arab members in each Knesset. As important as national elections has been the introduction of democracy at the grass-roots level, with the election of village councils and local authorities replacing the old system of appointed *mukhtars*, or village headmen, subservient to the local notables. There are now thirty-four such elected councils, whereas in 1948 there were only two.

The economic situation of the Arabs has also greatly improved. With such modern methods as crop rotation, contour ploughing and use of fertilizers, the produce of the Arab villages has increased sixfold. Today more than 80 percent of the Arabs own the land they till. Arab workers are now admitted as full members of the Histadrut, and their wage scales are the same as those of the Jewish workers and higher than anywhere else in the Middle East. The average income per family for Israel Arabs is about $1,600 a year,

44 •

THE HUMAN LANDSCAPE

as compared to $105 in Egypt. Arab and Druse villages are now being developed under a five-year plan.

A revolution has taken place in the education of Israel's Arab children, who are also subject to the law making schooling free and compulsory up to the age of fourteen. Aside from some fifty church and mission schools with almost 14,000 pupils, the figures for the growth of government schools in Arab areas in Israel's first nineteen years are revealing:

	1948	1967
Kindergartens	11	157
Primary schools	60	191
Secondary schools	1	15
Number of pupils	7,000	64,000
Number of teachers	250	2,022

Arabic is the language of tuition in these schools; Hebrew is taught as a second language. The most fundamental change in the school system is that it now includes Arab girls, something which was virtually unknown before the State of Israel. There are now more than 500 Arab students at the Hebrew University and the Haifa Technion.

The Arab villages have been included in the network of health and social-welfare services. Here again, the figures show striking advances—for instance, in the drop in the infant mortality rate. Malaria has been eradicated, trachoma and tuberculosis have been reduced to slight incidence, and vaccination against polio has been extended to all children. The Arab Scout movement has also been developed alongside the Jewish *Tsofim* (Scouts) and is affiliated with the National Scout Council. The Israel contingents at International Scout Jamborees invariably include Arabs as well as Jews.

PROFILE OF A NATION

In Israel the legal system has carefully preserved the principle whereby matters of personal status (mainly marriage and divorce) are dealt with by the religious law of each faith, administered by its own religious courts. For the Moslems, the government appointed a number of *cadis* (judges) who decide cases in accordance with *Shari'ah* (Moslem religious law). However, as with the Oriental Jewish communities, traditional ways have sometimes been amended by the Knesset in accordance with modern views. For instance, marriage of girls under the age of sixteen has been forbidden; and polygamy has been made illegal, even for Moslems.

Much is also being done to foster the language and culture of the Arab minority. Arabic has the status of an official language and it appears with Hebrew on coins, bank notes and postage stamps. In the Arab areas, Arabic is in general use in government offices, the courts and the schools, and for all other purposes. Arab Knesset members address the House in their own language and can listen to debates by simultaneous translation into Arabic. There are a growing number of books published in Arabic and a variety of Arabic newspapers and magazines. The State Broadcasting Service, Kol Yisrael, devotes fifteen hours a day to Arabic broadcasts, including daily readings from the Koran. Arabic television news programs have begun, and these will soon be followed by educational TV.

The Bedouin

Of the 22,000 Bedouin nomads in Israel, 15,000 live in the Negev, where they belong to 18 distinct tribes and sub-tribes. Their wandering desert life has produced a peculiar form of society quite different from that of the settled village communities. It is this Bedouin way of life which is closest to that of the Hebrew Patriarchs of the Bible and also resembles the accounts in T. E. Lawrence's *Seven Pillars of Wisdom*. But, shorn of romantic notions, the freedom and simplicity of Bedouin life is paid for in the currency of hardship and poverty. When drought hits their world, when the water holes run dry, the sparse grazing shrivels and the sheep and goats start dying, the tribesmen stare into the grim face of famine and tell themselves stoically that it is Allah's will.

There have been several such winter droughts in Israel; the government has taken emergency measures, supplying food, water and fodder to the Bedouin encampments and employing many of the menfolk on relief works. Apart from these abnormal drought measures, the authorities have been improving the basic conditions of the Bedouin. Their grazing grounds cover a million dunams (250,000 acres), and in addition they have 400,000 dunams (100,000 acres) of cultivable land. These nomads are accustomed to raising a thin crop of winter grain by sowing the seed on the bare ground and then ploughing it under with primitive wooden implements drawn by camels. This cultivation is now being improved by bringing water to some areas by pipeline, by using tractors and other improved agricultural implements, and by introducing modern farming methods. Meanwhile, the Bedouin flocks have increased sixfold since 1948.

Mobile health clinics serve these people regularly; and where the tribes have become seminomadic, remaining in a fixed area, it has been possible to set up elementary schools. There are already Bedouin children attending high school in Beersheba. The primitive Bedouin way of life is thus

PROFILE OF A NATION

slowly yielding to civilization, just as the open spaces of the nomad's arid world are yielding to green fields. Gradually these nomads are being encouraged to settle down as tillers of the soil, and thousands of the men are being employed as wage earners on such Negev construction as the new city of Arad and the road from Ein Gedi to Ain Feshka, along the Dead Sea. They remain a dignified and picturesque community, clinging hard to their ancestral folkways.

THE DRUSES

The Druses are another colorful minority in Israel. They number 23,000 and live mainly in Galilee in one town, Shfaram (or Shefar'am) and eighteen villages. They are a fine, handsome people, proud of their warrior traditions; the men are conspicuous for their big curling mustaches, baggy white trousers and headgear which is higher and more turban-like than the usual loose Arab *kheffiyah*. The Druses are Arabic-speaking, but constitute an exclusive religious sect which broke away from Islam more than a thousand years ago. Their faith contains elements of Christianity and Judaism grafted onto the Islamic stem; its tenets are kept secret, being known only to members. Their sacred shrine and place of pilgrimage is the tomb of the Prophet Shu'eib, whom they identify with Jethro, the father-in-law of Moses. It is situated near the Horns of Hattin, overlooking Tiberias.

Most of the quarter-million Druses in the Middle East live in Syria and Lebanon, mainly in the mountainous region of the Djebel Druze. They were always fiercely independent and gave a great deal of trouble to their Arab rulers. In the War of Independence hundreds of them

THE HUMAN LANDSCAPE

joined the Jewish forces against the Arabs and were afterwards allowed by the Israel army to form their own cavalry units, which still steal the show at Independence Day parades.

At the time of Turkish rule and during the British Mandate, the Druses in Palestine were simply treated as part of the Moslem Arab community, to their great dissatisfaction. In 1956, however, a law adopted by the Israel Knesset gave them the status of a separate religious community, authorized to deal with personal and family matters in accordance with their own traditions and through their own judges.

It is an exhilarating experience to be a guest at a feast in a Druse village. The main course is usually a whole lamb stuffed with meat, rice and herbs, served with cucumber and tomato salad, tachina (a thick sauce made of ground sesame seeds in oil) and pitta (the huge, circular, paper-thin Arab bread that one tears with one's fingers). The custom is for the hosts not to eat with their guests but to stand behind them and serve them. After the meal the company retires to the lounge, spread with straw floor mats and painted blue to ward off the evil spirits. The evening is likely to culminate in a spirited *debka*, a dance performed by the men to the accompaniment of the *oud*, a single-stringed instrument, and by the singing and clapping of the audience.

THE CIRCASSIANS

There are 1,200 Circassians in the Galilee, living in two villages: Kafr Kanna, near Nazareth, and Rihaniya, in Upper Galilee. They are Moslems who came to Palestine in the last century from the Caucasus Mountains. They still speak their own Circassian language, and the men wear distinctive gray Persian-lamb caps. Like the Druses, the Circassians are a stalwart people with a martial background. They, too, fought on the Jewish side in the Israel-Arab war, and a number of them serve today as volunteers in the army or in the border police.

In May, 1948, when Israel was born, the Proclamation of Independence hopefully declared that

> Even amidst the violent attacks launched against us for months past, we call upon the sons of the Arab people dwelling in Israel to keep the peace and to play their part in building the State, on the basis of full and equal citizenship and due representation in all its institutions, provisional and permanent.

Looking back over the two decades since then, it can be said that Israel's Arab minority is being steadily integrated into the national life of a modern progressive state while yet preserving its own religion, language and culture.

THE NEW TERRITORIES

At the end of the Six-Day War in June, 1967, the cease-fire left Israel in possession of new territories containing more than a million Arab inhabitants. Pending a peace settlement, these areas have been placed under Israel military government. The areas are:

Judea and Samaria (the West Bank area): the region south, east and north of Jerusalem, to the Jordan River and the Dead Sea, with 600,000 Arabs.

The Gaza Strip: the finger of coastal plain along the

THE HUMAN LANDSCAPE

Mediterranean that was under Egyptian occupation, with 400,000 Arabs.

The Sinai Desert: with 30,000 inhabitants in the coastal El Arish area and 50,000 Bedouin in the desert to the south.

The Golan Heights: the Syrian region east of the Huleh Valley and Lake Tiberias. Its Syrian and Palestinian inhabitants moved farther into Syria during the fighting, and only some 6,000 Druses, in six villages, remained.

The 65,000 Arabs in East Jerusalem are in a special position. Soon after the hostilities, the two parts of the city were united under a single municipal administration and Jerusalem's Arab citizens started integrating into the life and economy of Israel.

In the occupied areas generally, it is remarkable with what little friction ordinary life goes on and what a high degree of cooperation has developed between the inhabitants and the Israel authorities. Terrorist activity continues from Syria, Jordan and occasionally from Egypt and Lebanon, but without aid or encouragement from the local population. Visitors traveling through these areas find the villagers tilling their fields and bringing their produce to market; the shops full of customers and the churches and mosques open to worshipers; the children at school; commerce carried on as usual; transportation, water, electricity and other public services functioning; most of the Arab officials, teachers and policemen on their jobs; the same Arab mayors and village *mukhtars* still in office, and the local authorities continuing to run the affairs of their communities.

Restrictions on movement are practically nonexistent, and great numbers of Jews and Arabs alike are eagerly visiting areas from which they had been cut off for twenty years.

Across the Jordan River bridges flow truckloads of produce and goods, groups crossing to remain or visit in Jordan, and relatives returning to the West Bank under a family-reunion scheme.

Much anxious discussion goes on about the prospect of peace and the political future of the territories. Meanwhile the Israelis, and the Arabs in the occupied areas, coexist and mingle in a way which would not have been thought possible before the Six-Day War.

CHAPTER 3

Running the State

THE PRESIDENT

Israel is a republic headed by a President, who is elected for five years by a majority of the members of the Knesset (the parliament). The President is not the head of the executive branch as in the United States; his powers resemble those of a British constitutional monarch, as he stands above party politics and represents the nation as a whole.

THE KNESSET

The parliament is a single house of 120 members, called the Knesset (the Biblical name for an assembly or gathering). It is elected by secret ballot; every Israel citizen, male or female, from the age of eighteen upward, has the vote.

The electoral system for the Knesset is a remarkably pure form of what is known as proportional representation.

PROFILE OF A NATION

There are no constituencies. Each party puts up a list of candidates for the country as a whole. It will then get a number of Knesset seats proportionate to its percentage of the total national vote (with a 1 percent minimum).

After a Knesset election, the President consults the various party leaders before calling on one of them to form a government. Each government to date has been a coalition one.

In the crisis just before the Six-Day War in June, 1967, all the parties, except the Communists and a few dissident individuals, joined in a Government of National Unity under Premier Levi Eshkol. He died in office in Feburary, 1969, and was succeeded by Mrs. Golda Meir.

The country's largest party is the Israel Labor Party. At the beginning of 1968, the Israel Workers' Party (Mapai) joined forces again with two smaller groups that had previously broken away from it (Achdut Avoda and Rafi) to form the Labor Party, which holds 55 seats out of the total of 120.

A year later it negotiated an alignment with a leftist labor group, Mapam, with 8 seats.

A small Independent Liberal group (5 seats) is usually included in the coalition governments.

Gahal, usually in opposition, represents a more strongly nationalistic group, together with conservative middle-class urban elements. It has 26 seats.

There are four distinct religious parties that press for adherence to the traditions of Judaism. Some of them are combined in a National Religious Front that is included in government coalitions. The religious parties hold 17 seats.

There are 7 Arab members, belonging to several parties.

The Communist movement is legal in Israel; it submits

its own ticket in the elections. It concentrates its efforts mainly on the Arab minority. Its number of seats has varied from 3 to 6. In 1965, it split into two separate parties.

Each Knesset has had 10 or so women members, the most notable one being Mrs. Golda Meir, who was Labor Minister, then Foreign Minister (from 1956 to 1966), and then Secretary-General of the Labor Party until her retirement from the post in 1968. As Premier she remains a member of the Knesset.

THE LEGAL SYSTEM

Israel has no written constitution in the ordinary sense. Fundamental rights and freedoms (such as freedom of worship, speech, assembly and occupation) are safeguarded by the general law of the country. Certain statutes are regarded as basic laws which will at some future time be integrated into a final constitution and will meanwhile be amended freely in the light of experience.

The laws in force in Israel are a layer cake of different historical periods.

In the Ottoman Empire (up to the end of World War I) there were certain laws which applied to everyone, such as the Civil Code (*Mejella*) and the Land Law, but in matters of personal status—including marriage, divorce and inheritance—each religious community lived by its own set of laws, which were administered by its own courts. When Britain became the ruler of Palestine under the Mandate, the Ottoman system was not abolished but was adapted and enlarged to meet modern needs through Palestine Ordinances and the injection of English common law.

When Israel was established, all the existing laws were

PROFILE OF A NATION

retained except for those specially introduced under the White Paper to limit Jewish immigration or land settlement. But since then, the Knesset has passed a mass of legislation streamlining or altering the laws.

There are no jury trials in Israel. Judges are not elected; they are appointed from the legal profession by the President on the recommendation of a special nominating committee, ensuring that appointments are made strictly on merit and not through party patronage.

The system of religious courts in matters of personal status is still in force, and Israel as yet has no civil marriage or divorce. However, the Rabbinnical, Moslem or Christian religious law practiced by the various communities is not sacrosanct, but is subject to general reforms introduced by the Knesset in the light of modern ideas. For instance, there is the Women's Equal Rights Law (1951), abolishing discrimination in such matters as inheritance and guardianship of minor children; polygamy was stopped in 1951; and the marriage of child brides was forbidden in 1950. Furthermore, the district courts have been given concurrent jurisdiction with the religious courts in matters of personal status other than marriage and divorce.

Flogging was abolished in 1950, and the death penalty in 1954, except for two kinds of crime: treason in wartime; and war crimes, crimes against humanity and crimes against the Jewish people. It is under the second category that Adolf Eichmann was brought to trial; and his is the only case in which the death penalty has been carried out.

In the areas occupied in the Six-Day War, the existing legal and court systems were generally kept intact but are subject to the over-all authority of the military government.

RELIGION

Israel has no State religion and is not "theocratic," as is sometimes supposed. There is a government Ministry of Religions which is divided into Jewish, Moslem and Christian departments and provides help and facilities for all creeds in the country.

THE ARMED SERVICES

The defense map was completely transformed by the Six-Day War. Instead of being hemmed in by the old armistice lines, Israel's forces now stand on cease-fire lines along the Suez Canal, along the Jordan River and inside Syria; and Israel-held territory includes the whole Sinai Peninsula, the West Bank area, and the Golan Heights. But no peace settlement is yet in sight; Egypt is being rapidly rearmed by the Russians; and a million Arabs inhabit the occupied areas. The immediate threat to Israel has receded, but it has to remain a nation on guard.

In finding working answers to the security problem, Israel's army has taken on its own special qualities. It is a modern citizen army based on universal conscription. The only regular part of the army consists of a comparatively small cadre of commanders, staff officers and instructors. Young people are drafted at the age of eighteen—youths for three years and girls for two years, unless they are exempted because of marriage or to meet religious scruples. It is these conscripts who form the full-time army in uniform when conditions are normal. After completing their service they go into reserve units—men until they are forty-nine, women until they are thirty-four or have children. These units have an annual training period of more than a month. With no space (before June, 1967) for defense in depth, and liable to attack from different directions at the same time, Israel evolved the most rapid and efficient system in the world for calling up reservists: they can be taken out of civilian life and put into the field in forty-eight hours.

The first shock of a surprise attack on land would have to be borne by the border villages, which are constructed and sited with a careful eye to their defense role. Behind them, the conscripts in training are the mobile striking force, while the reserve units are being called up. This relationship between agricultural settlements and defense, which is a strong tradition in Israel, has produced one feature unique to Israel's army—*Nahal*, which stands for Pioneering and Fighting Youth. The Nahal groups are organized from the youth movements. When the members of a group reach military age, they go through the basic training period together and spend the rest of their army time settling new border kibbutzim. In this way, the army promotes farm settlement in order to meet the special needs of defense.

The army also sponsors education on a scale which makes it the country's biggest school. The emphasis here is on integrating the youth from the immigrant families by teaching them Hebrew and making them familiar with the country's history, geography and problems. A high proportion of the immigrants come from underdeveloped countries, and the youth from these families must be taught not only to use a rifle, but to understand democracy and even to brush their teeth regularly. After their years in uniform these young men and women come out better prepared for civilian life.

The women in uniform now have exclusively noncombatant duties. They are nurses, clerks and signalers; they operate Link trainers for the Air Force, run radar stations and pack parachutes. They no longer drive army trucks, as this was found to be too much of a strain for girls; nor do they do any army cooking. The women signalers, however, might find themselves right up with the front-line troops. The Sinai Campaign opened with a parachute battalion being dropped to seize and hold the vital Mitla Pass very far behind the enemy lines, and dropped with them were two girl signalers who had volunteered for this hazardous job. Though they are not part of the fighting troops, all girl recruits are taught to defend themselves with rifles, hand grenades and Uzis, the famous "made-in-Israel" submachine guns.

There is a single unified general staff and a single chief of staff, who commands all the armed forces. The senior service, and by far the largest, is the army, which in recent years has built up a strong armored spearhead. Then comes the air force, which maintains a very high professional standard, as indeed it should, with enemy airfields a matter of minutes away from the borders in terms of jet speeds. The navy is the smallest service, its main job being the protection of Israel's coastal waters. It has been augmented by submarines bought from Britain. Service unity is symbolized in the fact that there is no difference in the names of the ranks for army, air force and navy. These ranks carry Hebrew names which go back to Biblical times.

Israel's security rests solidly on one principle: making up in quality what it lacks in space and numbers. Foreign experts concur that the military training is as rigorous as any in the world. It concentrates on developing the speed, stamina and personal initiative of all ranks—traits which earned world headlines for the Israel army in 1956 and again in 1967. Morale is no problem, even among the newest recruits from Oriental communities. When the Israelis fight, they fight for their survival, and it is said that their secret weapon is the Hebrew phrase *Ain brerah*, which could be translated as "No alternative."

THE POLICE

Israel's police force has been built up into an efficient body of nearly 10,000 men. They are not controlled by city councils or other local authorities, as in the United States, Great Britain and other countries, but form a single national body directed from a central headquarters.

One unusual task of the police is to share with the army the guarding and patrolling of the frontiers between Israel and the neighboring Arab states. This is done by the specially trained mobile Border Police Force, which wears distinctive green berets and has its own commander. It operates against infiltrators and marauders and coordinates the local protective measures of the frontier settlements.

THE FOREIGN SERVICE

Even before the establishment of the State, the Political Department of the Jewish Agency carried on activities on the international front. With the Proclamation of Independence in 1948, the head of that department, Moshe Sharett, became Foreign Minister; the able group working under him formed the nucleus of the foreign ministry and provided the country's first ambassadors abroad. The foreign service is unusually large and widespread, because of the needs and pressures of Israel's diplomatic struggle with the Arab world, its special ties with Jewish communities elsewhere, and, in recent years, its extensive programs of co-operation with other new and developing states.

In 1968 there were 113 diplomatic and consular missions abroad in addition to a network of government offices dealing with trade, tourism, investment and defense needs. The number of embassies was greater before the Six-Day War, when the Communist countries, except Rumania, broke off diplomatic relations with Israel as a mark of political support for the Arab states.

THE JEWISH AGENCY

The League of Nations Mandate for Palestine stipulated that there should be a "Jewish Agency" as a recognized public body to cooperate with the Mandatory administration in the development of the Jewish National Home.

The agency set up for this purpose was based on the World Zionist Organization but included some non-Zionist elements. During the time of the Mandate it promoted the practical work of immigration and settlement and dealt with the Mandate's Administration and foreign governments abroad on issues of political policy. The Jewish Agency was officially invited to take part in the United Nations debates on the future of Palestine in 1947–48. In 1948, with the establishment of the sovereign State of Israel, the political responsibilities of the Jewish Agency disappeared. In coordination with the government, the Agency continued its practical work in immigration and land settlement and in the strengthening of cultural ties with the Jewish communities abroad.

Connected with the Jewish Agency are the main "national institutions." The oldest of these is the Keren Kayemet, (Jewish National Fund), which was founded in 1901 to acquire and reclaim land in Palestine for settlement. The other principal Zionist instrument is the Keren Hayesod (Palestine Foundation Fund), which was launched in 1921 to serve as the financial arm of the Jewish Agency. Its income is mainly derived from the funds raised by Jews throughout the world.

Another notable branch of the Jewish Agency is the Youth Aliyah, founded in 1934 to rescue children from Nazi Germany and bring them to Palestine. Since then, this unique institution has brought to Israel, cared for, educated and trained more than 110,000 children and youth from 60 countries. The emphasis has been on agriculture, and Youth Aliyah wards have already established nearly fifty farm settlements of their own; but it also provides training for industry. Recently Youth Aliyah has been adapted to care for and train some of the children of new immigrants.

CHAPTER 4

"Our Daily Bread"

ELEMENTS OF ECONOMIC GROWTH

Since 1948 Israel's population has more than trebled; the national income has increased threefold; and agricultural and industrial output has multiplied several times over. Israel's rate of economic growth is one of the highest in the world. Such advances would be impressive for a rich country which was at peace. But they are extraordinary for a small, new state, half-arid, with poor natural resources and with Arab enmity imposing boycotts and high defense budgets. What accounts for this surge forward? The clue lies not in the wealth of Israel's subsoil but in the will of its people. The most casual visitor is struck by a sense of national purpose which is deterred neither by the niggardliness of nature nor by the malice of man.

The drive towards economic independence is proceeding on a broad front. One of the major issues is an accommodation with the European Common Market, which is Israel's most important export area. An initial trade agreement was signed in 1964.

In 1966 a lull in immigration and a slump in building, coming on top of years of rapid expansion, rising wages and living standards, brought about serious economic strains and some unemployment. The government embarked on stiff reform measures, under the banner of the "economic restraint policy." The objectives were to halt inflation, limit local consumption and divert resources into export industries. The "restraint" was successful in stabilizing price levels, and the momentum of growth is quickening again.

In November, 1967, Israel followed Britain in devaluating its currency (IL 3.50 to $1.00 instead of IL 3). The effect on prices and exports has yet to be seen.

In agriculture the emphasis has shifted from food crops to such industrial crops as cotton, sugarbeets and groundnuts; to the expansion of citrus growing, and to the development of new export crops such as bananas, melons, grapes, avocados and flowers. Israel's farm program has been able to make such rapid progress because 90 percent of the farm land is publicly owned, and planning is therefore relatively easy.

The key to agriculture is water. Since earliest times Israel has been a thirsty land, with nomads wandering with their flocks from well to well, and the tillers praying for the rains, which usually fall only in winter. The main feature of an elaborate national water plan is the great 108-inch conduit which brings Jordan River water from the north to the dry south, linking up with regional projects like that which pipes water from the Yarkon River near Tel Aviv into the northern Negev. Even with the completion of all projects,

"OUR DAILY BREAD"

the available water will be enough for only about half the irrigable land. Israel's most exciting dream is of finding a cheap method for turning salt or brackish water into fresh water; important work is now being done on various processes.

Industry in Israel—essential to its present and future standard of living—today produces a volume and variety of manufactured goods undreamed of in 1948. The emphasis is on industries which exploit local raw materials—food products, chemicals and fertilizers, cotton, cement, glass sand, clay, phosphate rock—or which are little dependent on raw materials (rayon, plastics, pharmaceuticals), or where the local "added value" is substantial and skill and "know-how" is a key factor (diamond cutting and the making of paper, tires and fashion goods). The government pays particular attention to fostering industries in new development areas in order to disperse the population.

In Israel's economic growth, the sources of power and fuel are a special concern. The country has no coal or hydroelectric power. Local oil and natural gas production meet only 10 percent of its needs. An adequate supply of imported oil has been assured by means of a 16-inch pipeline from Eilat, by Israel-owned supertankers, and by the refineries at Haifa; and work has commenced on a 42-inch pipeline from Eilat which will provide a substantial oil-transit facility to Europe. At present the supply of crude oil purchased from other sources is augmented from the oil wells on the Gulf of Suez coast of the Sinai Peninsula.

It is obvious why Israel should be intensely interested in the prospect of developing reasonably cheap atomic power in the next decade or so. Joint United States–Israel engineering studies are in progress for a dual-purpose reactor to provide both power and distilled water. It will take several years to develop it on an experimental basis. Another exciting prospect for the future is the harnessing of sunshine, which is Israel's most plentiful resource. All over the country, solar heaters have sprouted on roof tops to provide domestic hot water; and a large solar-energy pilot plant has been erected in the south.

Israel's access to the Dead Sea opens up a great natural storehouse. Centuries of evaporation have made its waters a dense solution of chemical salts—five times the concentration found in ordinary sea water. At the southern tip, at Sdom (the Biblical Sodom), the Dead Sea Works were by 1968 extracting more than 500,000 tons of potash a year, as well as bromide and common salt. The growing market in the Far East, reached through the port of Eilat, has opened up a big future for this almost limitless source of chemical salts. An ambitious $100 million expansion program has been carried out, with a huge area of the Dead Sea enclosed by miles of dikes dividing the area into shallow pans so that the sun can quickly evaporate the liquid and leave the salts and minerals free to be pumped into the separating machinery.

Another "natural resource" is the open coastline of the Mediterranean. In 1948, the merchant fleet of Israel consisted of four old vessels adding up to only 6,000 tons. By 1968 the Israeli flag was flown by more than 100 modern vessels with a capacity of one and a quarter million tons, including transatlantic passenger ships, cargo vessels, citrus boats and oil tankers; and many more ships are on order. (The name of the national carrier is the Zim Line.) Haifa Port has been greatly expanded, and a second deep-water harbor has been built at Ashdod, south of Tel Aviv. At the

"OUR DAILY BREAD"

southernmost point of Israel, Eilat is being developed as the gateway to Africa and the East.

Israel has also taken to the air. The El Al National Airlines, which began with two small planes in 1948, has grown into a large concern. It was one of the first airlines to operate Boeing 707 and 720-B jets. Its staff and crew are almost entirely Israeli. There is also an internal airline company called Arkia.

The tourist industry is expanding rapidly. In this field Israel has obvious assets—its Biblical past, modern nation-building, superb climate, varied landscape and colorful blend of peoples. From 20,000 in 1950, the annual number of tourists swelled to nearly 500,000 in 1968. The inclusion of the Old City of Jerusalem and renewed access to Bethlehem and the West Bank area are an important fillip to tourism, which is one of the country's biggest earners of foreign currency.

As German reparations, American grants in aid and other intergovernmental sources of foreign capital have declined, the gap must be filled by a flow of private investment. Israel's Capital Investment Law offers attractive benefits and concessions to approved enterprises.

Israel's expectation is that science will overcome the poverty of nature. Dr. Chaim Weizmann, the first President of Israel, was also a brilliant scientist. It is related that Lord Peel, Chairman of the 1936 Royal Commission, asked him the purpose of his test-tube experiments while visiting Dr. Weizmann in his Rehovot laboratory. The answer was, "I am creating absorptive capacity." Today, in the Weizmann Institute, the Hebrew University, the Haifa Technion, the Agricultural Research Station in Rehovot, the Arid Zone Research Institute in Beersheba and the projects of the

Research Council and the Atomic Energy Commission, Israel's scientists restlessly seek the answers to the country's problems. In mastering scientific tools and using them to carve out its own progress, Israel may well become a natural bridge between the advanced technology of the West and the less developed nations. It was this hope that inspired the remarkable international conference at the Weizmann Institute in August, 1960, on the theme of "The Role of Science in the Development of New States." The conference was attended by 126 statesmen and scientists from forty-one countries. Three similar Rehovot Conferences have followed on specific problems of developing countries: one on agricultural planning, the second on fiscal and monetary questions, and the third, in 1967, on health.

AID TO DEVELOPING COUNTRIES

Israel has been sharing its own experience in development and nation-building with more than sixty other new states, and developing lands, which form an arc stretching from Southeast Asia through the Mediterranean and Africa to Latin America. The ties of practical cooperation take many forms: hundreds of Israel experts abroad; thousands of trainees and students in Israel; on-the-spot instruction courses in Africa; joint companies engaged in development of merchant shipping, construction, hotels, and water resources; model farm villages and planned rural projects; and the training of national security forces. Israel believes in self-help and mutual help for the new countries.

THE HISTADRUT

The Histadrut—the General Federation of Israel Labor—is the most powerful body in the country, next to the government itself. When it was formed in 1920 with 5,000 members, Palestine was undeveloped and just beginning the period of the British Mandate. It had no statehood, no industry and no real capitalist class. The new federation had not only to safeguard employees, but also to create jobs for them in cooperative enterprises as well as provide the housing, health and social services which could help them to survive in a difficult land.

Today, the Histadrut is a protean and pervasive organism. Its labor-union network embraces 70 percent of the earning population, from the *kibbutznik* to the self-employed professional man, and includes 300,000 housewives and 30,000 Arab members. Its medical fund, the *Kupat Holim*, serves two Israelis out of three and operates 15 hospitals, 12 convalescent homes, and about 1,000 clinics. The Histadrut's cultural activities cover adult education and language instruction, a daily newspaper called *Davar*, a book-publishing house, mobile libraries, a theater for new immigrants, and musical and theatrical activities in the kibbutzim. The industrial, commercial and financial enterprises associated with the Histadrut give it control of about one quarter of the country's economy.

COOPERATIVE FARMING

The Bible depicts the Hebrews first as nomads wandering with their flocks, and then as tillers of the soil and shepherds. In this later phase, their social and religious life fitted into the cycle of the agricultural seasons, and a man's dream of contentment was to sit at peace beneath his own vine and fig tree. During the centuries of the Dispersion the Jews were cut off from contact with the land, but in their synagogues they clung to the rituals once evolved by their farming ancestors.

The revival of Jewish agriculture in Palestine started less than ninety years ago. The first settlements, like Petah Tikvah (1878), and Rishon-le-Zion, simply followed the model of a European peasant village, where each person lived in his own cottage and cultivated his own patch of land. In 1909 a little group of new settlers—ten young men and two young women—were allotted a piece of land in the Jordan Valley just south of Lake Tiberias, and started to work it as a group, pooling their efforts and earnings. This was Degania, the first experiment from which evolved the *kibbutz*, the type of collective farming settlement which is unique to Israel, and which has attracted worldwide attention. Degania is sixty years old and still going strong. From its tiny seed there has sprouted a network of more than 300 kibbutzim from one end of the country to the other, ranging from the latest border outposts with about fifty young people, to old, well-established kibbutzim with populations of more than a thousand, in some cases including the grandchildren of the founders. Clearly the

"OUR DAILY BREAD"

kibbutz has long since ceased being an experiment and has become a permanent feature of the Israel landscape.

To understand its sturdy hold, the kibbutz must be seen not merely as a way of farming, but also as a complete way of life. At the beginning there were strong practical reasons for its existence. The newcomers of the Second Aliyah were burning with Zionist zeal to redeem the land, but they themselves had neither means nor training. The Palestine countryside of their dreams was a harsh and neglected land, their Arab neighbors were often hostile and the Turkish administration was corrupt and indifferent. If they wanted to venture on new and creative paths instead of just subsisting as the hired hands of the older Jewish farmers, it was obvious that they would survive better as groups than as individuals. This answer to the difficult challenge also fitted their own philosophy. They brought with them from Russia and Poland the Tolstoyan ideals of self-labor and equal sharing which were applied to Zionist pioneering. In the kibbutz there is no privilege, but absolute equality among all members. The system is voluntary—a new member can join if the kibbutz approves of him after a year of probation, and any member can leave whenever he wishes. It is democratic, functioning through a series of committees elected by a "town meeting" at which all the members gather, usually once a week, to make decisions. There is no private property—everything but personal belongings is owned in common, and the individual works for the group at whatever task is assigned to him by the works committee, while the group takes care of his needs.

In addition to the kibbutz, there are looser types of cooperative agricultural settlements. One such is the *moshav ovdim* (cooperative workers' settlement). The first moshav was set up in 1921, its kernel a group of dissidents from Degania who had made a painful decision to break away from their comrades and run their farming and their living in a way less tightly organized and less uncompromisingly pooled than that of the kibbutz. In the following years, scores of moshavim sprang up around the country. The moshav pattern lies between that of the kibbutz and the unrestricted private farming of the older villages. A member of the moshav lives in his own family house and farms on his own account. But the ground belongs to the Jewish National Fund, like that of the kibbutz; the holdings of all members are the same size; no member employs any hired labor; there is cooperative marketing and buying of supplies; grazing lands and the use of heavy farm equipment may be shared; and the settlement operates democratically through a village council and a system of committees.

After 1948 the kibbutz system continued to expand, but its relative importance in Israel's over-all development declined. The kibbutz was largely bypassed in the large-scale land settlement which followed mass immigration. For most newcomers, the ideals and mores of the kibbutz meant nothing, and the departure from conventional family life was incomprehensible. The smallholders' village of the moshav type became the standard pattern for the immigrants who were being funneled into the new areas. In the second decade of statehood, the number of kibbutzim increased by 70 percent, but the number of moshavim by 300 percent.

This trend, however, does not diminish the world-wide interest in the kibbutz, Israel's unique collective adventure. Nor can it detract from the dazzling role of the kibbutz

"OUR DAILY BREAD"

members in the years before statehood, when they were the elite of the Yishuv—the backbone of its self-defense, its pioneering and its leadership in every field of national effort. Now that there is a state, a government, an army and a rapidly swelling immigrant population, the kibbutzim are no longer as much in the center of things; but they remain the embodiment of *chalutziut*, of Israel's best pioneering qualities.

Part Two

From Dan to Eilat

CHAPTER 5

Jerusalem, the Golden

For out of Zion shall go forth the law, and the word of the Lord from Jerusalem.
—Isaiah 2:3

If I forget thee O Jerusalem, let my right hand forget her cunning.
If I do not remember thee, let my tongue cleave to the roof of my mouth; if I prefer not Jerusalem above my chief joy.
—Psalm 137:5–6

Ten parts of beauty were allotted the world at large [the Jewish Sages said]: and of these Jerusalem assumed nine measures and the rest of the world but one . . . ten parts of suffering were visited upon the world—nine for Jerusalem and one for the world.
—Talmud, Gemarah Kiddushim 49b

THE TURBULENT HISTORY

At Sha'ar Hagai (Gate to the Valley), which is still known by its Arabic name Bab-el-Wad, the highway from the coast cuts into the hills. As one's car climbs into the narrow gorge, flanked by the pine plantations growing between boulders, there are reminders of the 1948 siege—russet-painted remains of vehicles sprawling in the ditch like the skeletons of long-dead animals. They lie where they were burnt out, silent memorials to the truck convoys which battled their way through Arab ambushes to bring supplies to the starving city. At that time ordinary men and women suddenly found themselves at one with their stubborn Jewish ancestors whose bellies had been gnawed by hunger and thirst in this eternal city when the eagles of the Roman Tenth Legion were planted before its gates, nineteen centuries earlier.

Emerging from the Bab-el-Wad pass, the road winds up into expanding vistas of hill and valley with, on a clear day, a backward glimpse of the coastal plain and the Mediterranean. This ancient Biblical landscape of Judea has a bleak beauty which is hard to define, but catches one by the throat. Here is neither the alpine majesty of European mountains nor the soft domestic charm of English hill country. Eroded to the bone by centuries of storm and neglect, striated by horizontal lines of rock ledges, these hills usually have an air of brooding and a stony rejection of man's antlike husbandry.

Towards evening, however, the landscape is drenched with magic color, as the orange afterglow of sunset fades into soft and lovely shades of mauve and purple; and in the

JERUSALEM, THE GOLDEN

spring the starkness is briefly painted over with fresh green grass and the brilliant hues of wild flowers, until this enchantment is burnt away again by the *khamsin* wind and the summer sun. But the tenacity of the Jewish settlers is slowly reviving even these austere hillsides. The most regular travelers up and down the mountain constantly rub their eyes in amazement at the saplings which suddenly become visible between the rocks, the new stone-walled terraces climbing out of the valleys and planted with vines and fruit trees, and the hundreds of little red-roofed cottages which now crown the hilltops and march along the skyline ridges commanding the western approaches to Jerusalem.

Going to Jerusalem from the coast is an *aliyah* (going-up), a word which implies not merely a physical ascent but also a spiritual one. (It is used, for instance, in the synagogue service when one "goes up" to read a portion of the Torah.) As you sweep smoothly along the new four-lane highway in an hour's drive to the capital, what a goodly company you are in! Up this pass, in Biblical times, the Hebrew farmers and villagers rode or trudged, bringing the fruits of their fields to the Temple and coming to celebrate in Jerusalem the three festivals of Pesach, Shavuoth and Succoth. Through these mountains came swinging the spearmen of the Pharaohs, the centurions of Rome, the weary remnants of the Crusader armies, and many other fighting men before and since. And throughout the Middle Ages there passed Christian and Jewish pilgrims on their three-day trip from Jaffa, moving slowly along the rough mountain track on foot or on donkey or camel back, banded together in groups with armed guards to protect them from brigands and wild animals. The local Arab chiefs, like the notorious sheiks of Abu Ghosh, used to extract protection money from them in the form of a head tax called *ghafar*. In his well-known guide book, Zev Vilnay refers to the following question put to Rabbi ben Zimra, who settled in the Holy Land in the seventeenth century:

> "The pilgrims who have to pay ghafar, so much per head, are they entitled to change their clothes so that they shall be mistaken for Arabs and pay nothing?" On which the Rabbi ruled, "Since this only entails loss of money it is forbidden to Israel to wear Arab dress."

Later, the Turks built a line of seventeen guardhouses to protect the pilgrim road; the last of them still stands in a ruined state at the Bab-el-Wad corner. The first coach to make the trip was that of Emperor Franz Joseph of Austria, for whom the road was especially prepared in 1869; and the first motor vehicle was that brought by an American tourist in 1908.

Ten miles outside the city is the Hill of Kiriat Ye'arim (Kirjath-Jearim) where the Ark of the Covenant rested for twenty years after it was recovered from the Philistines and before King David installed it in Jerusalem. Today there is near this site a church and convent of Our Lady of the Covenant, surmounted by a huge concrete statue of the Virgin Mary.

On the other side of the road, looking like an old Italian painting, is the large Arab village of Abu Ghosh. In its center is a fine Crusader church. Set in the eastern wall of the church is a stone tablet inscribed in Latin, "Detachment of the Tenth Legion," left behind by the Roman forces which occupied this site and sacked Jerusalem in A.D. 70. This church is part of a Crusader castle built by the Knights Hospitalers and known as the Castle of the Spring or the Castle of Emmaus.

JERUSALEM, THE GOLDEN

A little farther on there are the ruins of a twelfth- to thirteenth-century Crusader monastery and church called Aquabella (Beautiful Water). It gets its name from the Roman occupation twenty centuries ago. Just beyond is a round hilltop still called Castel—from the Latin *castellum*, a fort—and the reason is obvious, for it completely dominates the bend in the road and the valley below. It was a fortified position for the Romans and the Crusaders, and in the early stages of Israel's War of Independence in 1948 it changed hands several times.

Over to the left, the most prominent object on the horizon is the tall minaret of the Mosque of Nebi Samuel, the site, by Moslem tradition, of the prophet Samuel's tomb. The Crusaders called this place Mountjoy and built a church there in the twelfth century.

From the settlement of Mevaseret Yerushalayim (Herald of Jerusalem), the first buildings of the Holy City suddenly come into view, spilling over a lofty ridge five miles ahead.

On entering the city for the first time, one cannot but feel the emotional impact of 4,000 years of continuous history which have given the very word "Jerusalem" a profoundly mystic sound to hundreds of millions of Christians, Jews and Moslems throughout the world. This is the city of David and Solomon, of Isaiah and Jeremiah, of Ezra and Nehemiah, of Judas Maccabaeus and his brothers. This is the city of Jesus' last ministry and His crucifixion. And Moslems hold this city to be the place from which Mohammed is believed to have ascended to Heaven, and which they accordingly regard as next after Mecca and Medina in holiness.

It seems as if there has always existed a Jerusalem cradled

in this high amphitheater, withdrawn from the busy traffic of the coastal plain and the desert caravan routes—closer to eternal things as it contemplates the rugged landscape and breathes in the pure mountain air.

Nothing about the serene air of Jerusalem today recalls its thirty-three centuries of turbulent history, including earthquakes, nineteen military sieges, two total destructions by conquerors and many rebuildings. The existence and stubborn survival of an important city at this spot at first seems to defy reason. It is far from the seacoast or any river basin, and off the great caravan routes of early times. Surrounded by bleak hills, it is difficult to reach and in past ages had scanty water sources—a single natural spring below the eastern wall, and underground cisterns hewn out of the rock to hold rain water. But its position on the great divide between the coastal plain and the Jordan Valley, and at the heart of the highlands of Judea and Samaria, has always made Jerusalem a strategic prize.

Its beginnings are lost in the mists of antiquity. It is already there when Abraham the Patriarch arrives in the Promised Land; Abraham accepts "bread and wine" from its king, Melchizedek (Genesis 14:18–20). Centuries later, when Joshua invades the country through Jericho, it is the King of Jerusalem, Adoni-zedek, who forms a coalition of five Canaanite rulers to block his advance (Joshua 10:1–23). (The word *zedek*—"righteousness"—as part of the names of these two Jerusalem kings suggests the early religious significance of the city.) Since the Book of Genesis, how often has Jerusalem been pagan, Jewish, Moslem and Christian; how many different men other than Jews have sat here in the seat of power—Canaanites, Jebusites, Egyptians, Babylonians and Persians; Greeks and Romans; Moslem

JERUSALEM, THE GOLDEN

Arabs, Seljuks, Fatimids, Crusaders, Mamelukes, Ottomans and British. Under King Solomon, Herod the Great, the Emperor Constantine and Sultan Suleiman the Magnificent its buildings burgeoned into splendor. At other times it was reduced to rubble, with the blood of the slaughtered citizens flowing down its gutters.

But throughout the flux of these thousands of years there runs one constant thread—the unique attachment of the Jewish people to Jerusalem. This attachment has remained unbroken from the time King David made Jerusalem the capital to the time David Ben-Gurion did likewise, 3,000 years later. Through all the centuries of dispersion, in the farthest corners of the earth, Jews have prayed for the return to Zion and built their synagogues with the Holy Ark pointing in the direction of the destroyed Temple of Solomon. History has no parallel to this mystic bond; without it, there would have been no State of Israel.

When Sir Moses Montefiore, the renowned Anglo-Jewish philanthropist, visited Palestine for the first time in 1827, he found some 2,000 Jews in Jerusalem, huddled together in the confined courtyards and alleys of the Old City's Jewish quarter and existing chiefly on the *halukkah*, the charitable funds donated by pious Jews abroad. Distressed at their condition, Montefiore built a new residential quarter for some of them outside the walls; it was called Yemin Moshe (Right Hand of Moses) in his honor. He also provided them with a windmill to grind their flour which still stands as a distinctive Jerusalem landmark. Yemin Moshe faces Mount Zion and the Old City across the narrow Valley of Hinnom (notorious as the site of the human sacrifices to the god-idol Moloch which took place in pre-Hebrew times). Its stone houses, with their cut-out rooftops echoing

FROM DAN TO EILAT

the design of the Old City wall, were destined to play an important part in the War of Liberation. Taking the full brunt of attack from the Jordanian Arab Legion (based in the Old City) and at times completely surrounded, Yemin Moshe held out for months and made possible the Israelis' retention of nearby Mount Zion.

After the founding of Yemin Moshe, the new area of Jerusalem expanded steadily and numerous other Jewish quarters were established. The largest of them were Mea Shearim and Mahne Yehuda, to which Russian and Polish Jews transplanted the life of the ghetto; while Oriental communities from Bokhara, Persia, Kurdistan and Yemen each set up its own distinctive quarter. To the southwest of the Old City Bavarian Templars built the small neat houses of the German Colony, and beyond them the Greek Colony was established and planted with cypress trees.

The Russians built a great compound for their pilgrims, with a large church standing in the center; and fine monasteries and hospices were erected by the French, the Italians, the Ethiopians and others.

This expansion took place in the last period of Turkish rule. The city was in bad shape, however, when General Allenby entered it in 1917. As an official publication later described it:

> The state of Jerusalem in December 1917 can hardly be imagined by those who see it now. No sanitary arrangements of any sort existed in the Old City and practically none in the new. The only water supply was derived from private rain-fed cisterns. There were no available food supplies in the city. Women and children were to be seen walking in the streets in every stage of emaciation and were besieging government offices for a crust of bread.

JERUSALEM, THE GOLDEN

Under the thirty years of British rule the New City grew steadily in size, dignity and beauty, due to the influx of Jewish immigrants and capital, the needs of the Mandatory administration, and a genuine official pride in Jerusalem. The city's planning department decreed that all new buildings should be built or faced with local stone, a pink-gold sandstone. The authorities brought in architects and experts, built roads and struggled with the problems of sewers that had to be channeled out of solid rock and a water supply that had to be pumped up from the Sharon Plain, forty miles away. The street names, in English, Hebrew and Arabic, were written on blue tiles baked in the Old City by Armenian craftsmen.

Far beyond the older Jewish quarters there sprouted a whole new perimeter of residential suburbs—Rehavia, an elegant middle-class quarter of villas and gardens; the northern quarters of Geula, Kerem Avraham and Sanhedria; Talpiot and Armona on the ridge to the south near Ramat Rachel; the garden suburbs of Beit Hakerem, Bayit Vegan and Yafeh Nof in the hills to the west. Affluent Arab merchants and professional men set up new quarters of their own in Katamon, Talbieh and Sheikh Jarrah. In the town itself, modern buildings started to give New Jerusalem something of a skyline—the business center contained the General Post Office, the Bank Leumi and the Assicurazioni buildings; the King David Hotel facing the towering Y.M.C.A., the Jewish Agency compound and the Yeshurun Synagogue next door and looking down from the heights were the Hebrew University, the Hadassah Hospital and Government House. Streets like Jaffa Road, King George Street and Ben Yehuda Street lost their sleepy look and turned into bustling city thoroughfares lined with mod-

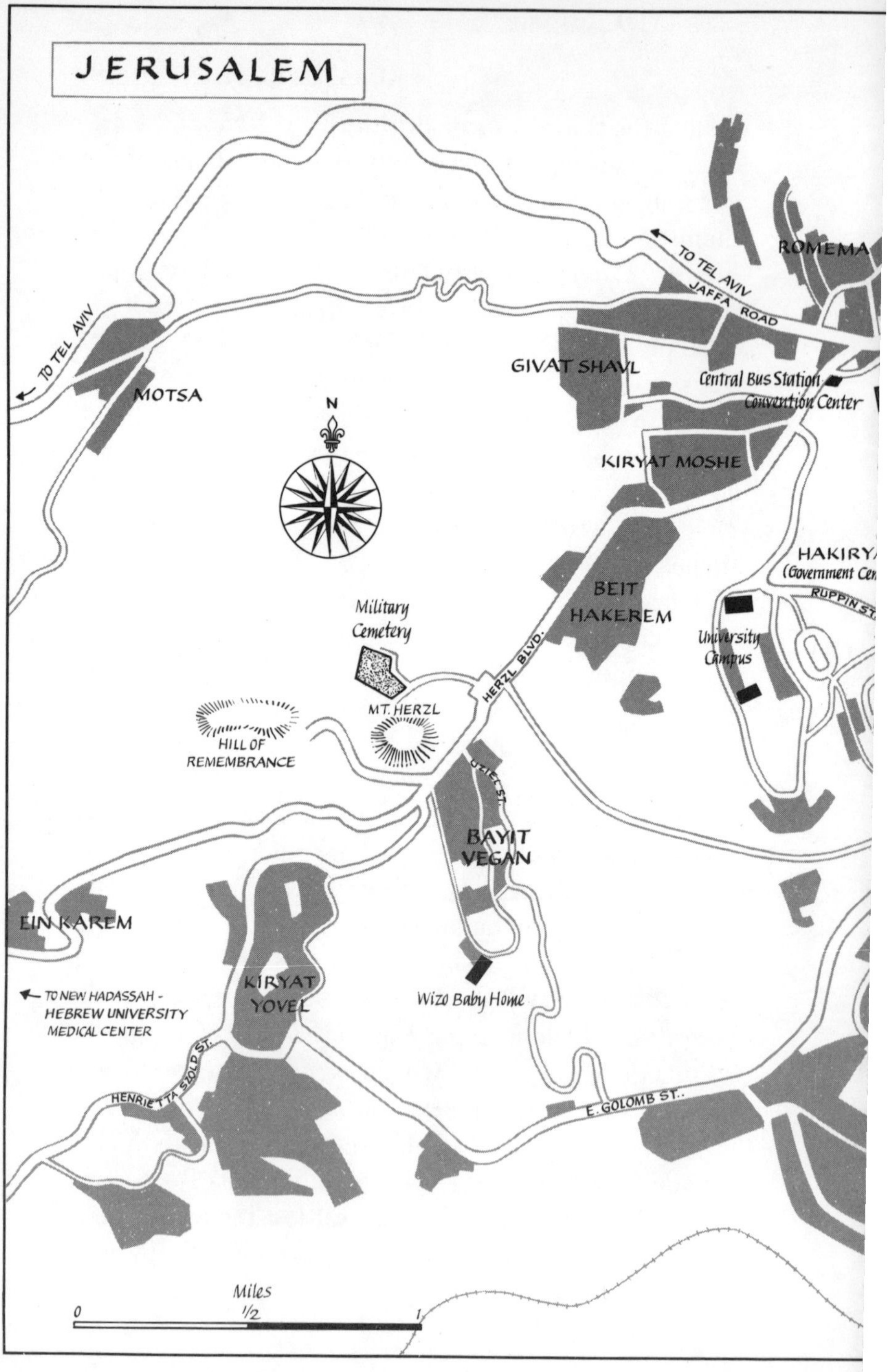
JERUSALEM
TO TEL AVIV
MOTSA
N
TO TEL AVIV
JAFFA ROAD
ROMEMA
GIVAT SHAVL
Central Bus Station
Convention Center
KIRYAT MOSHE
HAKIRY
(Government Cen
RUPPIN ST.
BEIT
HAKEREM
University
Campus
Military
Cemetery
HERZL BLVD.
MT. HERZL
HILL OF
REMEMBRANCE
UZIEL ST.
BAYIT
VEGAN
EIN KAREM
KIRYAT
YOVEL
Wizo Baby Home
TO NEW HADASSAH -
HEBREW UNIVERSITY
MEDICAL CENTER
HENRIETTA SZOLD ST.
E. GOLOMB ST.
Miles
0
1/2
1

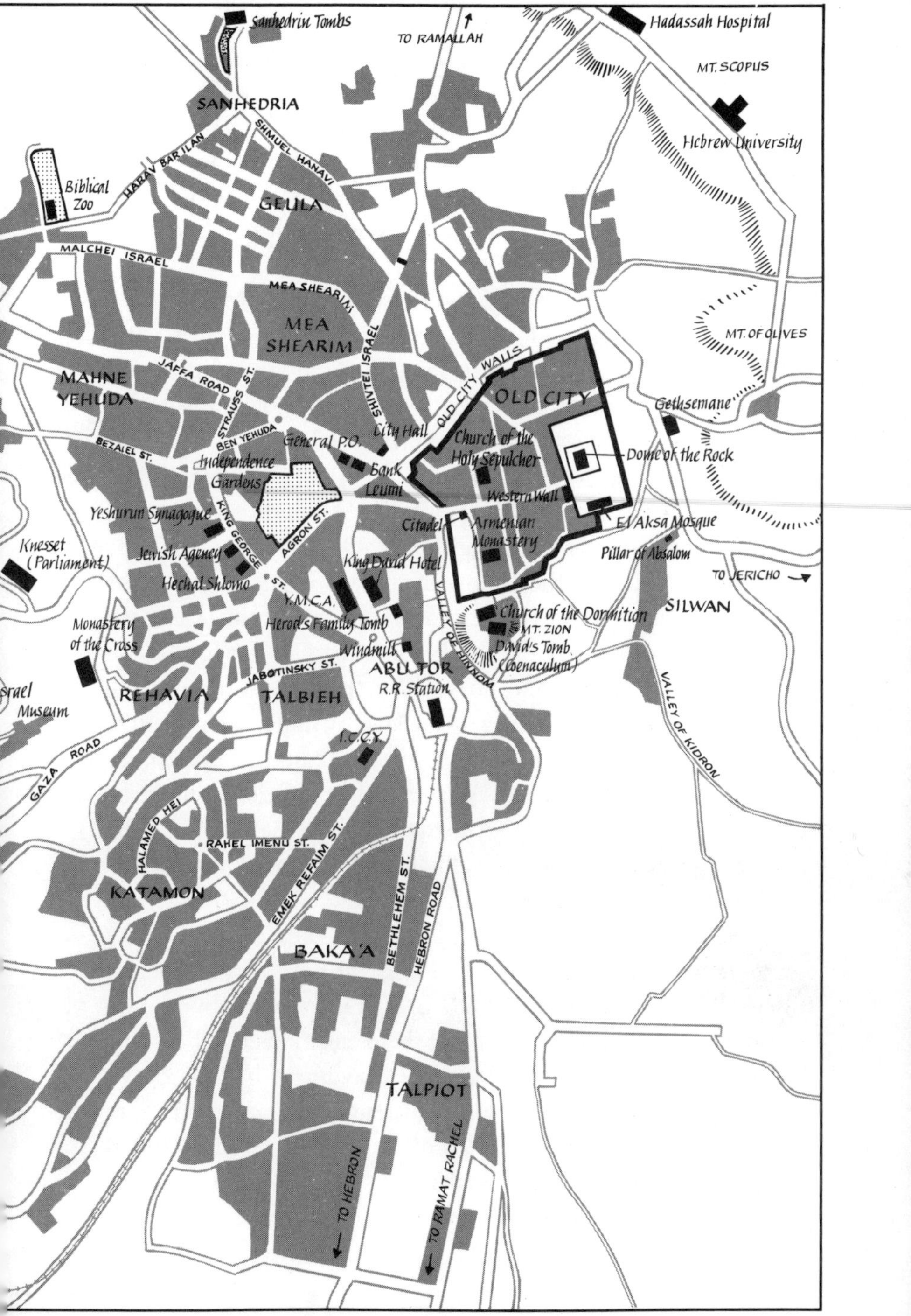
Sanhedrin Tombs
TO RAMALLAH
Hadassah Hospital
MT. SCOPUS
Hebrew University
SANHEDRIA
SHMUEL HANAVI
HARAV BAR ILAN
Biblical Zoo
GEULA
MALCHEI ISRAEL
MEA SHEARIM
MEA SHEARIM
SHIVTEI ISRAEL
MT. OF OLIVES
OLD CITY WALLS
MAHNE YEHUDA
JAFFA ROAD
STRAUSS ST.
OLD CITY
Gethsemane
BEN YEHUDA
City Hall
General P.O.
Church of the Holy Sepulcher
Dome of the Rock
BEZALEL ST.
Independence Gardens
Bank Leumi
Western Wall
Yeshurun Synagogue
KING GEORGE
AGRON ST.
Citadel
Armenian Monastery
El Aksa Mosque
Knesset (Parliament)
Jewish Agency
King David Hotel
Pillar of Absalom
Hechal Shlomo
ST.
TO JERICHO
Y.M.C.A.
VALLEY OF HINNOM
SILWAN
Church of the Dormition
Monastery of the Cross
Herod's Family Tomb
MT. ZION
Windmill
David's Tomb (Coenaculum)
JABOTINSKY ST.
ABU TOR
R.R. Station
Israel Museum
REHAVIA
TALBIEH
VALLEY OF KIDRON
I.C.C.Y.
GAZA ROAD
HALAMED HEI
EMEK REFAIM ST.
RAHEL IMENU ST.
KATAMON
BETHLEHEM ST.
HEBRON ROAD
BAKA'A
TALPIOT
TO HEBRON
TO RAMAT RACHEL

ern stores and restaurants. By the end of the Mandate in 1948, the new Jerusalem had become a handsome city of 150,000 people (two-thirds of them Jews), sprawled over a rolling expanse of ridges and valleys a dozen times the area of the walled Old City.

Jewish and Arab quarters were so interwoven in the New City that when the fighting broke out at the end of 1947, there was no defined "front line," but a confused intimacy of raiding and sniping. The communal geography during these months was further complicated by the "security zones"—sections of the city in which the British troops and officials had barricaded themselves behind barbed wire. Events moved swiftly to a climax. On May 14, 1948, the Mandate expired, the State of Israel was proclaimed and the Arab invasion armies advanced. In Jerusalem, the last of the British disappeared up the Nablus road to the north, on their way to Haifa and home. The thrust of Jordan's Arab Legion into the New City was halted by hand-to-hand street battles, while the Egyptian forces attacking from the south were stopped at Ramat Rachel. Most of the non-Jewish quarters of the New City, such as the German Colony, the Greek Colony, Baka'a, Talbieh and Katamon, were captured by small Haganah detachments, which thus established a solid and contiguous Jewish-held area.

A painful setback to Israel was the loss of the ancient Jewish quarter of the Old City. Surrounded by 20,000 armed Arabs, the quarter was heroically defended by just over 100 Haganah members. By May 27, it had been partially reduced to rubble, and a surrender to the Arab Legion was negotiated with the help of the Red Cross and United Nations officials. The male survivors were taken as prisoners to Amman, while 1,700 women and children, old people and wounded were evacuated to the Jewish-held New City.

Another serious Jewish reverse was the failure to oust the Arab Legion from Latrun, which would have opened the Jerusalem–Tel Aviv highway. (It was reopened only in 1967, after the Six-Day War.) For nearly four weeks after the State was proclaimed, Jewish Jerusalem remained isolated and was pounded by more than 10,000 shells from the Arab guns on the surrounding heights. Despite 1,738 casualties during these weeks, morale remained unshaken, tightly rationed food and water were distributed, medical services functioned effectively and school classes continued in air-raid shelters. The English daily newspaper, the *Palestine Post* (now the *Jerusalem Post*), under its courageous editor, Gershon Agron, did not miss a single issue.

Meanwhile, before the first truce (June 11, 1948), the siege had already been pierced by Israel's "Burma Road"—a rough and, in places, precipitous track cut through the mountains under cover of darkness, to skirt round Arab-held Latrun. At first supplies had to be carried over the worst stretch on the backs of Jerusalem's middle-aged Home Guard, holding each other's shirttails in the dark; but later, vehicles could get through with the help of tractors, and a hundred tons of precious supplies reached the beleaguered city almost every night. The "Burma Road" remained the only link with Jewish Jerusalem for months after the truce, until a new highway was constructed.*

In 1949 the armistice agreement between Israel and Jordan bisected the city with an armistice line from north to south that passed close to the Old City wall, with Mount

---

* For a full account of the siege, one should read *The Faithful City* by Dr. Dov Joseph, who was at the time Israel's Military Governor of Jerusalem.

Zion on the Israel side. The Hebrew University and the Hadassah Hospital on Mount Scopus remained an isolated enclave held by an Israel police garrison that was supplied every two weeks by a truck convoy under a United Nations flag. "Government House," on the Hill of Evil Counsel, to the south of the city (the former residence of the British High Commissioner), was in an "area . . . between the lines" and became the U.N. headquarters for supervising the armistice.

The only official crossing point between the zones was at the Mandelbaum Gate, where the meetings of the Mixed Armistice Commission took place. Once a year, at Christmas, special arrangements were made for Arab Christians from Israel to visit Bethlehem, eight miles away. Jews were denied any access to the Western Wall (the "Wailing Wall"); most of the Jewish quarter and its sixty synagogues and religious academies in the Old City were destroyed, and the ancient cemetery on the Mount of Olives was desecrated. From time to time, the peace of the city was broken by shooting incidents across the no-man's-land, or by conflicts concerning Mount Scopus.

The nineteen-year division of Jerusalem was abruptly and unexpectedly ended by the Six-Day War in June, 1967. It had been hoped in Israel that Jordan would not enter the war, or would at most make a token show of force. Israel's area of Jerusalem was only lightly held by a single infantry brigade of local reserves. On the morning of June 5, when fighting was already raging against the Egyptian forces in the Sinai Desert, Jordanian artillery, mortars and machine guns from the surrounding hills opened a heavy barrage of

JERUSALEM, THE GOLDEN

fire on the civilian Jewish quarters of Jerusalem. During the next forty-eight hours, tens of thousands of mortar bombs rained down upon these quarters, while their inhabitants remained crammed into basement shelters. More than 500 civilian casualties were inflicted in the first few hours.

Later that day, the Jordanian forces started moving forward. They occupied Government House, but were ejected by the Israelis two hours later. Other Jordanian troops massed for an attack on Mount Scopus. It was clearly the Jordanian plan to gain complete control of all the high ground dominating the city.

The Defense Minister, General Dayan, and the General Staff realized that Jerusalem was in serious danger. A reserve armored brigade was moved up from the coastal plain to Ma'aleh ha Hamisha, a kibbutz west of Jerusalem, and was ordered to advance through the mountainous country north of Jerusalem and then wheel south. It fought its way all night through fortified hill positions and minefields. By next morning it reached the Ramallah road and turned south toward Mount Scopus. Meanwhile, on the previous afternoon, a paratroop brigade that had been assigned to an operational jump in Sinai was rushed up to Jerusalem instead, and just after midnight was flung into a direct assault on the Jordanian positions in the suburbs of East Jerusalem. After the fiercest hand-to-hand fighting of the war, the paratroops broke through to positions close to the north wall of the Old City. On Tuesday night units of the armored brigade and the Jerusalem Brigade took the Arab-held ridges on the south and east, so that the Old City was virtually encircled. On Wednesday morning the ring was completed as the paratroops, with the help of air support, advanced along the ridge from Mount Scopus and also drove up the mountain road in a frontal charge and captured the Augusta Victoria area and the Mount of Olives.

The Israel forces then converged on the Old City, broke into it through St. Stephen's Gate near the northeastern corner, and fought their way through narrow, twisting alleys against pockets of resistance and rooftop snipers' nests. A few minutes later the brigade commander signaled GHQ: "The Temple Mount is ours," and went on to the Western Wall, where the first exhausted soldiers rested their heads on the venerable stones with tears of emotion running down their cheeks.

For the first time in nineteen centuries, the whole of Jerusalem was under Jewish control.

Jerusalem's domes, minarets, spires and towers mark the rich diversity of its religious life as a city holy to three great faiths.

Its population in 1969 comprised 210,000 Jews and 65,000 Arabs. Most of the Arabs are Moslems. The Christians (Arab and European) number only 13,000, but are divided among no less than twenty-five sects, in four main groups: Orthodox (Greek, Roumanian, Russian); Catholic (Roman, Greek, Maronite, Syrian, Armenian, Chaldean); Monophysite (Armenian, Coptic, Syrian Jacobite, Ethiopian); and Protestant (Anglican, Lutheran, Baptist, Mennonite and others).

Jerusalem is the seat of the Greek Orthodox, Latin, and Armenian patriarchs in the Holy Land, as well as of the archbishops and bishops of the Anglican, Greek Catholic, Coptic, Syrian and Ethiopian churches. Since the Crusades, the Franciscan Order has been the *Custos* of Catholic

JERUSALEM, THE GOLDEN

holy places, and its emblem, a form of Maltese Cross with four simple crosses between its arms, is a familiar sight.

The traditional garments of the pious of all faiths—Christian monks and nuns, Chasidic Jews and Moslem kadis—add their distinctive notes to a Jerusalem crowd.

The orthodox East European Jews, in their own quarters, preserve·intact the customs, the garb and the Yiddish language of the Polish ghetto and the Russian *shtetel* (village) of past centuries—the men with beards and *payot* (side curls), because of the Biblical injunction against shaving, and dressed on the Sabbath and Holy Days in silk kaftans and fur-brimmed hats. For them, Jerusalem was, is, and should remain a Holy City, where one ekes out a livelihood in order to pursue a life of prayer and study. To them, the recovery of the Western Wall came as an act of divine favor.

In the Yemenite, Bukharan, Persian and other Oriental Jewish quarters, the people lead equally pious lives in accordance with their own traditions and customs.

In the cobbled lanes and cramped courtyards of Mea Shearim or Mahne Yehuda, in the numerous synagogues and *yeshivot* (Talmudic seminaries), the orthodox Jew is fighting a rear-guard action in a modern, secular age. The oddest sight in Jerusalem is that of religious Jews in Sabbath or festival garb threading their way through the crowded Moslem bazaar on their way to the Wall.

Compared to Tel Aviv or Haifa, Jerusalem is basically a poor town, with little industry and not much arable land in the surrounding hill region. The "middle class" consists of intellectuals rather than businessmen: civil servants, university professors and students, and members of the free professions (such as doctors in private practice). The "work-

• 93

ing class" is made up of workers engaged in construction, the building trades and light industry, small shopkeepers and artisans, and employees in the hotel and tourist industry which has been booming since the Six-Day War.

More western immigrants now want to live in the capital, and there is a housing shortage. This will be relieved as new residential suburbs are developed, especially at Givat Hamivtar, the empty space between Sanhedria and Mount Scopus, to the north of the Old City.

THE OLD CITY

The walled Old City is only a small fraction of the area of Jerusalem, since today modern suburbs spread out in all directions. To the east, south and west the Old City is held in the fork of the Kidron and Hinnom valleys. Only from the north is there a level approach to the wall, and it is from that side that the city was usually attacked.

The wall is pierced by eight gateways: the Jaffa Gate next to the Citadel on the west; the New Gate on the northwestern corner opposite Notre Dame de France Monastery; the Damascus Gate and Herod's Gate to the north; St. Stephen's Gate (known in Hebrew as the Gate of Lions) and the walled-up Golden Gate to the east; and to the south the Dung Gate (near the Western Wall) and the Zion Gate leading onto Mount Zion.

The present wall of the Old City was built in the sixteenth century by the Turkish Sultan Suleiman the Magnificent and is two and a half miles in circumference. It follows the line of Emperor Hadrian's wall of the second century A.D.; and in parts of the present wall the masonry

JERUSALEM, THE GOLDEN

in the upper courses can be seen to rest on much older stonework.

In the twelve centuries between King David and Hadrian, the size and location of Jerusalem, and therefore the course of its ramparts, went through a number of changes. David's city remained substantially on the site of the Jebusite town he had captured. It included Mount Ophel, on the slope south of the present Haram-esh-Sharif, and curved down to the pool of Siloam (Shiloah) in the Kidron Valley. King Solomon enclosed the Mount Moriah area north of Ophel and there built the Temple, with his palace just below it. Later, the city spread westward to form the Upper City where the Jaffa Gate now is, and a new wall was looped around this expanded area.

There is some argument among the scholars as to where the north wall lay at the time of Jesus. On this depends the authenticity of the site of Calvary, located by tradition within the Basilica of the Holy Sepulcher. The original Hill of Calvary would have had to be outside the wall at that time.

The wall started by Herod Agrippa I, in A.D. 42, ran some way north of the present one so as to take in the then-new northern suburb of Bethesda. Its precise location is still a matter of argument.

The space inside the walls has for centuries been divided into four main quarters, each named for the religious community that has been concentrated in it. The Christian quarter is in the northwest, with the Church of the Holy Sepulcher as its hub. South of it is the Armenian quarter. The northeastern part of the Old City is the Moslem quarter, a good deal of it taken up by the great raised platform of the Haram-esh-Sharif, which contains the Dome of the Rock and the El Aksa Mosque. This is the Jewish Temple Mount, on which the First and Second Temples stood. Sandwiched between the Western Wall of the Mount, the Moslem and Armenian quarters and the southern city wall is the ancient Jewish quarter. After it was overrun by the Arab Legion in 1948, most of the quarter, including its famous old synagogues, was demolished by the Jordanians; even the name "Jewish Quarter" was taken off the Jordanian maps. Since the Six-Day War it is being restored and reoccupied.

The Western Wall

As the only surviving portion of the great retaining wall of the Mount from the time of the first Jewish Temple, the Western Wall is the most revered of Jewish holy places. (The name "Wailing Wall" was coined in the Diaspora and has never been adopted in Hebrew, which speaks only of the *Kotel ha-Ma'aravi*, which means "the Western Wall.") Until Israel's recapture of the Old City in the Six-Day War, the exposed part of the Western Wall was nearly sixty feet high, with nineteen courses of massive stone blocks; the lower courses dated back to Herod's Second Temple. A narrow lane ran alongside it. Since June, 1967, the old houses in front of the wall have been pulled down, creating a large open square which is being landscaped. At the same time, more courses have been dug out at the foot of the Wall and excavation is still going on. The Wall continues northward and southward along the side of the Temple Mount, though it is at present concealed under houses.

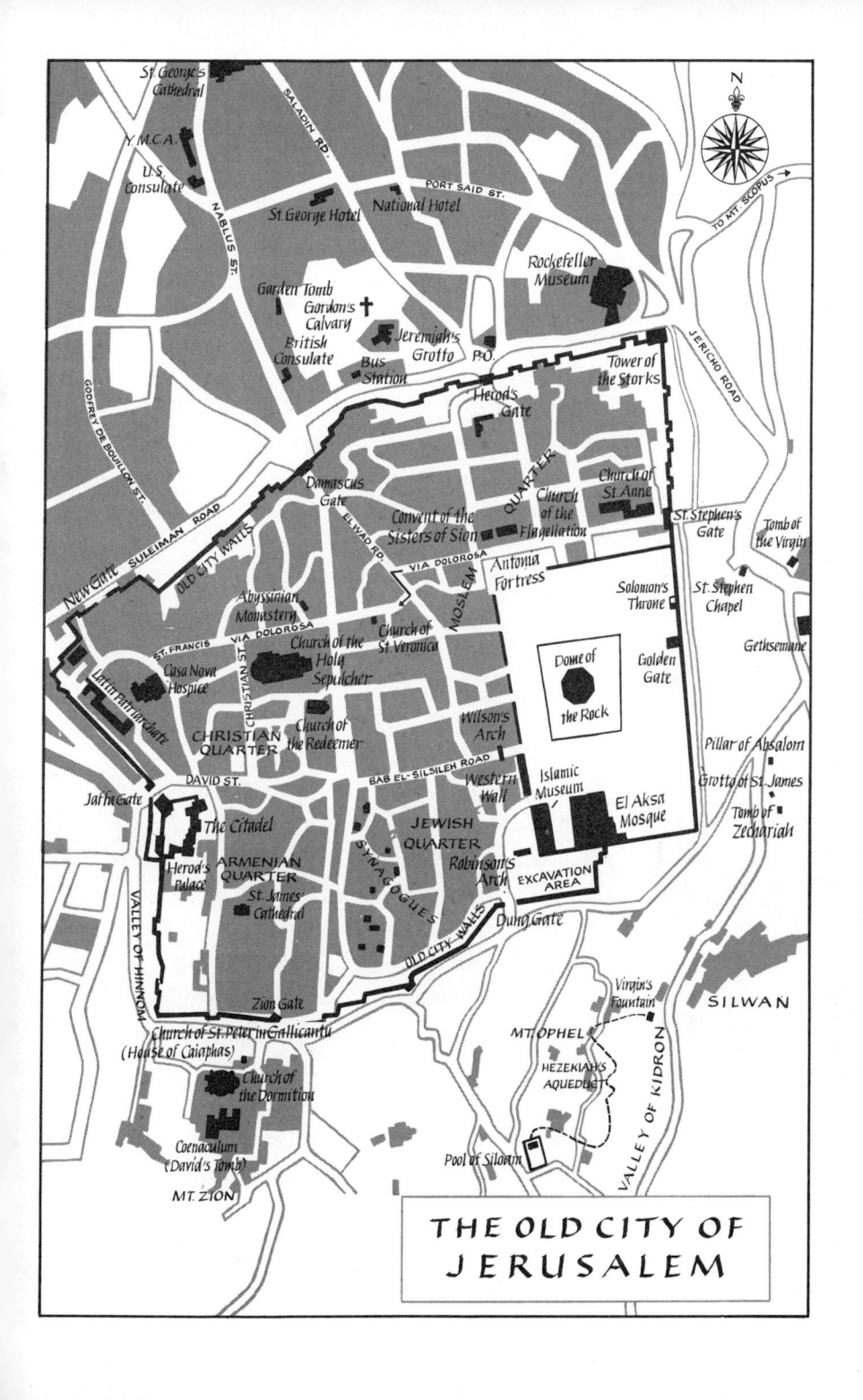

THE OLD CITY OF JERUSALEM

At the southern end of the Western Wall are the remains of two bridges or viaducts which linked the Temple Mount with the Upper City at the time of Herod. They are known as Robinson's Arch and Wilson's Arch, after the two men who discovered them in the last century.

An archaeological dig headed by Professor Binyamin Mazar was started along the southern side of the Wall in the spring of 1968. It has uncovered the foundations of Robinson's Arch and the Herodian pavement some thirty feet below the present level. It was part of a wide plaza laid down in the first century B.C. in front of the main entrance to the Temple compound. On the pavement were the huge stones, some weighing three-quarters of a ton, that had been thrown down by the Romans from the top of the wall when Titus destroyed the Temple in A.D. 70.

The excavations have uncovered thirteen levels of civilization. Coins have been found that were struck between A.D. 66 and A.D. 70 during the Jewish revolt against the Romans. The most exciting piece unearthed is a limestone pot with the word *Korban* (Sacrifice) in a beautiful Hebrew script. It is decorated with two birds and is a part of one of the ritual dishes associated with Temple sacrifice.

Another part of the excavation has reached levels dating from the eighth and seventh centuries B.C., the period of the Judean kings; pieces of pottery inscribed with the word *La-Melech*, Hebrew for "To the King," have been found.

The excavations will extend along the southern wall towards Mount Ophel, the Biblical site of King David's city. It is towards these ancient and emotion-laden walls of the Temple compound that every synagogue in the world is orientated.

The Church of the Holy Sepulcher

Standing on the site of Calvary or Golgotha, where Jesus was crucified, interred and resurrected, is the Church of the Holy Sepulcher, the most sacred shrine of Christendom. The original church was built in the fourth century by the Roman Emperor Constantine, after the site was chosen by his mother, Queen Helena (St. Helena), who like Constantine was a pagan convert to Christianity. She visited the Holy Land in A.D. 326 and, together with the Bishop of Jerusalem, claimed to have discovered the place of the tomb and relics of the True Cross. A temple of Venus, erected earlier by the Emperor Hadrian, was pulled down to make room for the new church, the conspicuous feature of which was a rotunda over the Sepulcher surmounted by a great dome upheld by massive columns. What still remains of Constantine's church in the present structure are the foundations of the rotunda and part of the entrance and steps. Under his mother's stimulus, Constantine also constructed the first Church of the Nativity at Bethlehem and another church on the Mount of Olives.

In later centuries the Holy Sepulcher went through the ups and downs arising from the country's disturbed history. The Persians destroyed the church in the seventh century, and after the Abbot Modestus had rebuilt it on a reduced scale, it was knocked down again by the Moslem Caliph Hakim of Egypt. It was repaired in 1048 by the Byzantine Emperor Constantine Monomachus. In the twelfth century, during the Latin Kingdom of Jerusalem, the Crusaders built a massive new church which included the shrines in that locality under a single roof. The church of today does not differ substantially from the Crusader structure, although the present dome is only a hundred years old.

For centuries different Christian sects contended over their rights to the church or a portion thereof, and their claims were backed by different foreign powers. These disputes were the spark that set off the Crimean War of 1853–56. After peace had been restored, the Ottoman Sultan reaffirmed an earlier status quo which still regulates the rights to the main Christian holy places.

In the Church of the Holy Sepulcher, six Christian communities exercise rights of possession and worship. The three major communities are the Latin, represented by the Franciscan Order, the traditional Roman Catholic "Custodian of the Holy Land"; the Greek Orthodox and the Armenian Orthodox. They have residence, individual chapels and rights over the main portion of the Basilica, where they succeed one another at fixed hours for part of the day and part of the night for the exercise of the liturgy. The three minor communities are the Coptic, who have their own chapel but the right to hold services therein only on certain days; the Syrians, who use a chapel which belongs to the Armenians, and who are permitted only certain ceremonies on the more solemn festivals; and the Abyssinians, who maintain a small shrine and rows of quaint cells for monks on the rooftop of St. Helena's Chapel. The rights of each community cover the use of lamps, decorations, pictures and candles and govern all cleaning and the carrying out of repairs—for repairing a roof or the decoration of a column implies recognition of exclusive possession of the item repaired or decorated. The keys for opening and closing the church remain to this day in the hands of a Moslem

JERUSALEM, THE GOLDEN

Arab family, Nusseibeh, under an arrangement drawn up in the thirteenth century.

When an earthquake left the church in a dangerous condition in 1927, inter-sect wrangling about repair projects went on for eight years until the British Mandatory government stepped in and carried out some temporary shoring up of the building. Work is proceeding on the proper restoration of the church.

Visitors to the most important of all Christian sanctuaries must be prepared to find little of magnificence or beauty. Just inside the entrance is a flat red stone in the floor, known as the Stone of Unction. It marks the place where Jesus' body was anointed before being buried. Straight ahead is the Crusader Rotunda, with a cupola supported on eighteen massive columns. In the center is the Holy Sepulcher.

From the Rotunda you enter another large church also under repair, the Greek Cathedral, in the center of which stands a small white marble hemisphere said to mark the center of the world.

An ambulatory passes a number of chapels belonging to different Christian orders and commemorating events leading up to the crucifixion. The chapel directly behind the Holy Sepulcher is the traditional tomb of Joseph of Arimathea, an Israelite who besought the body of Christ from Pilate and, aided by Nicodemus, swathed it in clean linen. (The caretaker will, for a small fee, provide the candles you need to examine these Jewish tombs.) The aisle leads to a steep flight of stairs going down to St. Helena's Chapel, where the walls are decorated with paintings of Armenian church history. To the right one descends further into an ancient cistern, the Latin Chapel of the Finding of the Cross.

To the right of the entrance to the Basilica is the site of the Hill of Calvary, with two chapels divided by great columns. The chapel to the right, heavily decorated with mosaics on a gold background, is the site of the Tenth and Eleventh Stations of the Cross. Before the altar on the left, the Twelfth Station, is a silver star in the floor with a hole in its center marking the place where the Holy Cross stood, with two black stars marking the crosses of the two thieves. On the right is a crack in the rock which allegedly was caused by an earthquake at the moment of the crucifixion— "The earth quaked and the rocks were rent." This crack goes right through the rock and can be seen from below in a natural grotto known as the Chapel of Adam. During the Easter festival the church is crowded with worshipers, and on Palm Sunday there is a Latin procession that commences in Bethphage, carrying palm branches in memory of Jesus' entry into Jerusalem.

The Stations of the Cross

The Via Dolorosa, or Way of Pain, is by tradition the route along which Jesus went on foot from His condemnation to His crucifixion. The sites where the events of this last sorrowful journey are supposed to have taken place are known as the Stations of the Cross and are fourteen in number. Nine of the incidents are referred to in the Gospels and the other five are handed down by tradition. The first two Stations are placed in Antonia, the great fortress built by Herod; the next seven are along the route to Calvary; and the last five are within the Church of the Holy Sepul-

JERUSALEM, THE GOLDEN

cher. Each Station is now marked by a church, a chapel, a fragment of column or just a number.

The Stations are:

First Station:	Condemnation
Second Station:	Jesus is made to carry the Cross
Third Station:	The first fall
Fourth Station:	Jesus meets His mother
Fifth Station:	Simon is made to bear the Cross
Sixth Station:	St. Veronica wipes Jesus' face
Seventh Station:	The second fall
Eighth Station:	Jesus consoles the women of Jerusalem
Ninth Station:	The third fall
Tenth Station:	Jesus is stripped of His garments
Eleventh Station:	Jesus is nailed to the Cross
Twelfth Station:	Death of Jesus
Thirteenth Station:	The body is taken down
Fourteenth Station:	The burial in the Sepulcher

Every Friday afternoon at 3 P.M. the Franciscans lead a procession down the narrow streets and mark the Stations with prayer. They are led by a *kavass*, an official wearing a blue frock coat with red binding and a fez and carrying a heavy stick. He keeps order and decorum. The procession consists of about fifty priests and nuns, and the prayers are conducted by a monk wearing a battery-fed loudspeaker.

The procession begins at the Antonia fortress, where the trial of Jesus is said to have taken place. Today this is the courtyard of the former Turkish barracks, now serving as the Umariya Boys' School. From two large barred openings on the east side of the courtyard is a spectacular view of the Temple Mount and the jewel-like Dome of the Rock.

The original Roman roadway is ten feet below the present Via Dolorosa, and adjacent parts of the paving can be seen below the Church of the Flagellation and Convent of the Sisters of Sion. In several places there the stones are marked with the games the Roman soldiers used to play. One can also peer down into the huge, ancient water cisterns that are still in use by the Sisters of Sion.

Haram-esh-Sharif

The great platform of Mount Moriah, which the Moslems call Haram-esh-Sharif (Noble Sanctuary), site of the Jewish Temple Mount, occupies the southeastern sixth of the Old City. It is this area, and the two mosques in it, which make Jerusalem a Holy City for the three hundred million Moslems in the world, next in importance to Mecca and Medina. This sanctity has a slender historical basis. The Prophet Mohammed never came here, nor is Jerusalem mentioned by name anywhere in the Koran; but it is related that one night in a vision the Prophet was carried from Mecca on his legendary horse El Burak to "a far distant place of worship," which is identified by tradition as Jerusalem, and from there his steed bore him aloft unto heaven.

By A.D. 638, six years after Mohammed's death, the conquering Arab armies had overrun Palestine, and the Caliph Omar entered Jerusalem on foot as a mark of respect. He built a wooden mosque on the ruined area of Mount Moriah. There is an old story that Omar had insisted on the Christian patriarch taking him to the site of the Jewish Temple, found it used as a refuse dump, and made the patriarch crawl through the garbage as punishment for the neglect of a place holy to another faith. The splendid Dome of the Rock, often erroneously called the Mosque of Omar,

JERUSALEM, THE GOLDEN

was actually built by a later caliph, Abd-el-Malik, and completed in 691. The large rock in the center, from which the mosque takes its name, is by tradition that on which Abraham was commanded to sacrifice his son Isaac; and later it became the site of the altar in the Jewish Temple. Moslems believe that Mohammed made his mystic ascent from this very rock, and visitors are allowed to touch the indentation (now perfumed) which was imprinted by the hoof of his horse.

Abd-el-Malik was prompted to build this superb shrine by a desire to draw prestige and pilgrim revenue away from Mecca, which was in the hands of a rival caliph. His son and successor, Caliph Walid, built a second mosque at the southeastern corner of the compound which was the forerunner of the present El Aksa Mosque. During the Crusader kingdom in Jerusalem, 1099–1187, the Dome of the Rock was converted into a Christian church, with a gold cross on the top of the dome; it was called Templum Domini (Temple of the Lord). The group of Crusader knights in charge of the compound became known as the Order of Templars; the order spread throughout Europe and built a number of churches on the circular design of the Mosque of the Dome. The best known of them is the Temple Church in the Strand in London. The Templars established their headquarters in the El Aksa Mosque, the site of King Solomon's Palace. The vaults constructed by Herod underneath the southeastern corner of the Temple Mount were used by the Templars to stable their horses; they referred to them as "Solomon's Stables," the name they still bear.

After the Saracen ruler Saladin had defeated the Crusaders and recaptured Jerusalem, he wiped out all traces of the

Christian occupation of the Temple Mount and restored the two mosques, which have remained Moslem shrines ever since.

The Dome of the Rock is an eight-sided building surmounted by a beautifully proportioned dome recently covered by shiny gold-toned aluminum. The outside walls are adorned with marble slabs and green and blue Persian tiles carrying inscriptions from the Koran. There are four doors, each facing one of the four points of the compass. The open space surrounding the building is a huge platform bounded by eight flights of steps. At the top of each stands an arcade. Underneath the platform are vast rock-hewn cisterns into which the rain water drains for storage. The eight arcades are known as *Mawazeen* (scales or balances). There is a belief that, on Judgment Day, a giant set of balances will be placed here to weigh the merits of each Moslem.

The interior of the mosque is divided by columns into three sections. The bare rock in the center forms a contrast to the exuberance of the decoration. The balustrade that surrounds the rock was put there by the Crusaders in 1196 when they made the mosque into a church. In one corner is an ornate box said to contain three hairs of the Prophet's beard; underneath it is the print said to have been left by the hoof of Mohammed's horse just before he ascended to heaven.

Just east of the mosque stands a small eighth-century building called the Dome of the Chain. It resembles the Dome of the Rock; it was built to serve as the treasury of the Haram. Legend has it that a heavenly chain once hung in the center of the cupola, hence the name.

The El Aksa Mosque was fully restored under the British Mandatory administration. It is a rectangular structure with a silver dome, and is large enough to hold 5,000 worshipers. The two rows of columns inside the mosque have Byzantine capitals which were probably taken from various Christian buildings. The ornate wooden beams were a gift from King Farouk of Egypt. The pulpit (*minbar*) at the southern end is made of ebony and was constructed without a single nail; it is decorated with inlaid ivory and mother-of-pearl. It was made in 1168 in Aleppo. There is a separate prayer hall for women to the right.

Church of St. Anne

Just inside St. Stephen's Gate is the Church of St. Anne, in the custody of the White Fathers. It is a beautiful Crusader church built in the twelfth century during the Latin Kingdom of Jerusalem. It occupies the traditional site of the home of Joachim and Anne, the parents of Mary, the mother of Jesus. Here Mary was born. A stairway to the right of the nave leads down to the crypt; and under the altar is a statue of Mary as a smiling child.

Within the courtyard of the church is the Pool of Bethesda.

> Now there is at Jerusalem in the sheep market a pool, which is called in the Hebrew tongue Bethesda, having five porches. . . .
> And a certain man was there who had an infirmity thirty and eight years. . . .
> Jesus saith unto him, Rise, take up thy bed and walk.
> And immediately the man was made whole, and took up his bed, and walked.
> —St. John 5:2–9

A Walk through the Old City

Apart from visiting the main religious shrines, every visitor should find time to stroll through the colorful bazaars and shopping streets of the Old City and mingle with the rich assortment of human beings that pass through them. The best way to spend an hour is to enter by the Damascus Gate, in the northern wall, and emerge through the Jaffa Gate that faces the New City to the west.

The Damascus Gate is the handsomest of all the portals to the Old City. It was built in 1537 by the renowned Turkish sultan, Suleiman the Magnificent, on foundations that go back to the Roman period. The massive stone blocks of Emperor Hadrian's gate have been uncovered along the side of the moat over which one crosses by a bridge. The higher courses of these Roman blocks were marked with simulated joints by Suleiman's architects, so that the building stones above them should not seem insignificant by comparison.

The roadway zigzags beneath the arch of the gate and emerges into an open shop-lined area where Hadrian erected a victory column that is depicted on the sixth-century mosaic floor map of Jerusalem uncovered at Madeba (ancient Medaba) in Jordan. The column vanished centuries ago, but to this day the Arabs refer to Damascus Gate as the Gate of the Column, which shows the tenacity of folk memory in the East. The road soon forks, and we take the right-hand *shuk* (market), which was called by the Romans the Cardo Maximum, or Great Hinge, since it was the main hub of the city. The Arabs call it after the Khan (inn) of the Olive Oil that can still be seen to the

JERUSALEM, THE GOLDEN

left through a gateway leading to a courtyard enclosed by a double arcade.

The lower half of the market alley is covered by a vaulted Crusader roof, and graceful arches which can still be seen along the side. Most of the stalls are little more than caves in the side walls. They sell a profusion of fruit and vegetables in season, groceries, toilet articles, pots and pans, bread, oil, candies, pastries, Turkish delight and the grilled meat which made the scornful Crusaders call this street *"malcuisinat,"* or "the street of rotten cooking."

On a busy day the exotic crowd jostling through the bazaar includes Moslems, Jews and Christians of every sort and garb; Arabs in traditional robes and kheffiyahs, or in modern business suits; veiled Moslem wives in black; village women with beautifully embroidered dresses, bearing baskets of farm produce on their heads; Greek Orthodox priests in high round hats; Benedictine and Franciscan monks in their brown and black habits with long ropes at their waists; nuns of various orders with distinctive head-dresses; Orthodox Jews in long black kaftans or striped golden silk, their faces framed in beards and side curls under round fur-brimmed hats; Western tourists and pilgrims; groups of Israel sightseers, many from the kibbutzim; and young Israel soldiers, with Uzi submachine guns casually slung over their shoulders, shopping with their girl friends; and laden mules and donkeys barging through the crowd.

At the back of the Church of the Holy Sepulcher, just before the stairway leading to the Ninth Station of the Cross, there is a pastry shop called Zaletimo, established in 1860, that serves a delicious pastry, called *m'tabar*, stuffed with goat's cheese and smothered in hot honey. The storehouse at the back of the shop leads to the original entrance to the Basilica, long since closed up.

Just beyond the pastry shop the street curves round to the right into the Christian quarter, passing between the Russian Church and the imposing white stone Lutheran Church of the Redeemer, inaugurated by Kaiser Wilhelm II in 1898. We emerge in front of the Church of the Holy Sepulcher and turn into the fine Muristan quarter, where there are elegant carpet and leather shops and the street of the gold and silver smiths. In this quarter stood the Crusader Hospital of St. John, from which the Order of the Hospital of St. John of Jerusalem (the Knights Hospitalers) took their name. (Muristan is a corruption of *bimuristan*, an old Arabic word for hospital.) In the center of this area stands a large, ornate fountain (that does not work) dating back to the time of the Sultan Suleiman.

Beyond the Holy Sepulcher we turn left into Christian Street, a more modern and expensive shopping center selling silk and brocade fabrics, shoes and jewelry. It leads into David Street, another narrow teeming bazaar, in which it is hard for the tourist to resist the burnished copper coffeepots, the green Hebron-glass beads or the brightly colored Bedouin embroidery. To the left David Street descends steeply by a series of steps towards the Western Wall and the Haram-esh-Sharif. To the right, the street mounts upward for a hundred yards to the square in front of the Jaffa Gate. Next to the gate is an opening through which cars can drive; it was cut through the wall so that the Kaiser could make a theatrical entrance in his carriage, dressed in a white cloak and a golden helmet topped by an eagle.

The square is dominated by the Citadel, originally built

as part of Herod's palace. Herod built three great towers to protect his palace. The largest, called Phasael, was named after his brother. It is the only one of which there are still remnants. The second was Hippicus, after his best friend; and the third was named for his wife Mariamne, a Hasmonean princess he married and finally murdered.

The different archaeological levels in this area have now been cleared up and restored and you enter the site across a bridge that used to be a drawbridge over the moat. The base of the great Phasael tower is to the right. The original portion is visible as several courses of large cut stones above the sloping face of stones which were added later by the Mamelukes. The different types of masonry tell the history of the Citadel for 2,000 years. It is the highest point in the Old City and almost every ruler made it his headquarters, beginning with the Maccabees. After Titus conquered and razed Jerusalem in A.D. 70, he left the towers standing and used the area as a garrison. Two of the three towers appear on the Byzantine Medaba map of the sixth century.

There is little sign of Moslem occupation, but during the Crusader invasion of 1099, the Citadel became the palace-fortress for the Latin kings. The enclosed area was extended and stables added. The Crusaders rode away forever in 1239, and after fifty years the Mamelukes swept in, strengthened the lower ramparts and built mosques. Suleiman the Magnificent, who rebuilt the city walls in the sixteenth century, garrisoned his troops here after adding the entrance to the east. During the thirty years of the Mandate, British troops guarded the city from the Citadel, as did Jordanian troops after the War of Independence.

The site, which is still erroneously referred to as "David's Tower," is well worth visiting. The different parts are clearly labeled, so that the tourist can spend a fascinating hour here.

OUTSIDE THE OLD CITY

Mount Zion

> Walk about Zion, and go round about her: . . . that ye may tell it to the generation following.
> —Psalm 48:12–13

Mount Zion is sacred to the pious Jew as the traditional burial place of King David, although the scholars are skeptical, since David's city lay a little farther to the east. At the top of the hill is a stone structure known as David's Tomb; and there, in a rock-hewn room, lies a huge sarcophagus covered by an embroidered shawl. The flickering candles lit by devout visitors are reflected in the row of fine Torah crowns that stand against the smoke-stained walls lined here and there with colored Armenian tiles. The room next door, often referred to as the "Hall of the Washing of the Feet," is used for prayer, and the chanting echoes through the heavy arched aisles of what had once been a Crusader structure, through which you reach the tomb.

Above the Tomb is the Coenaculum, the "upper room," which is the traditional site of the Last Supper. It was here that Jesus came with His disciples to celebrate Passover, and from here He went down into the Garden of Gethsemane. On entering the Coenaculum one finds a fourteenth-century Gothic hall whose pointed arches spring from two columns in the center that are built directly over the two great columns of the aisle below. This structure was built by Franciscan monks after the Saracens had destroyed the original building. Some time in the seventeenth century the Turks expelled the monks, and the site became the Mosque of Nebi Da'ud (the Prophet David), as David ranks in Islam as one of the major prophets.

The Dormition Monastery is the most impressive building on Mount Zion. It was erected by the Benedictine Fathers at the beginning of the twentieth century on a plot of ground that was presented to the German Kaiser by the Turkish Sultan. According to Christian tradition, this is the place where the Virgin Mary fell into eternal sleep—the *dormition Sanctae Mariae.* (Her tomb is near Gethsemane.) The mosaic of the circular floor under the dome has as its motif the months of the year, with their symbols and saints. On one side stairs lead down to the crypt, where a statue of Mary on her death bed stands in the center. The mosaics in the various chapels around the statue were designed and presented by different countries. The Coenaculum was visited by Pope Paul VI on his pilgrimage to the Holy Places in Israel in January, 1964.

The two excavation sites in the grove of pine trees on Mount Zion have, unhappily, begun to fall in. The one nearest the entrance to David's Tomb leads down to a Greek Orthodox underground church dating from Byzantine times. The excavation in the center of the grove has uncovered foundations from Herod's time, when Mount Zion was within the city walls. On the left going down is Bishop Gobat's School.

Work has now started at the Jaffa Gate on a strip of park round the outside of the walls.

On the slope beyond Mount Zion there is the large Church of St. Peter in Gallicantu, run by the White Fathers. It is built over the traditional site of the house of the

High Priest Caiaphas, where Jesus was first brought before being taken for trial by Pontius Pilate the next morning. Underneath the present church is a courtyard where Peter denied his Master. Below that is a cavern where Jesus is said to have been imprisoned that night. Next to the cavern is what may have been an ancient jail, for in the rock are still the loops to which the chains were fixed. There are also two round pots, still lined with plaster, in which vinegar and brine may have been kept.

In the grounds of the church are the remains of early Jewish storehouses and caverns; a first-century roadway and steps lead down to the Pool of Siloam.

Mount Scopus

The name Mount Scopus (in Hebrew *Har ha-Tzofim*) means Hill of Observation. From here there is a commanding view over Jerusalem to the west and the Dead Sea valley to the east. During the period of the British Mandate the Jews built the Hebrew University and the Hadassah Hospital on this splendid site. These buildings were cut off from the rest of Jewish Jerusalem in the 1948 fighting and remained an Israel enclave, manned by a small police garrison and supplied every two weeks by armored trucks brought up under United Nations auspices.

Although the 1949 armistice agreement provided for free access to the institutions on Mount Scopus, this provision was not respected by the Jordanians; the cluster of imposing buildings, with their invaluable library, scientific instruments and medical equipment, remained disused and decaying. With the reunion of Jerusalem in 1967, Mount Scopus is once more part of the living city. During the nineteen-year armistice the Hebrew University developed its new campus and Hadassah, its great medical center, to the west of Jerusalem. Now that the Mount Scopus buildings have been recovered they are being brought back into service and new ones erected. Among them is the Truman Peace Center.

Close to the entrance of the Hadassah Hospital is the well-tended British Commonwealth Military Cemetery, with 2,500 graves of the soldiers who died in the Palestine Campaign of 1917 against the Turks. Their regimental crests are carved on the surrounding wall.

Farther along the ridge, between Mount Scopus and the Mount of Olives, is the Augusta Victoria Hospital, with its square tower standing out against the skyline. It belongs to the German Lutherans, and is named after the wife of Kaiser Wilhelm II.

Mount of Olives

The road continues along the top of the ridge to the Mount of Olives, past the small Arab village of Et Tur on the eastern slope, sometimes identified with the Bethphage of the Gospels, and reaches a Russian church with a very tall tower that is the most prominent object on the ridge— either from the west, or from the east by way of the Jericho road. It is worth toiling up more than 200 steps to see the view. In the same compound is a convent of Russian nuns and another church, which is supposed formerly to have held the severed head of John the Baptist. (The head is also said to have been found at Sebastia, near Nablus.) The old mosaics are worth a look.

The Mount of Olives, or Olivet (in Hebrew *Har ha-*

Zeitim) derived its name from the great groves of olive trees that draped its flanks in ancient times. For Jews all over the world it is best known as the site of the sacred burial ground where every pious person wanted to be interred with his forefathers. Jewish tradition has it that on the Day of Judgment the dead will rise first of all from the Mount of Olives; and according to one legend, the Lord will on that day cause tunnels to be created from burial grounds elsewhere in the world, so that the spirits of the departed may more easily assemble at the Mount. After 1948, access for Jews to the cemetery was cut off and it was neglected and desecrated by the Jordanian authorities; most of the tombstones were overthrown and broken, or carted off for building purposes. The cemetery is now being restored; and the roadway that had been driven through it to the Intercontinental Hotel on top has been closed off.

For Christians, the top of the Mount is the place from which Jesus ascended to heaven after His resurrection. A fourth-century church stood here. It was succeeded by a Crusader building, of which some remains can still be seen. It became a mosque after the Moslem occupation of Jerusalem in the twelfth century. The present church is Moslem-owned, but the different Christian sects have permission to set up altars and hold Mass at specified times. The Arab guard allows visitors to go up a staircase to the roof.

Other Christian religious edifices nearby are a Carmelite Convent, the Church of the Paternoster (with tablets bearing the Lord's Prayer in thirty-two languages) and the excavated remains of the Eleona, an early Byzantine church also built in the fourth century. There is an underground tomb which the Jews believe is that of the prophetess Hulda, the Christians that of Saint Pelagia, and the Moslems that of

JERUSALEM, THE GOLDEN

a pious lady, Sit Adawia—an encouraging example of coexistence among the faiths. The road ends at the Intercontinental Hotel, with the seven arches of its dining room facing towards the Old City below.

A short distance to the east is the village of Bethany, which can be reached from the Jericho road. Here, according to the Gospels, Jesus was entertained by Lazarus and his two sisters, Mary and Martha, and later returned to perform the miracle of restoring Lazarus to life four days after his burial. From the Church of the Paternoster a path descends to a series of ancient rock-hewn tombs, held by some to include the burial places of the last two Hebrew prophets. Inscriptions indicate the tombs were also used in Byzantine times.

From here the old Roman road descends to the Garden of Gethsemane.

The view from the Mount of Olives at sunset is an unforgettable one. To the east, the khaki-colored Judean wilderness falls down in wave after wave to the Dead Sea, its gleaming surface 1,300 feet below sea level, with the great blue rampart of the Mountains of Moab beyond it. To the west, across the narrow Valley of Kidron, the Old City sprawls across its hilltops like a medieval painting. Seen from here, it looks as though only its great stone walls prevent it from sliding down into the ravine. In the gathering dusk the ancient wall, the golden and silver domes of the mosques and the huddle of flat roofs broken by church steeples and minarets are bathed in an unearthly pink light. At that moment Jerusalem comes into its own as one of the world's most beautiful cities.

The Garden of Gethsemane

The name Gethsemane is derived from the Hebrew *gat shemen*, meaning an olive press—a reminder of the groves of olive trees that once spread across these slopes. The garden where Jesus was betrayed by Judas Iscariot and arrested is at the foot of the Mount of Olives, across the valley from the eastern wall of the Old City. In it eight olive trees still survive, twisted and gnarled by age.

In the garden is the fine Franciscan Church of All Nations. It has a façade of Corinthian columns surmounted by a pediment of richly colored mosiacs that represent Jesus weeping over the fate of Jerusalem. The interior glitters with mosaics and colored marble. Before the altar is the large fenced-in Rock of Agony on which Jesus and the disciples are said to have rested. Parts of the old Byzantine foundation can still be seen, as can the original mosaics on the floor.

On the left of the entrance to the garden is the Tomb of the Virgin, with a twelfth-century Greek church built over it. A steep flight of steps leads down to the church, which contains several Christian altars and a Moslem prayer alcove. A chapel near the entrance is said to contain the tomb of Mary's parents, Joachim and Anne.

Behind and above Gethsemane is the Russian Church of St. Mary Magdalene, topped by a cluster of green onion-shaped domes. It was built by Czar Alexander III in 1885.

A little higher up the slope is a charming small church of black and white stone called Dominus Flevit (The Lord Wept). It belongs to the Franciscans and was built in 1955 by the Italian architect Antonio Barluzzi. It stands in a

JERUSALEM, THE GOLDEN

spacious garden dotted with Hebrew rock tombs, some from the late bronze period and others used from 135 B.C. to A.D. 300. The church has a Byzantine marble and mosaic floor. Behind the altar a picture window frames the beautiful view of the Old City.

Valley of Kidron

Below the Garden of Gethsemane, the Valley of Kidron continues southward, curving to the southwest at the corner of the Old City wall. To the left of the road is a group of venerable monuments, the best known of which is the Pillar of Absalom, which marks the traditional burial place of King David's rebel son. Actually the pillar dates from many centuries later, from the period of the Second Temple.

Next to Absalom's Pillar are several cave tombs hewn out of the hillside. One is the Tomb of Jehosaphat. Another, called the Grotto of St. James, was the family tomb of the priestly house of Hezir, referred to in the Book of Nehemiah. This is verified by the Hebrew inscription still legible over the entrance, on the pediment supported by two columns. Nearby is an odd-looking monument with a pyramid-shaped top which the Jews believe to be the Tomb of the Prophet Zechariah.

The steep slope rising to the left of the Valley of Kidron is covered with the stone houses of the Arab village of Silwan (or Siloam, or Siloah). In the bed of the valley is the Spring of Gihon (the Virgin's Fountain), known even before the capture of Jerusalem by King David as the only permanent water source in the area. As in the days of the early Kings of Judah, the spring lies outside the walls of the city, which then occupied the southern slope below the

• 119

present wall. (Part of the original Jebusite city has been excavated nearby.) About 700 B.C., when the city was threatened by the Assyrian army, King Hezekiah had a tunnel cut through into the city to ensure access to this vital water supply. One can still wade through the 1,730-foot-long tunnel which follows a zigzag course from the Gihon spring to the Pool of Siloam, which was at that time inside the walled city. The workmen started tunneling from each end and met in the middle, a remarkable feat of engineering recorded on a tablet that was fixed to the wall at that spot and is now in the Istanbul Museum. The inscription is in classical Hebrew.

A little farther along the floor of the valley is the Well of Job, still used by the villagers. Here the Valley of Kidron meets the *Valley of Hinnom* (sometimes Ben-Hinnom), that curves round the foot of Mount Zion and northward up to the Jaffa Gate. The valley was notorious in early times for idol worship and child sacrifices to the god Moloch, and was cursed by the Prophet Jeremiah. The word Gehenna, derived from *Ge-Hinnom* (Ravine of Hinnom), became a synonym for Hell.

Another local spot with an unsavory past is the top of the hill above the village of Silwan. Here King Solomon was said to have laid out a garden with different altars for several of his pagan wives, each according to her cult. It was called the Mount of Corruption (in Latin, *Mons Scandali*). Today it is a respectable Benedictine monastery and pilgrim's hostel.

The Rockefeller Museum

The Rockefeller Museum, (Palestine Archaeological Museum) is a handsome buff-colored building with an octagonal tower, on a promontory north of the Old City, almost opposite Herod's Gate. It is built around a courtyard and lily pond and stands in a garden of olive trees and flower beds.

The ten-acre site was once occupied by a Byzantine cemetery and church. In the shadow of an ancient pine tree in the garden is a mosaic floor from the original church. Later the Crusaders had a farm at this site. The museum was built in 1929 by the British Mandatory administration with a two-million-dollar grant by John D. Rockefeller, Jr.

In spite of heavy fighting in and around the museum during the Six-Day War, the exhibits suffered little damage. They are arranged chronologically from the Stone Age through the Bronze Age and down to Turkish times. The museum is open to the public at the same hours as the Israel National Museum in West Jerusalem.

The Tombs of the Kings

The name of this rock-hewn necropolis is misleading. It was cut for Helen, Queen of Adiabene in Mesopotamia, who came to Jerusalem about A.D. 43 with her children, and converted to Judaism. It lies half a mile north of the Old City, at the end of Saladin Road. A monumental rock staircase, with drainage channels at the side that take the rain water into cisterns, leads down to a large courtyard. The entrance to the tombs is to one side, through a decorated vestibule. Having crawled inside, you will find yourself in the first of eight connected chambers with twenty-two burial niches in the walls. The necropolis has belonged to the French Republic since 1886. The carved sarcophagi it once contained are in the Louvre in Paris.

Behind the Tombs of the Kings is the charming American Colony Hotel, which gives its name to this suburb. It was established as a charitable mission by a Chicago lawyer called Horatio Spoffard. The mission was later joined by a group of Swedes.

Farther along the road to Mount Scopus there is a signpost that reads "Shimon ha-Zadik" (Simon the Just). Here in a cliff on the side of the valley is a rock tomb traditionally held to be that of a high priest who lived in the third century B.C. The Oriental Jews seem to have a special veneration for Simon; at the late-spring festival of Shavuoth they come with their families to pray and picnic at this spot.

Herod's Family Tomb

Herod's family tomb lies practically next door to the King David Hotel. Its discovery at the end of the last century came as no great surprise, as the historian Flavius Josephus gives the exact location of this burial place. The mausoleum, built out of huge stone blocks, is entered through a sunken court. The tunnel leading into the burial chambers can be blocked by a "rolling stone," that is, a door and its hinges cut from a stone slab. The burial chambers lead off from a central corridor. Three stone coffins were found at the time of the discovery; these are now in St. Constantine's Monastery in the Old City, where they were taken during World War II, when the necropolis was converted into what must have been a rather eerie air-raid shelter. It is interesting to note that Herod's own burial place (a hilltop near Bethlehem) is a long way from his family tomb, but that is understandable, as many of his immediate family were killed by his order.

Tombs of the Sanhedrin

On the northern edge of Jerusalem, in a charming little park, lie the cave tombs of the members of the Sanhedrin dating back to the first and second centuries B.C. Israel's Sanhedrin was the supreme religious and legal council of seventy-one members, who sat in judgment in the Temple area.

The Jewish Agency

The U-shaped building in Keren Hayesod Street is the headquarters of the Jewish Agency, the World Zionist Organization, and the National Institutions—the Keren Hayesod (Palestine Foundation Fund) and the Keren Kayemet (Jewish National Fund). The Golden Books of the Jewish National Fund are also kept here, as is the Register of Tree Certificates. There is also a Hall of Remembrance in the Keren Hayesod building in which is kept a book listing the names of those who contributed towards Israel's immigration and absorption. The first plaque on the wall was in memory of the late Senator Herbert H. Lehman, who also served as Governor of New York.

Hechal Shlomo

A block farther down Keren Hayesod street, facing the public gardens, is the lofty stone building of the World Religious Center which houses the Chief Rabbinate. It is named Hechal Shlomo in memory of the father of Sir Isaac Wolfson, of England. In the Center are offices of nearly fifty organizations and departments concerned with almost every aspect of religious life in Israel; they are in constant contact with Jewish communities throughout the world. The visitor will be interested in the small synagogue on the left of the entrance. The arch and the *bimah* (pulpit) were brought from Padua, Italy; they are more than 240 years old. The stained-glass windows were designed by David Hillman, of London. The central rabbinical library has more than 60,000 books covering every aspect of Judaism. The religious historical museum is on the fourth floor; it has a fine collection of illuminated manuscripts. The view from the observation platform on the roof is magnificent.

The Khan

An old Turkish *khan* (inn) opposite the railway station has been restored and converted into an attractive small theater, combined with a bar and a night club. It is used not only for plays in English, Hebrew and Arabic given by a resident troupe, but also for folklore, tourist evenings and other cultural events. The Khan is a welcome addition to Jerusalem's rather meager night life.

International Cultural Center for Youth

This center was opened in 1960 in the German Colony. It was built by an interfaith group in America, helped by friends in other countries, in order to bring the cultural values of the world to Israel's youth. This is done through study groups, films, exhibitions, dance workshops, concerts and discussion forums with visiting youth. Traveling exhibitions extend its resources to youth institutions throughout Israel. The building stands in spacious gardens donated by Spyros Skouras in memory of his daughter. The synagogue tour which takes place at three o'clock every Friday starts in the hall of this center.

Ramat Rachel

To the west of the Government House area, on the same high ground, is the kibbutz of Ramat Rachel (Hill of Rachel). This is the only kibbutz within the confines of Jerusalem. It occupies a strategic position as the city's southern bastion, commanding the approaches to Jerusalem on that side. In the 1948 War of Independence, Egyptian forces twice captured the settlement and were twice expelled. The old dining hall is still pockmarked with the scars of battle. In October, 1957, trigger-happy Jordanian soldiers on the next hilltop a few hundred yards away opened fire on a group of Israel archaeologists examining the remains of Biblical fortifications at this spot. Twenty-two of them were killed or wounded.

FROM DAN TO EILAT

Excavations at Ramat Rachel have uncovered seven levels of settlement, from the seventh century B.C. to the seventh century A.D. The royal Judean citadel at this spot, destroyed by the Babylonian King Nebuchadnezzar, was rebuilt by the returning Jewish exiles. The site was later taken over by the Romans, who built a bathhouse and palace. It was occupied by the Tenth Legion; many of the floors bear their seal. A Byzantine church and monastery were erected in the fifth century A.D., and one can see today the remains of the mosaic floors, the oil presses and the water cisterns.

The Knesset

The center of the national capital is an expanse of high ground on the western edge of the New City, dominated by the square structure of the Knesset (parliament). There are some fine works of art in the Knesset. The state room intended for receptions was decorated by Marc Chagall. The outstanding feature is the Gobelin tapestry designed by Chagall as a triptych telling the story of the Jewish people from the creation of the world to the establishment of the State of Israel. On the entrance wall is a Chagall mosaic which shows Jews praying at the Western Wall, and on the floor are twelve mosaics of ancient Jewish symbols.

The magnificent entrance gates were designed by an Israeli sculptor, the late David Palombo.

Check the newspaper for the times of the tours, which depend upon whether the House is sitting or in recess. The tour also includes time spent in the visitors' gallery.

Farther along the ridge are several large stone government office buildings set in rock gardens and pine groves.

The Hebrew University

Across the valley from the government area, on a long narrow ridge called Givat Ram, the new campus of the Hebrew University has been constructed out of stone quarried on its site. With its clean functional architecture, lightened by panels of color and held together by the great central building of the National Library, the university has become one of the showplaces of Jerusalem.

There are two important impulses behind the creation of the Hebrew University: first, it satisfies the traditional love of learning to be expected from the People of the Book; second, it must provide the intellectual manpower needed by a struggling new country. It tries to hold a balance between scholarship and practical need. Together with courses in the humanities, Jewish studies, Asian and African studies, and education, it carries out teaching and research in the natural and physical sciences (both theoretical and applied), medicine, agriculture, law and the social sciences. The faculty of agriculture is in Rehovot.

The students—more than 12,000 of them—are older and work harder than those elsewhere. Between high school and university they have had to do their military service. In addition, most of them are without means, and more than 80 percent have part-time jobs to help them through college. There are about 250 Israel Arab students at the university; they are scattered through various departments, and find Hebrew no problem. An intensive *Ulpan* (full-time course in Hebrew) eases the language barrier for 2,000 foreign students who come from the United States, South America, Western Europe and many African and Asian states. A special medical course for students from the developing countries has been organized by the Hadassah–Hebrew University Medical School with the aid of the World Health Organization (WHO). In this course the instruction for the first years is given in English.

On the southern slope of Givat Ram, the Friends of the Hebrew University have helped to build hostels housing some 1,800 students. Near the hostels is a small synagogue that looks like a permanent white bubble.

The Israel Museum

In 1965, on a hilltop opposite the university, the Israel Museum was opened. It is composed of the Bezalel Art Museum, a fifty-year-old institution; the Samuel Bronfman Biblical and Archaeological Museum; the Shrine of the Book, housing the Dead Sea Scrolls; and the Billy Rose Sculpture Garden, designed by Isamu Noguchi. The museum complex consists of interlocked square pavilions at different levels; it can be enlarged as the collection of art treasures increases. The art wing also contains a children's museum. The initial project was made possible by grants from the governments of the United States and Israel. Jacob Epstein's widow has given the museum all her husband's original casts. Another great sculptor, Jacques Lipschitz, has also made a gift of his casts. In addition to normal hours the museum is open two nights a week.

By far the most precious exhibit in the Israel Museum is the seven complete parchment Dead Sea Scrolls. Most of the Shrine of the Book, which houses them, is underground, capturing the feeling of the cave in which the scrolls were found. Above ground can be seen a distinctive white

JERUSALEM, THE GOLDEN

dome shaped like the lid of an earthenware jar. This faces a shiny black slab. It has been suggested that the sharp contrast of the colors symbolizes the wars of the Sons of Light against the Sons of Darkness, an account of which is in one of the scrolls.

The story of how these unique records came to light has been told by Professor (formerly army general) Yigael Yadin in his book *The Message of the Scrolls*. In November, 1947, Yadin's father, Professor Sukenik of the Hebrew University, heard that an Arab antiquities dealer in Bethlehem had some old Hebrew manuscripts for sale. Having seen a fragment of one of them, Sukenik became convinced of their importance. On the very day of the United Nations partition decision, with Jerusalem in the grip of tension, he made a hazardous trip to Bethlehem in an Arab bus and bought three scrolls, carrying them back under his arm wrapped in a piece of newspaper. On being unrolled, they were found to be about 2,000 years old. There was a copy of the Book of Isaiah, a "thanksgiving" scroll and an allegorical account, hitherto unknown, of the War between the Sons of Light and the Sons of Darkness. The scrolls had been found in a rock cave near the Dead Sea by some Bedouin passing by with their goats. A few months later, in February, 1948, Professor Sukenik secretly negotiated for four more scrolls that were in the possession of the Syrian Orthodox Metropolitan in the Old City. Sukenik actually brought them to his home on loan, but in the confusion of the fighting going on in the country, he could not immediately raise a relatively small sum in ready cash to make an offer and had to hand them back—a fact he lamented until his death in 1953.

A year later, while on a lecture tour in the United States,

his son Yigael Yadin heard that the Syrian Metropolitan had brought the scrolls to the United States and was trying to sell them. After a month of anxious negotiation through intermediaries, the scrolls were bought for $250,000 through the generosity of the late Samuel Gottesman, whose family has since erected the Shrine of the Book. The four scrolls of this purchase include another Isaiah manuscript, a Habakkuk Commentary, the Manual of Discipline and the Genesis Apocryphon. It is now generally accepted that the seven scrolls formed part of the library of the ruined monastery at Qumran, on the shore of the Dead Sea.

Museum Hill runs eastward down an olive-clad slope and at the bottom is an ancient stone building, the Monastery of the Cross. According to legend, a tree in this valley was used for the cross on which Jesus was crucified. This medieval building has heavily buttressed walls in striking contrast to the museum buildings above. A courtyard leads to the church, a twelfth-century Crusader basilica with a vaulted ceiling and high dome over the altar. Original mosaics still cover portions of the nave floor, and one can see traces of frescoes on the walls.

The Wizo Baby Home and Child Care Centre

From the Hebrew University campus you can see the square stone building of the Wizo (Women's International Zionist Organization) children's center. Here, set in beautiful gardens, is a home for underprivileged infants and preschool children, with a nurses' training school attached. The center was built and is supported by the Wizo members of Great Britain.

Mount Herzl

Not far from the university, to the north of the highway, is Mount Herzl, on the crown of which lies buried Theodore Herzl, the man who was first fired by the vision of Jewish statehood and launched the movement which brought it about. In 1949, forty-five years after his death, the body of Dr. Herzl was brought in state from Vienna to Jerusalem. In the Herzl Museum to the left of the gate is a replica of his Vienna study, with the desk at which he wrote *Der Judenstaat* (The Jewish State).

On the slope of the mount, in serried ranks, lie buried the thousands of Israel men and women who died in battle. The soldiers and sailors drowned in the Mediterranean are poignantly remembered by tablets under the water of a pool, with a quotation from Psalm 69:

> I will bring my people from the depth of the sea.

After climbing up through the formal terraced gardens you get a sweeping view ranging from the stone walls of the city to wave after wave of mountain ridges stretching out. A thousand yards away on the same ridge is the Hill of Remembrance, dedicated to the six million European Jews killed by the Nazis. On it stand the buildings erected in 1957 by the organization known as Yad va-Shem (literally Place and Name), a phrase taken from the prophecy of Isaiah (56:5):

> Even unto them will I give in mine house and within my walls a place and a name.

The main memorial is a square building of uncut boulders with a superstructure of rough concrete. The iron doors, with their abstract design suggestive of barbed wire, lead into the bare chamber where an eternal flame casts its flickering light on the names of the Nazi extermination camps set into the mosaic floor. The rugged simplicity of this memorial is deeply moving. Nearby is a memorial column symbolic of a death-camp chimney. There is also a synagogue dedicated to the memory of the thousands of European synagogues destroyed during the Holocaust. A few hundred yards away is the imposing library, which holds the vast archive of material relating to the Holocaust and the individual records of the dead, who have posthumously been given "memorial citizenship" of Israel. Yad va-Shem supplied much of the detailed evidence for the trial of Adolf Eichmann in 1961.

Hadassah–Hebrew University Medical Center

Five miles west of Jerusalem, along the Henrietta Szold Road, the magnificent Hadassah–Hebrew University Medical Center has been built overlooking the village of Ein Kerem. It includes an eleven-floor, 500-bed teaching hospital, the Hebrew University–Hadassah Medical School, and also nursing, dental and pharmacy schools. In 1948, Hadassah (the women's Zionist organization of America) lost the use of its buildings on Mount Scopus, which had housed the finest hospital and postgraduate medical school in the Middle East and had served Jews and Arabs alike. Hadassah reacted to this shattering blow by planning an even larger and finer medical center, and year by year has raised funds to build it. It was opened officially in 1961. The Medical Center also provides training facilities for medical and nursing students from African and Asian countries as part of a program to help developing countries overcome their pressing public health needs.

A small synagogue holds the famous stained-glass windows by Marc Chagall, each depicting one of the Twelve Tribes of Israel.

Ein Karem

From Hadassah, a detour can be made through Ein Karem (Spring of the Vineyard), the attractive cypress-framed hamlet from which, according to tradition, came St. John the Baptist. Here among the vineyards and olive trees he was born to Elisabeth and Zacharias, a Jewish priest, when they were old. According to the Gospel of Luke, Mary paid her cousin Elisabeth a visit when they were both pregnant:

> And it came to pass, that, when Elisabeth heard the salutation of Mary, the babe leapt in her womb; and Elisabeth was filled with the Holy Ghost.
> —Luke 1:41

In 1948, when the Arabs fled across the border, the village filled with new Jewish immigrants, many of them from Oriental countries. But the monasteries continue to function undisturbed and the bells of the churches still ring out across the valley.

CHAPTER 6

Judea and Samaria*

*Since its occupation in the June 1967 War, the "West Bank of the Jordan"—the area to the south, east and north of Jerusalem—has become known in Israel by the Biblical names of Judea and Samaria (Yehuda and Shomron in Hebrew).

BETHLEHEM

Bethlehem, like Nazareth, is an Arab hill town dominated by the belfries of Christian churches and the red-tiled roofs of monasteries and convents. Along its steep streets and lanes flows the daily life of any Arab town; here are the market place, the little retail shops, the children pouring out of school, and the cafés where the menfolk haggle and gossip over little cups of Turkish coffee. But the main concern of Bethlehem is the happening of nearly 2,000 years ago—the birth of Jesus.

The year's highlight here is Christmas. There are actually three Christmases: the Latin (Western) one that is cele-

JUDEA AND SAMARIA

brated on December 25, according to the Gregorian calendar; the Orthodox (Eastern) Christmas thirteen days later, by the older Julian calendar; and the Armenian Christmas on Epiphany, January 19. On these three days the town is festive with lights and banners, the churches are full of worshipers and visitors, carols pour from loudspeakers in the crowded Manger Square, and brisk trade is done in the carved olive-wood and mother-of-pearl souvenirs for which Bethlehem is renowned. The climax on Christmas Eve, December 24, is the sumptuous midnight Mass, which is attended by dignitaries and diplomats.

To a Western visitor, Christmas in the city of the Nativity is oddly lacking in many of the traditional Yuletide symbols. There is no Santa Claus, with his plump, pink cheeks, white beard and red suit, for he is a pagan figure out of the dark forests of Teutonic Northern Europe. From there too came his sleigh and reindeer, as well as the holly and the mistletoe. The Christmas tree with colored lights, the greeting cards, the turkey and plum pudding and the gift-wrapped presents are all later European trimmings. They have little to do with the original story of the Babe born in a cowshed in the stony Judean hills, to a working-class Jewish family from the Galilee.

Starting at the Jaffa Gate in Jerusalem the road to Bethlehem is four miles long. There is also a ten-mile detour through East Jerusalem, built by the Jordanians when Jerusalem was a divided city. The roads meet outside Bethlehem, a few hundred yards from the prominent Greek monastery of Mar Elias (Elijah) with its pierced steeple.

On a clear day you get a glimpse of the Dead Sea from here. A cone-shaped hill rising to the left on the fringe of the Wilderness of Judea, is Herodium (Mount of the

Franks, in Crusader times), the site of the palace-tomb of Herod the Great. Josephus tells us that there were "twin hills like a woman's breasts" and Herod cut one down and piled the rock and earth on the other. From the top, this strange tyrant king could look down on Bethlehem, the city whose infants he ordered killed for fear of a future rival.

Near the entrance to Bethlehem, you see a small white dome on the right. This is the traditional Tomb of Rachel, the beloved wife of Jacob, who died giving birth to their son Benjamin. Over the gray tomb the Crusaders built a square structure with twelve arches and a cupola. In 1788 the arches were filled in; in 1841 Sir Moses Montefiore added the rather ugly square vestibule. Superstitious Jewish women hang threads round the tomb of "Our Mother Rachel" and then wind them round the wrists of their daughters, to bring them healthy sons.

The majority of Bethlehem's 20,000 inhabitants are Christian. The Arabs call the city *Beit Lahm* (House of Meat) while the Jews call it *Beit Lehem* (House of Bread). The inhabitants, many of whose names are French and Italian, claim to have Crusader blood, and the Bethlehem women tend to bear this out; for on special occasions they wear a short jacket of embroidered velvet over a full skirt and a tall pointed headdress from which a white veil falls, producing a medieval effect.

Bethlehem is an ancient town, first mentioned in the Bible in connection with the death of Rachel and then as King David's birthplace. Bethlehem was also the background to the romantic story of Ruth the Moabite and Boaz, in whose fields she gleaned. These were probably the same fields in which the shepherds heard the news of Jesus' birth from the herald angels.

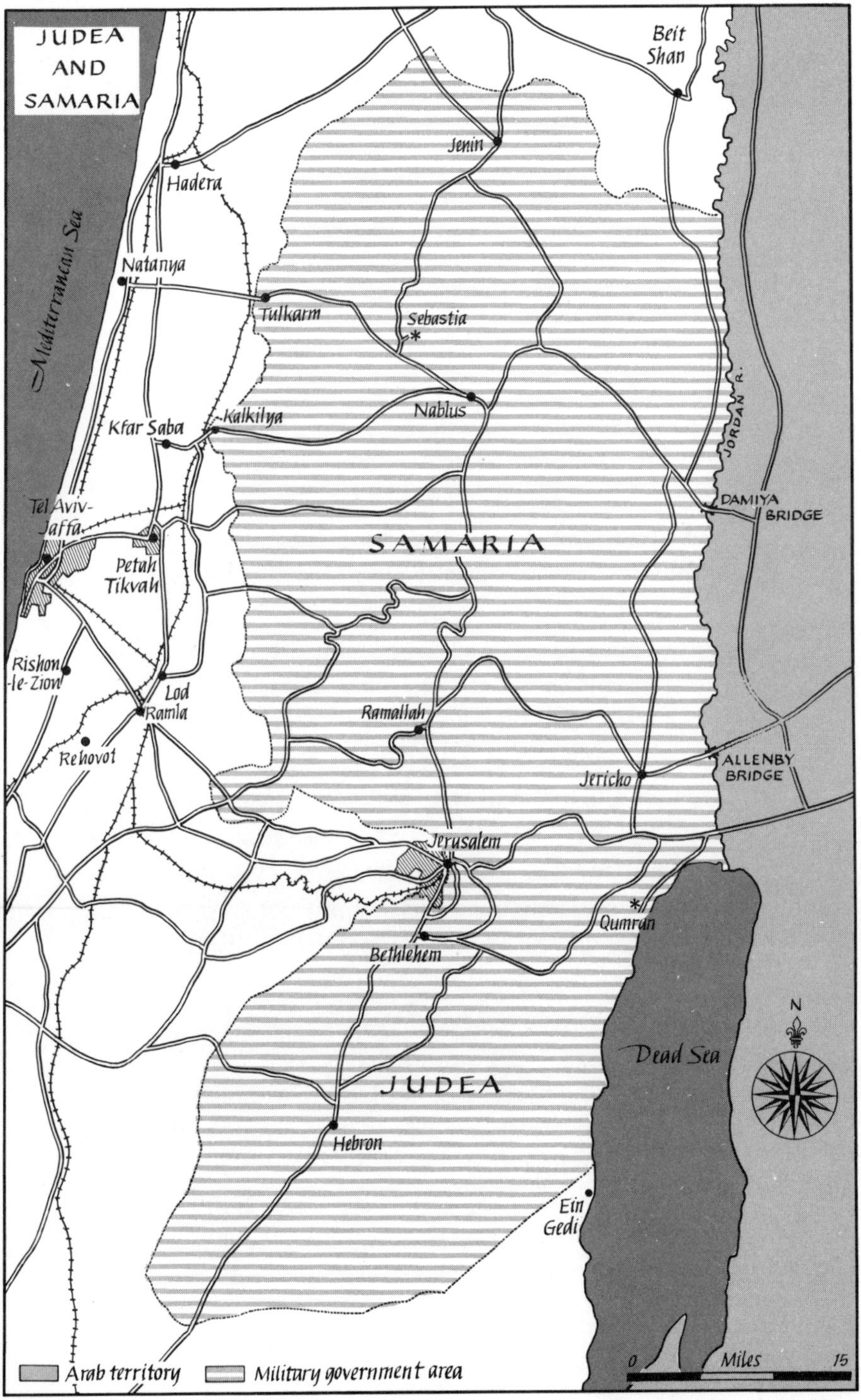
JUDEA AND SAMARIA
Mediterranean Sea
Beit Shan
Jenin
Hadera
Natanya
Tulkarm
Sebastia
Nablus
Kfar Saba
Kalkilya
JORDAN R.
Tel Aviv-Jaffa
Petah Tikvah
DAMIYA BRIDGE
SAMARIA
Rishon-le-Zion
Lod
Ramla
Rehovot
Ramallah
ALLENBY BRIDGE
Jericho
Jerusalem
Qumran
Bethlehem
N
Dead Sea
JUDEA
Hebron
Ein Gedi
Arab territory
Military government area
0 Miles 15

FROM DAN TO EILAT

The Church of the Nativity is rather like a citadel, with its thick stone walls. It stands at the southern end of the curved limestone ridge along which the city is spread. This site was established in the fourth century as the birthplace of Jesus. The original basilica was built over the site by the Emperor Constantine, prodded by his pilgrim mother, St. Helena. The present church belongs mainly to the Greek Orthodox Church, with shares and rights reserved for the Latin and Armenian churches. The Protestant sects (latecomers to the Holy Places) are allowed to hold a service on Christmas Eve in the open courtyard.

The interior of the church is Byzantine. Rows of Corinthian columns support massive beams of Lebanon cedar, and images of medieval saints line the walls. A section of the floor is open to show a portion of a mosaic dating back to the reconstruction of the church by the Emperor Justinian in the sixth century. The grotto is reached by a stairway through the bronze Crusader doors. Below, a silver star marks the site of the Nativity, and down two more stairs is the stone manger, with a fourth-century silver crib donated by Helena. The vault is small, blackened by smoke and lit by flickering candlelight. It has asbestos tapestry on the walls as protection from fire, a present from French President MacMahon in 1874.

Next to the Church of the Nativity is the Franciscan Church of St. Catherine, built in 1881. It is from here that the Latin Mass is broadcast and televised on Christmas Eve. Underneath is the tomb of St. Jerome, the fifth-century Bible savant.

Down the lane along the side of the Church of the Nativity is the Milk Grotto. The story goes that while Mary was nursing her child in the cave a few drops of milk spilt on the rock, thus giving it a chalky appearance.

HEBRON

The highway from Bethlehem to Hebron twists through hills sprinkled with olive and fig trees and terraced for grapevines. Along this road Abraham came with his flocks of sheep on his way to stay in Hebron; and later his great-grandson Joseph traveled this way in his coat of many colors, on his way to Shechem (Nablus) to visit his jealous brothers (Genesis 37:14). This is the road King David took from his first capital at Hebron to capture the Jebusite city of Jerusalem; and later his son Absalom raised the standard of rebellion against his father in Hebron. The Holy Family of Jesus passed through here, fleeing to Egypt from the wrath of Herod. All around this countryside the echoes of the past can be heard, and every village and hilltop claims its hero and its event.

Three miles from Bethlehem lie the Pools of Solomon, three reservoirs partly hewn out of the rock. Popular tradition attributes their construction to King Solomon, though they are probably of later date. They act as a catchment basin for the surrounding hills and for several springs in the area. Below the third pool are the pumping station and pipelines that take the water to the Temple area in Jerusalem. These pipes replace two ancient aqueducts. The rather decrepit fortress nearby was built by the Turks in the seventeenth century to guard the pools.

A little farther along, a road turns off to the right to Gush Etzion, a group of four Jewish religious kibbutzim that were wiped out by the Jordanian Arab Legion just before the birth of the State of Israel in 1948. After the area was occupied by Israel forces in 1967, a Nahal farming group resettled one of the villages, Kfar Etzion, that had been turned into a Jordanian military camp.

Hebron is one of the oldest cities in the world. Its Jewish community existed in Biblical times, and it was one of the four Jewish Holy Cities of medieval Palestine, the others being Jerusalem, Safad and Tiberias. In the Arab riots of 1929, the pious and peaceful ghetto was overrun by a bloodthirsty mob of Arabs, and more than sixty men, women and children were massacred and as many more wounded. Since that episode the town until 1967 had no Jewish residents.

The two most famous sites at Hebron are associated with the Patriarch Abraham. After leaving Lot in the region of Bethel, "Abram moved his tent, and came and dwelt by the oaks of Mamre, which are at Hebron"—Genesis 13:18. A centuries-old tree about a mile west of Hebron is known as the Oak of Mamre. It is barely alive and its branches are propped up on iron stakes. It may have been while sitting under this tree that Abraham saw three men approaching him, and having offered them hospitality, found he was entertaining angels unawares.

According to the story in Genesis, when his wife Sarah died, Abraham sought a tomb for her and went to see Ephron the Hittite, who offered him the use of his own family sepulcher. Abraham declined, and bought the cave and the field of Machpelah for 400 silver shekels. In the Machpelah cave tomb, tradition has it that Abraham and Sarah, Isaac and Rebecca, Jacob and Leah, and also Joseph, are buried. This was probably the first piece of property acquired by the Hebrew nomads in the Holy Land.

JUDEA AND SAMARIA

The cave of Machpelah is enclosed by a huge rectangular building (the Haram) whose foundations and lower courses date from the time of the Second Temple and may have been built by Herod. The distinctive crenellated parapet is more recent, as are the lofty minarets. Today it is a mosque. You climb a steep flight of stairs to the left of the building and, turning right, find yourself in a carpeted hall with six great cenotaphs. Joseph is in a separate enclosure. Through a grating in the floor you are permitted a glimpse into the original cave, to which entrance is forbidden. On the left of the entrance is the prayer hall, which only Moslems may enter. It was once a Byzantine church, then a Crusader one; the pulpit is a fine example of twelfth-century wood carving, recently restored.

The monuments are covered with costly tapestries embroidered with Koranic verses and pious inscriptions, the gifts of Turkish sultans. To the west of the enclosure is the women's prayer hall.

Probably nowhere else in the world do the Moslem and Jewish faiths intermingle so intimately as here in the Machpelah, where the Hebrew Patriarchs are revered as prophets by the followers of Mohammed. The tribal wanderer from Chaldea, to whose seed God promised the Land of Canaan, is claimed as their ancestor also by the Moslem Arabs, who call him *El Khalil* (the Friend of God), which is also the Arabic name for Hebron. The Jaffa Gate in the Old City of Jerusalem, from which one sets out for Hebron, bears an Arabic inscription that reads, "There is no God but God and Abraham is the friend of God."

JERICHO

At the entrance to Jericho is a sign which says, "Welcome to the oldest city in the world." The reason for this distinction can be stated in one word: water. You come down the mountain east of Jerusalem (2,600 feet above sea level) through the bleak Wilderness of Judea to emerge into an equally bleak plain (800 feet below sea level); and suddenly before you is an oasis town smothered in lush vegetation—bananas, oranges, dates, papayas, brilliant poincianas and bougainvillea, green grass and running water, which comes mainly from a gushing spring named after Elisha the Prophet, who is said to have "healed these waters" with a cruse of salt (II Kings 2:21).

Across the street from the spring is a mound where the British archaeologist Kathleen Kenyon has excavated portions of a tower, wall and staircase dating back 9,000 years. Jericho was, therefore, an ancient city when Joshua and the Children of Israel crossed the fords of the River Jordan five miles to the east and entered the Promised Land, after Moses had died. That was in the thirteenth century B.C. The Bible relates that Joshua sent two spies to the city, which was strongly fortified and surrounded by a heavy wall. They were hidden by a harlot called Rahab, who dwelt in a house on top of the wall. They arranged with her to mark the house with a scarlet thread hung from the window, so that she and her family would be spared. The walls fell flat before the blast of the rams' horns blown by seven priests, and the town was captured and razed. It was rebuilt and has changed hands many times in the more than thirty cen-

JUDEA AND SAMARIA

turies since Joshua, the last time being its occupation by the Israel army in June, 1967.

A little north of the Spring of Elisha there is an Arab house built over the mosaic floor of a fifth-century synagogue. Some years before the end of the Mandate, Professor Sukenik of the Hebrew University learned that the floor had been discovered by the Arab owner of the land while digging the foundations for his house. Sukenik, unable to raise the money to buy it, obtained a promise from the Arab owner that the floor would be preserved in his cellar. More than twenty years later, when Jericho was taken in the Six-Day War, it was found that the Arab family had remained faithful to the trust. A menorah, the seven-branched candelabrum which is the national symbol of Israel, is pictured in the center of the mosaic, and below it is the Hebrew inscription *Shalom al Israel*—"Peace be upon Israel."

Hisham's Palace

In the eighth century A.D. the Caliph Hisham ibn Abd-el-Malik, of the Omayyad dynasty in Damascus, was captivated by Jericho's balmy winter sun, desert air and oasis greenery—just as an American millionaire might "discover" a winter resort in the Bahamas.

A little more than a mile north of the Spring of Elisha, he built a palace within a walled estate. The two-story living quarters were grouped around a cloistered courtyard with an ornamental pool in the center. On the north side was the luxurious bathhouse, with a swimming pool, and hot and cold rooms and a brick furnace were in the basement. The baths were lavishly decorated by imported craftsmen

• 143

and the floors of the pools were covered with beautiful mosaics. Alternate male and female figures were set in the niches of the entrance porch. (Islam had not yet adopted the Hebrew prohibition against portraying the human image).

But Allah decreed otherwise. In the earthquake of A.D. 747, the palace was partly demolished, apparently before it was ever occupied. In 1936 the excavation of the palace began, and since June, 1967, a great deal of restoration has been carried out by the Israel authorities.

The showpiece is the mosaic floor of one small room in the bathhouse complex. It depicts a tree with gleaming fruit, underneath which three gazelles are being attacked by a ferocious lion. The effect is that of a Persian carpet.

Pieces of the intricately carved plaster from the pavilion and some of the palace decorations have been reconstructed; they can be seen in the Rockefeller Museum in Jerusalem.

High above Jericho, clinging to the mountain, is a Greek Orthodox monastery known as the Monastery of Temptation. Its site is believed to be the place where Jesus spent forty days and forty nights, being tempted the while by the devil (Luke 4:2). According to tradition, Jesus spent the forty days of temptation in a grotto which is today a chapel.

Ten miles south of Jericho, on a small barren plateau overlooking the Dead Sea, are the ruins of Qumran, a spot which became world-famous when the Dead Sea Scrolls were discovered in nearby caves. It is generally believed that Qumran was the home of a community of Essenes, an ascetic Jewish sect in existence at the time of Jesus. The archaeological evidence indicates that the buildings were occupied by the Essenes from the second century B.C. They

JUDEA AND SAMARIA

had an elaborate system of water supply: cisterns were fed with rain water by an aqueduct from a dam across the wadi. The place was sacked by the Roman legions around A.D. 68; the inhabitants were probably put to the sword. Before the end came they had succeeded in hiding their precious collection of sacred scrolls in caves in the surrounding cliffs. The scrolls were preserved in pottery jars.

On the Dead Sea shore two miles away, the spring and stream of Ain Feshkha have created a startling patch of green in the otherwise silent and lifeless landscape. It is here that the Essenes grew their food.

The ford of Bethabara lies five miles southeast of Jericho, reached through a flat and sandy wilderness. It was here on the River Jordan that by tradition "cometh Jesus from Galilee to Jordan unto John, to be baptized of him"—Matthew 3:13. From the earliest centuries of the Christian era, pilgrims have journeyed here to bathe or to be baptized in the river. The day of the Epiphany is especially associated with this observance.

Bethabara is a pleasant spot where the river flows strongly between acacia, tamarisk and flowering reeds before entering the Dead Sea. There is a Franciscan chapel on the shore, and a shallow amphitheater. A little higher up is the Greek Orthodox Convent of St. John the Baptist. The Arabs call this place *Qasa el Yahud* (Castle of the Jews) in the mistaken belief that it was here that Joshua led the Children of Israel dry-shod across the river.

NABLUS

The road from Jerusalem to Ramallah, ten miles north, is lined with expensive-looking stone villas, many of them built with money earned in Kuwait and other oil-producing countries. They are usually rented to affluent Arabs spending the summer in the hills.

Ramallah, meaning Height of Allah, is the largest town in the area; it is 3,000 feet above sea level. A prosperous Christian town of 40,000 inhabitants, it adjoins a smaller Moslem town called Birah or Al Birah. The surrounding ridges and valleys are steeped in Old Testament history.

From Ramallah a road winds southwest down to the plain, joining the Jerusalem–Tel Aviv highway at the Latrun Monastery. The main road from Ramallah to Nablus continues northward for thirty miles through the hills of Samaria (Shomron), which become more rugged and picturesque as you go on. Arab villages cling to the high ground, and on the terraced slopes and valley bottoms the villagers tend their olive groves, fruit trees and small, stony fields of wheat, barley and vegetables by the same primitive methods they have used for thousands of years.

Halfway to Nablus a road turns off to a mound of ruins called in Arabic *Seilum*. This marks the site of Shiloh, where the Tabernacle and the Ark of the Lord rested from the time of Joshua to the days of Samuel 300 years later.

The town of Nablus (called Shechem in Hebrew) is contained between Mount Gerizim and Mount Ebal. Shechem was an ancient Canaanite town; its earliest walls date from 2000 B.C. The Biblical patriarchs camped in Shechem and Joseph was buried there, though it is doubtful if his tradi-

JUDEA AND SAMARIA

tional tomb is authentic. In later years Shechem was overshadowed by Samaria just to the north, though Mount Gerizim remained sacred to the Samaritans. In 72 B.C. Vespasian founded the nearby "new city," Neapolis (later turned into Nablus by the Arabs), and it became an important Roman center, though most of the inhabitants remained Samaritans. The Crusaders conquered the city in 1099; a part of one of the churches built then still survives as a mosque. In 1187 it was taken by Saladin and the population became overwhelmingly Moslem, although a tiny Samaritan community still remained. Nablus has always been noted for its turbulence, and in the eighteenth century was the storm center of intertribal wars. Under the British Mandate it remained a headache to the authorities, as it did to its Jordanian rulers after 1948.

Today Nablus contains 30,000 Moslems, 700 Christians and about 150 Samaritans. It is the center of the Arab olive-oil soap industry, and continues to export this soap to the neighboring countries.

The group of Samaritans lives on the western edge of the city in great poverty. Their synagogue is bare of decoration and the worshipers squat on the floor on straw mats, using small wooden stools to hold the Torah, from which they read in turn. It is written in the Samaritan script, which is rather like ancient Hebrew, and consists of the Five Books of Moses only, as the Samaritans do not recognize the rest of the Bible as holy. Even the Samaritan Pentateuch has variations from the Jewish one. According to their tradition the Samaritan version of the Torah was written by Abishua, a contemporary of Joshua.

From the time of the return of the Jews from the Babylonian captivity, enmity prevailed between the Jews and the

Samaritans, who even at that time were a dissident Jewish sect. The Samaritans tried to prevent the rebuilding of the temple in Jerusalem, and Josephus records their insults to the Jewish state. The Samaritans offered assistance to Alexander the Great and were allowed to build a temple on Mount Gerizim, where they sacrificed as the Jews did in Jerusalem. Their temple was destroyed by John Hyrcanus. The Samaritans were troublesome to the Romans, who treated them with harshness and at times killed off numbers of them. The Procurator of Judea, Pontius Pilate, was recalled from his post after such a massacre in A.D. 36. A generation later many more Samaritans were put to death, and a temple to Jupiter was built on their sacred mountain.

The bad blood between the Jews and the Samaritans is revealed by the rather bitter remark of the woman from whom Jesus asked water at Jacob's Well: "How is it that thou, being a Jew, askest drink of me, which am a woman of Samaria? for the Jews have no dealings with the Samaritans" —John 4:9. This well can be seen just before you enter Nablus, where an unfinished church stands over it.

The antagonism continued between the Samaritans and another dissident Jewish sect, the Christians, who were allowed by a later Roman emperor to build their own church on Mount Gerizim. After the Samaritans were expelled, interfaith relations were seldom a pretty affair in the history of the Holy Land. Today, a small community of Samaritans still survives in Nablus, and another small group is settled in Holon, near Tel Aviv.

On the eve of the Passover festival, the entire community goes up Mount Gerizim and remains for a week in stone houses which are closed up for the rest of the year. They have an altar on which they sacrifice seven sheep as the

Torah demands—"Your lambs shall be without blemish, a male of the first year." The high priest stands on a rock and reads aloud chapter 12 of Exodus, which describes the Passover ceremonies; as he does so, his flock obeys each command quite literally.

SEBASTIA

After the death of King Solomon, the Hebrew kingdom split into two: Judah in the south, with its capital remaining in Jerusalem; and Israel in the north, with a new capital at Samaria, eight miles northwest of present-day Nablus. The Book of Kings records that Omri, King of Israel in the ninth century B.C., "bought the hill Samaria of Shemer for two talents of silver, and built on the hill, and called the name of the city . . . Samaria"—I Kings 16:24. Here on this lofty hilltop, commanding major strategic routes, Omri and his son King Ahab developed their new capital. From their palace they had a clear view of the Mediterranean more than twenty miles to the west.

On the summit Omri built a rectangular citadel protected by a wall of hewn stone carefully bonded, with header and stretcher courses laid on beds of natural rock. Remains of these walls can still be seen today on the site. Ahab's carved ivories are exhibited at the Rockefeller Museum in Jerusalem. Hundreds of *ostraca* (inscribed potsherds) with Hebrew writing have also been found, as well as a plaster-lined reservoir which might well be the "pool of Samaria" in which Ahab's chariot was washed after his death in battle against the Syrians.

In 722 B.C. the Assyrians conquered Samaria, the Israelites were exiled, and the city declined in importance. The Hellenistic period saw the revival of Samaria, between 331 B.C. and 107 B.C. The remains of magnificent buildings of that period, as well as great circular towers which were built on the Israelite walls, can easily be identified today. In 25 B.C. King Herod was given Samaria by the Roman Emperor as a reward for services rendered, and he set about beautifying the city. He changed its name to Sebaste (Sebastos is Greek for Augustus, the name of the emperor), and on the summit he built a temple with a spacious plaza round it. Its shining walls and columns of polished limestone were visible from Caesarea on the coast. The wide stairway that led to the entrance of the temple still exists, as do the remains of the fine forum. The stadium can be seen in outline among the olive trees on the eastern slope. Two great towers still stand at the entrance to the city.

Two hundred years later, the Roman Emperor Septimus Severus repaired the walls, rebuilt the temple and added a fine new theater, which is still in a good state of repair. He also added hundreds of columns to support the covered ways on either side of a wide street; many of these remain, as do the foundations of shops built between the columns.

Three and a half centuries later, in the Byzantine period, a legend took root that the body of John the Baptist had been buried in Sebastia. This led to the erection of two churches—the Cathedral of St. John, over what was said to be his tomb on the edge of the city, and a church near the top of the hill which is connected with the legend of the discovery of his head. In the twelfth century the latter church was rebuilt with a crypt. There are Crusader crosses cut in the stone stairway, and a faded painting of St. John. The Crusaders also rebuilt the cathedral; much of their massive masonry still stands on the original great paving

JUDEA AND SAMARIA

stones. Saladin conquered Sebastia in 1187, and part of the cathedral was subsequently converted into a mosque still used by the local Arabs, who live in the small village on the lower slopes.

Nearly thirty miles north of Nablus, the road reaches the Arab town of Jenin (or Janin), at the rim of the great Valley of Jezreel. It goes back to the Biblical Hebrew town of En-gannim (Spring of the Gardens) in the territory allotted to the Tribe of Issachar. From here one road continues northward across the plain to Afula and another turns left along the edge of the Hills of Ephraim to Megiddo, in the direction of Haifa.

CHAPTER 7

The Shefelah

The Shefelah (Lowlands) was the name generally used in Biblical times for the undulating foothill region of southern Judea. The term is sometimes loosely used to include the southern coastal plain as far as Gaza—that is, the whole of the ancient land of the Philistines, with whom the hill-dwelling Hebrews were in chronic conflict.

The region dealt with in this chapter extends from the Jerusalem–Tel Aviv highway southward between the mountains and the sea, until it opens up into the northern Negev.

FROM JERUSALEM TO TEL AVIV

The main road from Jerusalem emerges out of the mountains at Sha'ar Hagai (Bab-el-Wad)—the Gate to the Valley. Here it forks into two roads: the original Latrun highway, cut off by the 1948 war was reopened by the 1967 war. The detour highway, constructed after 1948 and swinging sharply to the left, is today used mainly by trucks and buses. It is 8 miles longer than the old road, which it joins near Ramla.

The Latrun Highway

Soon after leaving the exit from the hills, the road passes the beautiful Italianate building of the Latrun Monastery set into a slope among olive groves and vineyards; it belongs to the French Trappist Order. Above it are the remains of a Crusader castle, called Le Toron des Chevaliers, which was built by the Templars and used by Richard the Lion-Heart. (The Arabs derive the name of Latrun from "Le Toron.") The Trappist monks, who observe the silence of their Order, produce excellent red and white wine and brandy that can be bought by passing travelers who go up through the gateway.

The road continues through the soft wheatlands of the Vale of Ayalon (the Biblical Ajalon), which has a stirring martial history. It was here that the Lord hearkened to the cry of Joshua, "Sun, stand thou still upon Gibeon; and thou, moon, in the valley of Ajalon," when he wanted to destroy the defeated Amorites who might otherwise have escaped under cover of darkness (Joshua 10:12). Here Judas Maccabaeus routed his enemies and here the Roman legions assembled for the advance towards the Holy City; and it was in the same field that the Crusader army unfurled their banners a thousand years later.

A few miles before Ramla, a road turns off to the left to the kibbutz of Gezer, near the *tel*, or mound, of the ancient city of that name, fortified by Solomon. The *tel* was excavated more than sixty years ago and walls and structures like those of Megiddo were revealed. A unique find was a farming calendar nearly 3,000 years old. It divides the year among the seasons for olives, grain, flax, grapes, barley and summer fruits, and, rather sensibly, leaves a month for feasting.

Excavations of this important site were resumed in 1965 by the Hebrew Union College of Cincinnati and Harvard University; and plans are to continue this work for several years.

The Hartuv Highway

From Sha'ar Hagai, the detour highway (the main route from 1948 to 1967) runs southward along the foot of the hills to the Hartuv crossroad, also known as the crossroad of Samson, the local hero. At this point one road continues southward to Beit Guvrin and Kiryat Gat, in the Lachish area, while the Hartuv highway to Ramla and Tel Aviv turns sharply to the right and heads westward towards the coast.

Through miles of undulating vineyards, fruit orchards and carob groves in this pleasant Shefelah countryside one reaches the large town of Ramla, thirteen miles from Tel Aviv. It was built by the Caliph Suleiman in A.D. 716, and remained the capital of Arab Palestine until the eleventh century, when the Crusaders swept through it on their way to Jerusalem. Most of the city was destroyed, including the great mosque which lies to the west of the main road. The "White Tower" was added to this mosque in the thirteenth century as a minaret.

THE SHEFELAH

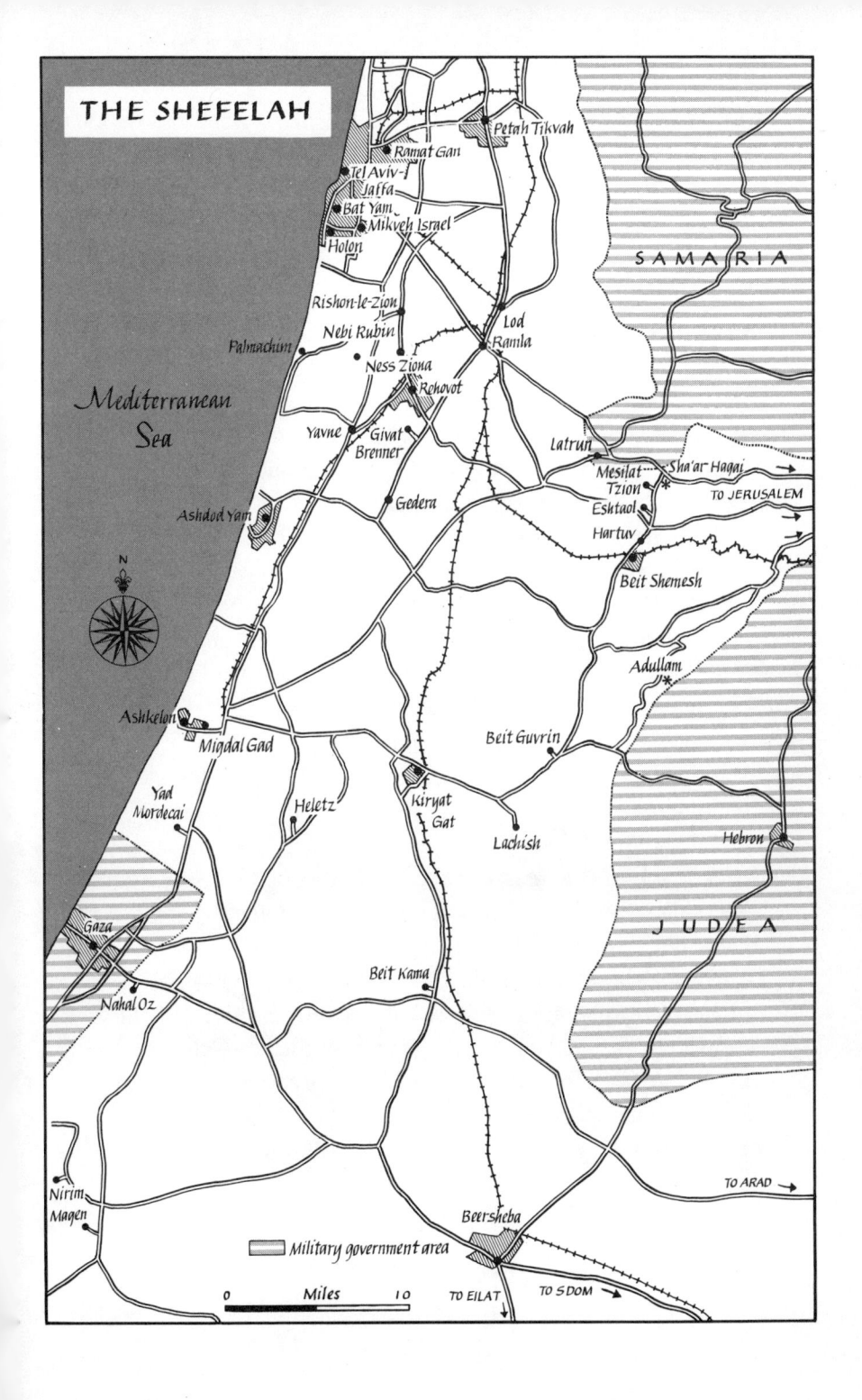

It is said that Napoleon watched his troops' attack on Jaffa from the top of this tower in 1799; looking the other way at the massive sweep of the Judean hills lying twenty miles to the east, he decided not to march on Jerusalem but to go north and attack Acre, where he failed and was forced to retire.

In the field around the White Tower are the remains of Suleiman's eighth-century mosque. It was destroyed by the Crusaders and rebuilt by Saladin at the end of the twelfth century. Under this field are three enormous underground vaults, reached by three stone staircases, with high, arched ceilings resting on stout stone columns. They are grouped around a square cistern with arched bays. In 1960, on the other side of the main road, there was uncovered another eighth-century cistern that was once known to the pilgrims as the Pool of St. Helena (the mother of Emperor Constantine). For a token fee you can go down an ancient stone staircase, step into a small gondola manned by a young Ramlaite, and glide along the three bays between the giant columns.

A few hundred yards east of the "White Tower," at the back of Ramla's marketplace, is a rectangular building known as the Great Mosque. This was originally a large Crusader church and it is beautifully preserved.

During the War of Independence in 1948, the two Arab towns of Ramla and Lod were the forward positions of the Arab Legion that had cut off Jerusalem and were threatening Tel Aviv. When the tide of battle turned against them the inhabitants of these two towns fled, leaving ghost towns which filled up with the medley of Jewish immigrants pouring into the country.

Ramla comes into its own on Saturday evening, when the

THE SHEFELAH

traffic to or from Jerusalem is forced to pick its way through the main street brimming with a festive crowd of shirt-sleeved burghers, their wives and their innumerable white baby carriages.

From the center of Ramla, a road branches off to the right to the international airport, passing through the small town of Lod, standing in a sea of gnarled old olive trees.

Lod, also known as Lydda and once as Diospolis (as it is marked on the sixth-century Madeba map), is first mentioned in the Bible as having been built by grandsons of Benjamin (I Chron. 8:12). The New Testament relates that St. Peter "came down also to the saints which dwelt at Lydda," and that he cured here the sick man Aeneas (Acts 9:32–35). The Romans sacked it in A.D. 70 and later rebuilt it and gave it the name Diospolis (City of Jupiter). The checkered later history of Palestine is summed up in masonry by the church and the mosque standing beside each other on Crusader foundations which were themselves erected on the ruins of the sixth-century Byzantine church.

The "local boy who makes good" of Lod was St. George who, according to legend, was born and buried here in the third century A.D. It is hard to think of any other saintly figure who has undergone such curious transformations. The story is that he became a tribune in a Roman legion and was put to death for his Christian faith. Somehow he later came to be depicted as a medieval knight on horseback slaying a dragon—a tale which seems to echo the legend of Perseus killing the sea monster to rescue the maiden Andromeda at Jaffa, a few miles away on the coast. In an equally mysterious way he became transmuted into St. George of Merrie England, after his fame had presumably been carried to that distant isle in the baggage of Crusaders returning from the Holy Land. At some stage, St. George of Lydda also became a holy man to the Moslems in much the same way as did the Prophet Elijah.

The capture of Lod in 1948 was one of the dramatic exploits of the War of Independence. Led by Moshe Dayan, a small column of open jeeps made a daring surprise attack on the town, tearing through the main street with machine guns blazing at the buildings on either side, like a sheriff's posse in a Western film.

In the nearby foothills to the east (on the old pre-1967 border) is Modi'in, the place of the origin of the Maccabeans, with whom eighteen tombs cut into the rock are associated. Each year at Chanukah, the Feast of Lights, a torch is kindled at this spot and carried by relay runners to Mount Herzl in Jerusalem, where it is used to light a great menorah (candelabrum) symbolizing that which was relit by Judas Maccabaeus in the Temple in 164 B.C.

Two miles outside Tel Aviv is Mikveh Israel, the first agricultural school in the country. It was established in 1870 by French Jews, who were granted the land by the Turkish Government. As you pass the school gates you can see the red-roofed buildings at the end of an avenue of tall palm trees. Here at this gate, Theodor Herzl had a conversation in 1897 with the German Kaiser, who was on his way to visit Jerusalem. Herzl reports in his memoirs that the Kaiser was dressed in a Crusader's outfit.

THE REHOVOT AREA

Just south of Tel Aviv–Jaffa lies a cluster of towns and villages which were the heartland of modern Jewish settlement before the end of the nineteenth century. The center of this area is the market and citrus town of Rehovot, and along the road leading through it are other towns and villages whose names echo with the early struggles of the pre-Herzl eighties, such as Rishon-le-Zion, Ness Ziona and Gedera.

Rishon-le-Zion lies five miles to the north of Rehovot. The small group of Russian Jews who founded it as a farm village in 1882 simply and proudly called it "The First to Zion." But things went hard with them until Baron Edmond de Rothschild helped them to find water and to build the wine cellars. Their synagogue had to be erected without permission from the Turkish authorities and was, therefore, disguised as a warehouse. The oldest inhabitants still tell with pride that Dr. Herzl visited the village in 1898, and that the national anthem "Hatikvah" (The Hope) was composed here by N. H. Imber and sung for the first time in the communal hall. Rishon today is a center of Israel's wine-making industry and still possesses the old cellars, with thick walls and sweet-smelling wine casks. Nesher (Eagle), Israel's first brewery, is next door to the cellars. (The local beer is mild.)

Less than three miles away is Ness Ziona or Nes Tsiyona (Standard towards Zion), founded two years later than Rishon-le-Zion. At that time the blue and white Zionist flag was unfurled for the first time in Palestine, and the settlement was given its name from the phrase in Jeremiah, "Set up a standard towards Zion."

Rehovot was founded by Polish Jews in 1890. Its chief pride is the Weizmann Institute of Science, the gleaming functional buildings of which stand in fifty acres of trees, lawns and flower beds. A small hill at the northern end of the grounds is crowned by the fine residence designed for Dr. Chaim Weizmann, Israel's first president, by the famous German architect Erich Mendelssohn. Dr. Weizmann used to enjoy taking his guests onto the terrace, sweeping his arm around the panorama of shiny green orange groves and telling how he stood on this very spot with General Allenby during the 1917 advance and declared he would make his home here one day. Allenby gazed at the sandy wasteland all round, and most likely decided that the Zionist leader was just a crazy dreamer.

The Institute, with its research facilities in applied mathematics, biophysics, electronics, experimental biology, isotope research, plant genetics and nuclear sciences, has a growing reputation abroad.

At the Jack and Eva Feinberg Graduate School, young scientists receiving more advanced training include a number of foreign students from Africa, Asia and Latin America.

The guests of the Institute are lodged at the handsome San Martin Hostel. Other noteworthy buildings are the Wix Auditorium and the Haber-Goldenberg Library, with its oddly pointed rooftops.

Dr. Weizmann died in 1952 and his wife in 1966; they are buried in simple graves in a shady corner of the garden. The government declared his house, his grave and the

Weizmann Institute of Science a national memorial site called Yad Chaim Weizmann.

Close to the Weizmann Institute is the Government Agricultural Research Station, operated jointly with the Faculty of Agriculture of the Hebrew University in Jerusalem.

The main road from Rehovot to Gedera runs through an intensively cultivated area passing Givat Brenner, one of the largest settlements in Israel, hidden behind orange trees. It has a beautiful rest house, surrounded by gardens, and a cultural house named after Enzo Sereni who, during World War II, was parachuted into Italy and killed by the Germans.

Uriel, farther south, is a village established in 1951 by Malben (American Joint Distribution Committee) for families whose breadwinners are blind. Here they are taught to make brushes, baskets and mattresses and to lead a normal life. Uriel, the name of an archangel, means "My light is God."

The old main road to Beersheba now leaves the citrus belt and traverses a rolling and spacious plain filled with farm villages that draw water from the eastern arm of the big irrigation pipeline to the Negev from the Yarkon River near Tel Aviv.

THE COAST

The village of Yavne (The Biblical Jabneel or Jabneh), six miles southwest of Rehovot, is on the coastal road that runs southward from Tel Aviv to Ashkelon. This area must have been inhabited from time immemorial, for it always had water from springs. Tradition has it that before the destruction of the Temple in A.D. 70, Rabbi Yochanan ben

Zakkai came before the Roman commander of Jerusalem and asked to be given Yavne as a safe place for himself and his fellow scholars. This request was granted, and a great school of learning was established here, called Kerem Yavne (Vineyard of Yavne), "for the scholars sat on the floor in rows, just like the vines of the vineyards." It was here that the sages established the Canon (authorized version) of the Old Testament. The Mishnah, the codified Jewish precepts and laws, was also begun here and was ultimately completed in Galilee in the second century.

Some of the nearby settlements were established by Orthodox Jews. They include Kerem Yavne, with its domed Yeshiva (Talmudic school) and B'nai Darom (Sons of the South). You are very likely to see farmers working in the fields with *yarmulkes* (skullcaps) on their heads, and the farmers' wives wearing the traditional *sheitlen* (wigs).

Six miles west of Ness Ziona lies a stretch of beach which has become the favorite swimming place of the foreign diplomatic corps. On Sundays, while the rest of the country is at work, they drive out beyond Palmachim, a communal settlement of ex-soldiers of the Palmach (commando force of Haganah), and along the stretch of coastal road that runs past the ruins of Yavne Yam (Yavne on the Sea), the ancient Greek port of Jamnia, where Judas Maccabaeus fought and vanquished the Greeks in 156 B.C.:

> He came upon the Jamnites also by night, and set fire on the haven and the navy, so that the light of the fire was seen at Jerusalem two hundred and forty furlongs off.
> —II Maccabees 12:9

All that is left of the port is crumbling pieces of masonry showing above the water, the remains of the harbor, and, on the shore, ancient walls partially covered by sand.

THE SHEFELAH

Just south of Palmachim, at Nebi Rubin, a strange edifice rises from sand dunes. Looking like a flat-topped, many-sided temple, this is the experimental atomic reactor of the "swimming-pool" type, built with the assistance of the United States government; the building was designed by the eminent American architect Philip Johnson. The reactor produces radioactive isotopes for research in medicine, agriculture and industry.

Fifteen miles farther down the coast is the new town of Ashdod Yam, which has been developed as Israel's second major Mediterranean seaport (after Haifa) to serve the southern part of the country. It was an ambitious project. There is no natural harbor, and, after long and exact studies of the winds and tides, one was constructed outwards from the flat sandy coast. The port is concentrating on developing mechanical means of loading citrus, potash and phosphates directly from shore to ship.

The plans for future development call for the building of a garden city of a quarter-million inhabitants and an industrial zone. All this is easier to visualize today than it was years ago, when there was nothing here but a stretch of windswept sand dunes. The scene is now dominated by what looks like a squat cathedral but is actually the largest power station in the country; it is operated by crude oil which reaches it through the pipeline from Eilat.

The avenues of young date palms along the sea front could serve as a symbol of the new Ashdod Yam. These were transported here wrapped in sacks and have taken root in the bare sand to provide shade and beauty for the inhabitants, who have also quickly taken root on the empty dunes. Here, as elsewhere in Israel, it is exciting to start from scratch and to see the paper plans become a living city.

Ashdod Yam is actually being revived as a port, for in ancient times it served as the sea outlet for the important Philistine city of Ashdod. This city became a thorn in the flesh of the Hebrews, and the prophets continually forecast its doom. It was finally conquered by the youthful King Uzziah of Judah:

> And he went forth and warred against the Philistines, and brake down . . . the wall of Ashdod, and built cities about Ashdod.
> —II Chronicles 26:6

The *tel* marking the site of the ancient city is being excavated, confirming layer by layer its turbulent history.

Five miles south of the site of ancient Ashdod is the site of another and even more famous Philistine city, Ashkelon. An American real-estate agent would be intoxicated with Ashkelon—ocean, beach and sunshine straight off a Caribbean cruise poster; antique cities half buried in the sand dunes; and all scarcely an hour's drive from Tel Aviv. The gently tilted land is fanned by cool sea breezes which mingle with the warm wind from the African coast, just around the corner. Through a break in the cliffs (out of which old Roman columns stick like the guns of a fort), the mouth of a stream, long silted up, used to form a small harbor. There has always been a plentiful supply of fresh water from springs and wells, and fruit and vegetables could grow in profusion in the fertile soil—including the scallions or small onions for which the place became famous in Roman times. (The word "scallion" comes from the Latin *caepa Ascalonia*, or onion of Ascalon.)

It is not to be wondered that this delightful corner of the coast was sought after throughout history. Ashkelon, like Jaffa and Acre farther north, is among the oldest cities in the world. The Tel-el-Amarna Letters (fourteenth century B.C.) mention Ashkelon as a rich but rebellious city. A little later the capture of the city by Pharaoh Rameses II was recorded on a thirteenth-century B.C. bas-relief at Karnak in Upper Egypt. The carving shows the Egyptian soldiers storming the fortified city with the help of ladders, while the bearded Ashkelonite defenders man the walls.

About the time of Joshua this coastal area was settled by the Philistines, a seafaring Greek people who worshiped Dagon and Ashtoreth (Astarte). There followed centuries of struggle between them and the Hebrews, who had established themselves in the rest of the country. As might be expected, Ashkelon is repeatedly referred to in the Old Testament as an enemy stronghold, one of the five main Philistine cities (the others being Gaza, Ashdod, Gath and Ekron). When the Philistines killed King Saul, David cries out in lament:

> Tell it not in Gath, publish it not in the streets of Askelon; lest the daughters of the Philistines rejoice.
> —II Samuel 1:20

There are records of the tribute paid by Ashkelon to the Assyrians and the Babylonians, of its conquest by the Persians, and its revival as an important commercial center by the Greeks. Prosperity continued under the Romans and Josephus records that Herod adorned the city with many fine buildings. Under the Moslems, Ashkelon retained its appeal and was known as "the Betrothed of Palestine."

The Crusaders fought many battles in and around Ashkelon until it was taken by Baldwin III in 1153. After it was destroyed by the Sultan Baibars in 1270, it never recovered. Sand blocked the mouth of the river and the gardens and fruit trees, fed by the underground wells, grew freely through the ruins, creating an emerald-green wilderness.

Legends grew up about buried treasure at Ashkelon. Lady Hester Stanhope, the adventurous niece of England's Prime Minister William Pitt, found a treasure map in 1851, organized an expedition, and dug in the Ashkelon area. She unearthed no riches, and there is a story that in feminine fury, she broke her one archaeological find, a colossal marble figure.

In 1960, part of the ruined site was turned into a charming national park. The trees were trimmed, the undergrowth cleared, where possible the walls reconstructed, some columns restored, and stretches of lawn laid down to the edge of the cliff.

The main outlines of the ancient city are clearly discernible—the massive outer walls with their four gates which faced Jaffa, Jerusalem, Gaza and the sea; the higher *tel* in one corner, near the cliff, which was the site of the Philistine Ashkelon; the ledges down to the port; and the lumps of crumbling masonry, battered by winter storms, which are the remains of the old sea wall and harbor moles.

The center of interest for the visitor is the excavated portion of a Herodian building in a corner of the park. In it are now grouped pieces of the colonnade from Herod the Great's Stoa of a Hundred Columns and several sculptured figures found during the 1920 archaeological expedition. The sculptures include a headless winged goddess of victory (Nike) standing on a globe of the world supported by a diminutive Atlas; a goddess of peace carrying a palm branch; and a fine mother and child bearing the crown of Isis. The relics also include tablets from ancient synagogues, with inscriptions in Hebrew.

Today you can climb to the top of the old Crusader wall and, looking towards the Mediterranean, let the tide of time sweep you back through recorded history. You can also walk along the seashore and, with luck, pick up one of the old pottery shards that the waves roll endlessly back and forth, or a piece of ancient glass holding all the colors of the rainbow.

Afridar, adjoining ancient Ashkelon, is an attractive model township established in 1953 by the South African Jewish community and the Ministry of Labor. The focal point of Afridar is the tall, slender clock tower of the shopping center. All the houses have gardens gay with flowers and there is great rivalry to win the coveted annual gardening prize.

Afridar has one of the most wonderful stretches of beach in Israel. It has six hotels, including the Holiday and Vacation Villages, which consist of gaily painted houses for rent to visitors and tourists. This is a joint project of Histour and the French C.E.T. Travel Agency. Another charming hotel, the Dagon, houses its guests in semi-detached cottages facing the sea. (It is named after Dagon, the Philistine sea god whose temple at Gaza was pulled down by the blinded Samson.) About a mile from the hotel is a well-preserved little Roman tomb, its walls and ceiling covered with delicate colored frescoes.

Just to the north of the Gaza Strip, opposite Ashkelon, is Israel's main oil field at Heletz. The first oil strike was made in 1955 and oil wells can be seen among the orange fields.

THE GAZA STRIP

During the 1948 war, Egyptian forces occupied the Gaza Strip, an Arab-inhabited finger of the Palestine coast 25 miles long and an average of five miles wide, with its southwestern end resting on the old Egyptian border. By the 1949 armistice agreement the Strip remained under Egyptian military control pending a final settlement. During the ensuing years it became a base for murderous raids into Israel by small squads of *fedayeen* (terrorists). The chain of Jewish villages around the perimeter of the Strip learned to live and plough their lands within a stone's throw of a turbulent frontier.

In the 1956 Sinai campaign the Gaza Strip was cut off and taken by the Israel army. Four months later it was handed over to a United Nations Emergency Force, which promptly handed it back to the Egyptians, while remaining stationed along the border.

In the Six-Day War of 1967, the Gaza Strip was again isolated and captured in some of the fiercest fighting of the war. Since then it has been under Israel military government. Its future remains to be decided in a peace treaty; but it is hardly likely to be returned to Egyptian rule.

The Strip today is crammed with 400,000 Arab inhabitants, of whom a majority—260,000—are refugees of the 1948 war and still live in eight refugee "camps" that have long since become permanent townships. They continue to get assistance from UNRWA, the United Nations refugee agency, in the form of supplementary rations, schooling, and health services.

The main city is Gaza. Smaller towns are Jabaliya, to the

north of Gaza, and Deir el Ballah, Khan Yunis and Rafah, to the south. From Rafah the coast turns westward and the old railway line parallels it through the town of El Arish and reaches the Suez Canal at Kantara (El Qantara).

The situation Israel found in taking over the Gaza Strip was a bleak one. Under the Egyptian military regime the territory was a stagnant concentration camp for the inhabitants, refugees and nonrefugees alike. Absorption into Egyptian life and economy was not permitted, and the inhabitants were discouraged from going elsewhere. The Israel authorities are making great efforts and assuming heavy financial burdens to sustain economic activity and to provide employment and social services. The citrus and date exports, which existed before the war, are now handled through Israel's marketing channels. Gaza residents are allowed to travel freely to Jerusalem, the West Bank area (Samaria and Judea), to cross the river to Jordan, and to visit the Arab community in Israel.

The history of Gaza stretches back for thousands of years. It was the southern gateway to the Land of Canaan and a key center along the Via Maris, the ancient caravan and trade route along the coast from Egypt. The Egyptian Pharaoh Thutmose III (fifteenth century B.C.) used Gaza as a fortified base; and in the Tel-el-Amarna Letters dating from a century later, the king of Gaza is described as a vassal of the pharaohs.

Gaza became one of the principal Philistine cities. It figures repeatedly in the Old Testament, notably as the scene of Samson's dramatic death. For 3,000 years since then it has remained a strategic prize, constantly changing hands between Egypt, Babylon, Assyria, the Greeks, the Hebrews and the Romans. It was captured by the Caliph Omar in

FROM DAN TO EILAT

the seventh century, by the Crusaders in the twelfth century, by the Turks in the sixteenth century, by Napoleon in 1799, and by General Allenby in 1917. The present-day Israelis therefore have illustrious forerunners.

There is very little for the visitor to see in Gaza that might recall such a long history. The large mosque stands on the foundations of a Crusader church. The tomb said to be that of Mohammed's grandfather gives Gaza a religious interest for Moslems. The name of another saint, Abu al-Azam (Father of Strength), whose tomb is here, may be a dubious reference to Samson. The British war cemetery, with more than 3,000 graves, is a real reminder of Allenby's heavy losses in wresting Gaza from the Turks.

The historical Gaza remains buried, awaiting serious archaeological excavation. Above the surface, the vista of sand and red soil and crowded towns and camps is redeemed by sunshine, the glittering Mediterranean, the greenery of fields, orange groves and palm trees nourished by plentiful wells and springs, and the brilliance of bougainvillea and poincianas.

THE LACHISH-ADULLAM AREA

The Lachish area, to the east of Gaza and Ashkelon, is the first part of Israel to be planned as an integrated region. The skeptics rub their eyes now at the sight of the blueprint made visible on the ground. Kiryat Gat, the urban center, is already a thriving town of 15,000 with functional shopping centers, a community center, a cinema, schools, an amphitheater and clinics. The industrial zone includes a cotton gin, a cellophane-tape factory, a refinery for beet sugar and a textile plant. Agricultural activity has been just as carefully

THE SHEFELAH

planned. The eastern branch of the Yarkon River pipeline passes through the area, providing irrigation for the main crop—cotton—as well as for other industrial or export crops such as groundnuts and sugar beets.

In the hillier parts of the Lachish area, cultivation has concentrated on grapevines and fruit trees, which can be grown on the terraced slopes.

The villages are in groups of four or five, each a mile or two from a rural center containing the stores, school, clinic, agricultural implement depot and homes of the instructors. This grouping was the result of a compromise between the argument that immigrants from the same country should be kept together in their own national groups, to give them a familiar environment, and the opposing argument that if all groups were mixed together, they would integrate more quickly into the life of the country. Under the Lachish plan, each small village is made up of people from one country, but each rural center serves several different villages; in the center the different groups meet and mingle with each other. What is more important for the future is that the children from the village communities mingle in the same school at the center. This integration pattern seems to have worked very well.

The Lachish area has become the pilot project for development areas in other parts of the country, where empty spaces are being settled in a systematic way.

Adjoining the Lachish area to the north is the Adullam development area, extending along the old Jordanian border in the direction of Jerusalem. This rugged region was opened up by the new Nes Harim (Miracle of the Mountains) highway from Jerusalem, which cuts through some fine hill scenery. A number of the narrow defiles have been spanned by a succession of flat stone terraces for fruit growing. In the Adullam area there are more than ten hill villages.

The main thoroughfare through the Adullam-Lachish area is the Beit Guvrin road, which branches off from the main Jerusalem–Tel Aviv highway at the Hartuv crossroad and continues southward through the foothills, along the old Jordanian border and through Beit Guvrin, until it reaches Kiryat Gat. A few miles south of the Hartuv crossroad, the new Nes Harim road emerges from the hills and joins the Beit Guvrin road.

In Biblical times this was a well-settled region of Southern Judea and contained three major cities—Beit Shemesh, Mareshah and Lachish. The site of the first of these is marked by a few remains which can be seen on the right-hand side of the valley shortly after leaving the Hartuv crossroad. Opposite the site, to the left, is the new town of Beit Shemesh, with the large Shimshon cement factory (named after Samson).

Farther south along the road is the kibbutz of Beit Guvrin. This was the site of a fortified Roman town, then a trading post of Phoenician merchants, and later the site of a Crusader citadel. The remains of one Crusader building are still preserved. At the top of the hill there is a locked shed (the key is kept in the kibbutz), erected to preserve the remains of Roman and Byzantine mosaic floors that mainly depict hunting scenes, animals and birds.

The ruins on a hilltop a mile to the south of Beit Guvrin, which can be reached by a dirt track, have been identified as the Biblical Mareshah, the probable birthplace of the prophet Micah. Mareshah is first mentioned in the Bible as one of the cities fortified by King Rehoboam for the de-

THE SHEFELAH

fense of Judah (II Chronicles 11:8). The Greeks settled here in the third century B.C. and called the place Marisa. The remains of the thick outer wall and some houses can still be traced; there are also water cisterns scooped out of the hill and a fine columbarium (from the Latin *columba*, dove), so called because of the dovecote effect of the tiers of burial niches.

Halfway between Beit Guvrin and Kiryat Gat, some way to the south of the road, the kibbutz of Lachish (or Lakhish) stands beside the *tel* excavated some thirty years ago by the British archaeologist John L. Starkey and identified by him as the Biblical Lachish, a Canaanite city conquered by Joshua. Centuries later, in 701 B.C., the Hebrew Lachish was sacked by the Assyrian Sennacherib. The resistance was so spirited that the event was depicted in Sennacherib's palace in Nineveh in a special bas-relief which is now in the British Museum. This vivid battle scene shows the columns of bearded Assyrian soldiers attacking the walls with the help of battering rams, while the defenders try to repel them with bows, stones and burning torches. Several captives are being hanged by the Assyrians.

Lachish and Azekah are mentioned by Jeremiah (34:7) as the last Judean cities, apart from Jerusalem, to hold out against the Babylonian army under Nebuchadnezzar in the seventh century B.C. An extraordinary piece of corroborating evidence came to light twenty-six centuries later, when John Starkey dug up some inscribed potsherds, known as the Lachish Letters, which are reports on the military situation written on the eve of the final battle. Shortly after his discoveries Starkey was killed by Arab robbers on his way to Jerusalem, and the digging of this site has not been resumed.

Five miles farther on, at the edge of Kiryat Gat, there is a mound which has been generally regarded as the site of the ancient city of Gath ("Tell it not in Gath . . ."). Some recent digging has revealed traces of early settlement dating from 3000 B.C. It has not been definitely established that this was the site of the important Philistine city from which Kiryat Gat has taken its name.

It is not merely chance or sentiment that is locating new towns and villages in the Lachish-Adullam region near the ancient sites whose names they revive. To a remarkable extent the recurring factors of strategic defense, travel routes and cultivable soil are recreating in modern Israel the ancient map of southern Judah.

CHAPTER 8

The Negev and the Sinai Desert

THE OPEN FRONTIER

The Negev is Israel's open frontier, its fondest dream and its toughest challenge. In the national imagination it holds a place like that of the American West of over a century ago, but there the comparison ends abruptly. Instead of vast grassy plains teeming with buffalo herds, Israel's southland is mostly a bone-dry, eroded and lifeless landscape which would daunt any human intruder less inured to hardship than the wandering Bedouin, or less compulsive a pioneer than the Israeli of today. There are easier places in Israel to live and work, but talk to the sun-browned, khaki-shirted young men who come riding into Beersheba on their dusty trucks and jeeps, and you find them caught up in the strange spell of taming a wilderness. This is a new desert breed of Jew, piping water into a thirsty land, making stubborn green patches to appear upon it, forcing it to yield up phosphates, oil and copper ore, binding it with undulating ribbons of road, setting regiments of trees marching across the dun-colored waste, and ever pushing southward the rim of habitation. The difficulties of colonizing the Negev should be heart-breaking, but in fact, this is one of the most exciting battles between man and nature being fought anywhere in the world.

And as the pioneer breaks through and the tourist follows in his wake, he finds that this harsh country can have its own beauty, with its painted cliffs and purple mountains, the great canyons which brim with color at dusk or dawn, the sense of space and freedom, the dry air, the brilliant skies at night and, as one nears Eilat, the startlingly blue waters of the Gulf of Aqaba.

Historically, the Negev has never been altogether cut off from human contact. Beersheba, with its perennial supply of drinking water from wells and springs and its key position on the trade routes, was a town in Abraham's time; and recently, underground cave dwellings have been found which date back 2,000 years before him. But it is likely that even in Biblical times the wild country farther to the south was sparsely occupied, or traversed only by Bedouin tribes. In the Roman period the area was occupied by the Nabataeans, an Arab people from farther east. They built a number of towns which prospered from caravan routes, and they became very clever at storing water and at irrigating small fields.

After the Nabataeans were crushed by the Romans in the second century A.D., a few of their towns, which lay astride important trade routes, were revived by the new Byzantine rulers of Palestine. Two towns, Avdat (Abde) and Shivta

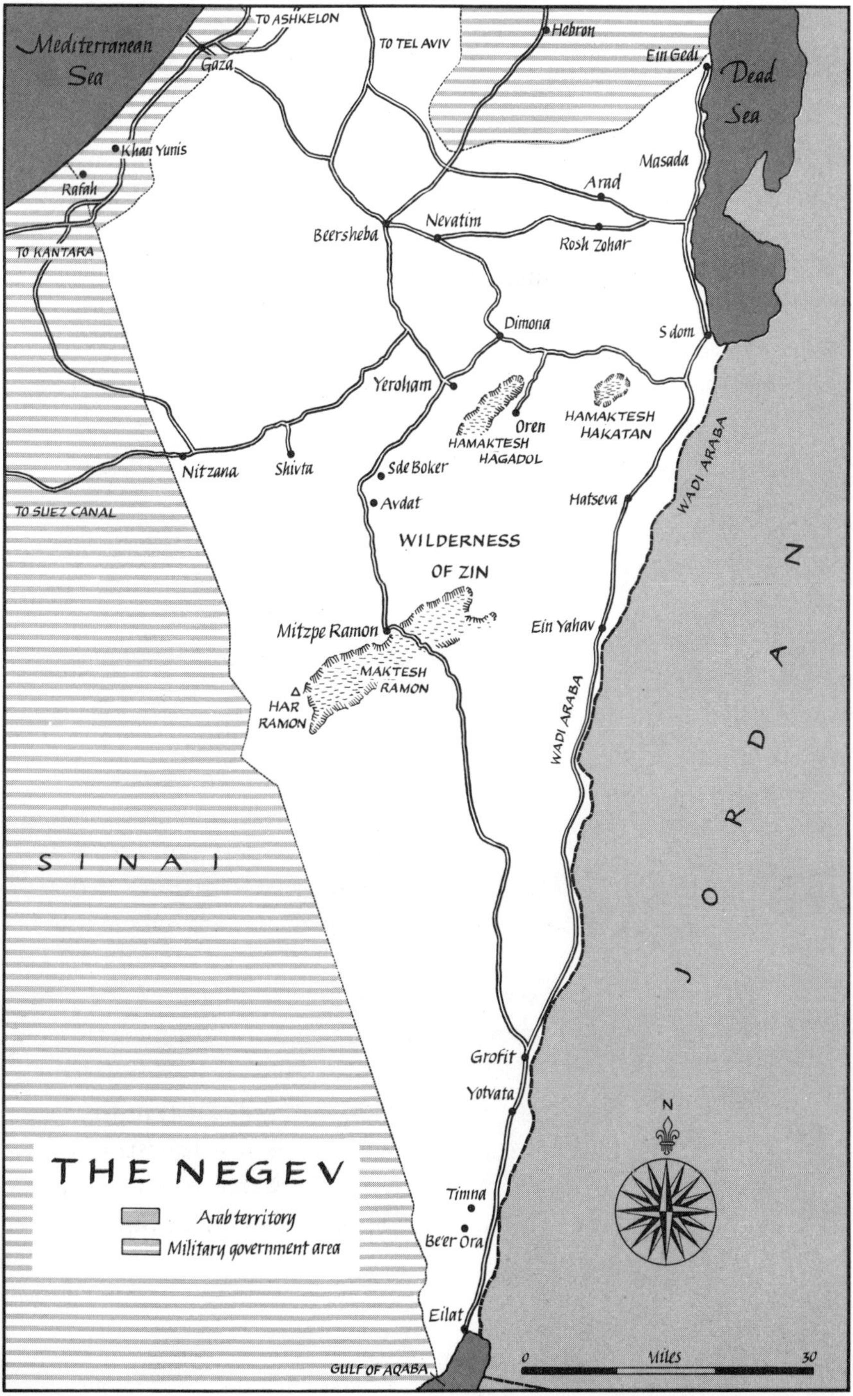
THE NEGEV
Arab territory
Military government area
Mediterranean Sea
TO ASHKELON
TO TEL AVIV
Hebron
Ein Gedi
Dead Sea
Gaza
Khan Yunis
Rafah
TO KANTARA
Masada
Arad
Beersheba
Nevatim
Rosh Zohar
Dimona
S'dom
Yeroham
Oren
HAMAKTESH HAKATAN
HAMAKTESH HAGADOL
Nitzana
Shivta
Sde Boker
Avdat
TO SUEZ CANAL
Hatseva
WADI ARABA
WILDERNESS OF ZIN
Mitzpe Ramon
Ein Yahav
MAKTESH RAMON
HAR RAMON
WADI ARABA
JORDAN
SINAI
Grofit
Yotvata
N
Timna
Be'er Ora
Eilat
GULF OF AQABA
0
Miles
30

(Subeita), have remained in a fair state of preservation and have been restored by the Israel government.

Under Arab rule, and later under the Turks, civilization disappeared again from the southern Negev, which relapsed into a domain of sun and sand, peopled only by poor and forgotten nomad groups living off their camels and goats; and by the big redheaded lizards that scurried between the scattered building stones.

So it would have remained but for the Jewish pioneer settlers. Under Arab pressure, land acquisition by Jews was harshly restricted. The Negev was the only big empty space in the country. During World War II, in 1943 the Jewish Agency set up three small pilot settlements south of Beersheba, at Revivim, Gvulot and Beit Eshel, in order to test the research work being carried out on soil analysis and crops. In 1946, with the Anglo-American Committee of Enquiry in the country and talk of a political *fait accompli*, the time had come for a bolder venture. One night, after the Yom Kippur fast, convoys of secretly loaded trucks went rumbling in the dark into the barren area, and by daylight next morning, the whole country was astonished to find eleven new settlements, each complete with prefabricated wooden huts, stockade and watchtower, carried down in sections and assembled during the night.

When the United Nations Special Committee toured Palestine in the summer of 1947, it found that, under conditions of physical hardship and danger, the tiny settlements were taking root. Impressed by this gallant desert pioneering, the Committee recommended that the Negev should be part of the Jewish State under its partition plan; and this was sponsored by the United Nations in its historic resolution of November 29, 1947.

THE NEGEV AND THE SINAI DESERT

But the question of the Negev's future still had to face an even severer test. When the Arab armies invaded Palestine at the end of the Mandate, in May, 1948, the Egyptian forces occupied Beersheba and cut the Negev off from the rest of the country by establishing a line from the coast north of Gaza to the southern edge of Jerusalem. They thus cut off and left isolated the Jewish settlements in the Negev which by then numbered twenty-seven. But these little villages became miniature Stalingrads and fought back waves of Egyptian attackers. Later, the Egyptian line was smashed and the armistice agreements confirmed Israel's hold on the southern part of the country as far as Eilat, at the head of the Gulf of Aqaba.

The Negev was again in danger in May, 1967, when Nasser massed his Egyptian forces in the adjacent Sinai Desert to the west, expelled the United Nations Emergency Force and declared a blockade of the Straits of Tiran. One formation of 200 tanks was poised near the border to cut off Eilat and the southern end of the Negev. The threat was smashed in the Six-Day War.

The opening of the Gulf of Aqaba in the 1956 Sinai Campaign meant the opening of Israel's back door, giving it free access for the first time to the Indian Ocean, East Africa and the Far East. This gave the Negev a new dimension and immediately quickened the tempo of its development. The limiting factor is water. It is now brought by pipeline from the north; but the great dream remains desalination at a cost that will make it economically feasible. Together with the development of irrigation goes constant experimenting with strains of crops, fruits, animals and poultry which are adapted to semiarid conditions. The approach of the Negev experts is today a less idyllic and more ramified one in which local farmsteads are auxiliary to new towns, mining, industry, transportation and services.

BEERSHEBA

To sense the antiquity of Beersheba you should arrive there on a Thursday morning, which is market day for the Bedouin tribes of the area. In their sweeping robes and white *kheffiyahs* (Arab headdresses), and with their veiled, black-garbed womenfolk, they come to sell camel colts, lambs and goats and to buy cloth, flour, coffee, sugar and the other basic needs of their primitive way of life. Watching their lean, weather-etched faces, the unhurried bargaining in the camel market, the animals being watered from the immemorial wells, the black flecks of the goat-hair tents against the distant ridges—one is suddenly looking upon the figures of the earliest Hebrews coming to this place for water and a little shade.

It was at Beersheba that Abraham, coming up from Egypt, dug a well for his thirsty flocks and swore to a pact with Abimelech, the formidable King of Gerar, giving him seven ewe lambs as a pledge so that he would not be driven away by the King's servants. The Book of Genesis continues that Abraham called the place Beersheba (Well of the Swearing) and planted a grove of trees there.

Centuries later, when the Land of Canaan was parceled out among the Twelve Tribes after Joshua's conquest, the southernmost area was given to the Tribe of Simeon; and Beersheba heads the list of towns and villages which came within its inheritance. Afterwards the settled area of Canaan became accepted as extending from Dan in the north to Beersheba in the south. The town obviously remained an

THE NEGEV AND THE SINAI DESERT

important center along the overland caravan routes for several centuries after Joshua. We read in the Bible about Samuel's two sons, Joel and Abiah, being corrupt judges in Beersheba.

Down the nameless centuries after the Biblical era, Beersheba remained a watering place for the nomads and a strategic outpost for the successive masters of Palestine. The Romans had a small fort here, as did the Crusaders. Under the Turks, Beersheba never became more than a small market and garrison town. The local population was only a couple of thousand when General Allenby's Australian cavalry captured it in the summer of 1917 (their neat military cemetery is still maintained at the edge of the town). More than thirty years later there were only 3,000 Arab inhabitants, who fled when the Israel army took the town by assault from the Egyptian forces which had occupied it at the end of the Mandate in May, 1948.

Now, over twenty years later, the sleepy, sand-swept little Arab border town has been engulfed in a modern boom town of more than 60,000 polyglot immigrants. Housing quarters have spread out across miles of naked, reddish earth faster than streets, water, electricity or shade trees can keep up with them. Off to one side a planned industrial zone is turning out sanitary ware, glassware and other products using Negev raw materials. The town has mushroomed so fast that it still has a raw and unfinished look, and some of its houses, hurriedly constructed, are unattractive. But nobody can escape Beersheba's personality: it has the tingling vitality and the cocky self-assurance of youth, the easy mingling of a border society, the distilled flavor of Israel's new frontiers. In its apartments, its streets and cafés and nightclubs, its movie houses and community center (with

FROM DAN TO EILAT

a swimming pool), a cross section of the whole "Ingathering" mingles with the virile young men who run the army units and the factories or who come into town from the potash works, the phosphate mines, the oil wells and the road construction camps.

Beersheba now has the beginnings of its own college in the Negev University, with 550 students. It has no campus yet and uses the HIAS hostel for classes in the humanities, biology and engineering, with the help of its two elder sisters, the Hebrew University and the Haifa Technion.

The best place for tourists to stay is the Desert Inn (air conditioned and with a swimming pool). There are now several other modern hotels. If you have an hour to spare after driving round the town, it is worthwhile to visit the Arid Zone Research Center, where vital experimental work is being carried out in connection with solar energy, artificial rain-making, desert soils and crops. If you have a taste for archaeology, you will also be interested in the excavations just to the south of the city. Here archaeologists have uncovered relics of inhabitants of the Chalcolithic period, at least twenty centuries before the time of Abraham. These are collected in the local museum.

BEERSHEBA TO SDOM

The tarmac road from Beersheba to Sdom, on the Dead Sea, runs for forty-seven miles southeast through a brown and barren landscape in which occasional camels or black goats crop hungrily at the patches of scrub in the wadis; and a large desert crow or two wheel against a sky drained of color at noonday, when the horizon melts into haze and

THE NEGEV AND THE SINAI DESERT

mirage. But even in this empty world there are the bones of old inhabited places, and now the new habitations of Israel.

Twenty miles southeast of Beersheba you reach Dimona, a town which started in 1955 with a handful of immigrants in tents and wooden huts. It now has several thousand people, sturdy stone houses, electric light, a water supply and sewers, a textile plant and an atomic reactor. It serves also as a dormitory suburb for the workers who commute by truck to the phosphate mines at Oron, in the Hamaktesh Hagadol (Big Crater), a few miles to the south. Until now Dimona has also housed the workers from the Dead Sea Works at Sdom, but they are to be absorbed by the new township of Arad, closer to Sdom. From Dimona a road cuts back southwest to join the Eilat highway at Yeroham (Yerucham).

Continuing eastward on the road to Sdom for another six miles, you note on the high ground to the right a square stone blockhouse of the deserted police post of Kurnub and some mounds of rubble that mark the site of the Nabataean and Byzantine town of Mamphis (*Mamshit* in Hebrew), which appears on the mosaic floor map, dating from the sixth century A.D., found at Madeba in Jordan. In the deep gorge behind Kurnub you can still see the massive dams used by the Nabataeans to store water. These masterpieces of ancient engineering were described in detail by Leonard Woolley and T. E. Lawrence in their *Wilderness of Zin*. The site was also excavated in 1967 by an Israel archaeologist, Dr. Avraham Negev, who made exciting finds, including an unprecedented hoard of more than 10,000 well-preserved Roman silver coins dating from the second and third centuries A.D. They were found in a large bronze jar

• 183

which had been hidden in a specially built cache beneath the staircase of a two-story Nabataean house that was still intact. This historic site is being reconstructed by the National Parks authority.

Beyond Kurnub the road starts dropping sharply, and all of a sudden, round a bend, you look down upon what is probably the most spectacular view in all Israel—the southern end of the Dead Sea, lying 3,000 feet below you in the floor of the vast canyon known as the Wadi Araba (Arid Valley); the opposite wall rises again sheer thousands of feet to form the Mountains of Moab. During the day this is a pallid and lifeless lunar panorama, but at sunset the violet dusk wells up from its depths, while the higher slopes still flame with orange-red.

The pass was carved out of the cliff faces of the escarpment by surveyors and workmen who often dangled dizzily at the end of ropes. This valley is part of a giant crack in the earth's surface, the Great Rift Valley, which runs for thousands of miles beyond the Red Sea into the heart of the African continent.

Sdom

The potash works at Sdom (or Sodom) squat on the shore like a primeval monster sucking up the sludge from the evaporating pans or turning out bromides in yellow-stained structures. The products of the Dead Sea Works are stored in what look like cubist tents. This extraction of the unlimited chemical wealth locked in the Dead Sea salts was started more than thirty years ago by a Russian Jewish engineer, Moshe Novomeysky, who had once been

THE NEGEV AND THE SINAI DESERT

exiled to Siberia by the Czarist regime. The industry has a promising future and is being expanded at a cost of a hundred million dollars. Huge earthen dikes have been constructed in the water to form evaporating beds.

The salts, which seep in with the water from underground springs, and the high evaporation rate in this arid region make this the densest water on earth—25 percent solid matter, compared with 5 percent in the Atlantic Ocean. You can bathe in this water, but you cannot sink or drown in it.

Going north along the shore from Sdom, the road skirts eroded cliffs of salt; one tall salt pillar is, by local legend, Lot's wife. It was in this vicinity that the Lord destroyed the wicked twin cities of Sodom and Gomorrah by raining down fire and brimstone upon them—probably a reference to an actual volcanic catastrophe. The Bible relates how Lot was told by two angels to flee with his wife and two daughters, with an injunction not to look back; but Mrs. Lot's curiosity or fear overcame her and when she could not resist turning around, she thereupon became a pillar of salt. Lot's comment is not recorded.

Two miles along the water's edge are living quarters for the workers and, beyond them, a guest-house and restaurant, a youth hostel with a tilted roof that looks like a ski jump, a museum of the Dead Sea area, and a post office which will stamp on your letters "Lowest Post Office on Earth."

A few miles south of the Dead Sea Works, where the sedge-covered salt flats meet a low red bluff, there stands one of the most isolated and remarkable settlements in the country, Neot ha-Kikar. Its dwellings are constructed in fortress fashion around an internal courtyard—partly as a carefully devised answer to the fierce heat, and partly for defense reasons, for the Jordanian border is literally only a stone's throw away. Their settlement supports itself by growing the earliest tomato crop in Israel, marketing dates from groves flourishing in the layer of sand and silt washed down and spread out by winter flash floods, and providing desert safaris in command cars and jeeps. These tours visit places of interest in the Negev and the tourists cook out, spend the nights in sleeping bags under the brilliant stars and, for a brief while, taste the simple life close to nature. Since the Six-Day War, five-day tours to Sinai have also been organized.

Arad

Three thousand feet above the Dead Sea, on the edge of the plateau overlooking it, stands the development town of Arad. It can be reached from the south, through Sdom; or from the west, by a new road through the settlements of Dvira and Lahav, intersecting the highway from Hebron to Beersheba. The road from the west traverses what is still a desert landscape, dotted with Bedouin encampments. But the air on the plateau is dry and bracing, with chilly nights, and Lahav, surprisingly, grows some of the best apples in the country.

From Arad the road zigzags down the escarpment to the edge of the Dead Sea, making 125 sharp curves in a distance of 17 miles. This Nahal Zohar defile was used in ancient times, and at a certain point, near the bottom, one looks

THE NEGEV AND THE SINAI DESERT

down from the road on the remains of a Byzantine fort that guarded the route to Edom (now Southern Jordan).

The economists plan a bright future for Arad as the center of a petrochemical industry utilizing Dead Sea minerals, the natural gas found at nearby Rosh Zohar and the phosphate rock deposits which have been located not far away. For the Dead Sea Works down below, Arad is the perfect "dormitory suburb" to which the workers can return after a day's labor in the sticky heat 1,300 feet below sea level. Much thought has gone into the planning of the town and its homes, to adjust them to the desert conditions and the prevailing winds. There are two new air-conditioned hotels here, with a stupendous view over the Dead Sea.

As the walls of the new Arad rise, the archaeologists are digging up the ancient Arad, five miles away across the desert. The Bible speaks of a King of Arad slain by Joshua and of the vicinity's being settled by a group of Kenites, a tribe related to Moses. King Solomon was known to have a fortress here to guard the caravan route down the Wadi Araba to Ezion-geber at the head of the Gulf of Aqaba. The excavation of Tel Arad was started in 1962 and has revealed a number of layers of building, starting with a fortified early Bronze Age town which stood here more than 1,000 years before Father Abraham forded the Jordan River into Canaan. On a mount close by, King Solomon's citadel is being excavated, and here the focus of interest has been the sanctuary built exactly according to the description in the Bible of the Holy of Holies in King Solomon's Temple in Jerusalem.

In a tiny museum in modern Arad the visitor can see some of the remarkable Egyptian-type jars from the early Bronze Age dwellings. Scientifically, the most important finds are *ostraca* (inscribed potsherds) from the Israelite period. One such fragment has the name Arad cut into it seven times.

Masada

Twenty miles up the Dead Sea shore north of Sdom, where the high ground recedes from the water's edge, a great flat-topped mount projects from the rest of the range and rises a sheer 1,300 feet; its plateau measures about 650 yards by 220 yards. This is Masada (Fortress), a natural and almost impregnable stronghold which played a dramatic part in the early history of the Jews. It can be reached by road from Sdom, or by way of the new road through Arad, to the west.

Jonathan the High Priest, in the second century B.C., was the first to fortify this rock. Herod fled here in 40 B.C. when the Parthians took Jerusalem. He became king in 37 B.C. and a few years later he erected a defense wall with thirty-seven watch towers round the rim of the Masada plateau. At the northeastern corner, looking out across the Dead Sea, he built a most extraordinary three-tiered, hanging palace-villa. Access to the middle and bottom terraces was by a staircase invisible from the outside, enclosed in a shaft scooped out of the rock. He kept the top of the mountain clear for cultivation and stored water from the winter flash floods in large rock cisterns which were filled by way of aqueducts from the escarpment behind. The smooth plaster lining of these cisterns is still intact. Storage chambers for oil and food were also constructed. The whole fortress was designed to withstand a long siege, and for almost 100 years it served all who fled the tyrants in Jerusalem to carry on the struggle in the Wilderness of Judea.

When Jerusalem fell to Titus in A.D. 70, a band of Jewish patriots, called Zealots, numbering about 1,000 with their women and children and led by Eliezer ben Yair, fled to Masada. They were pursued two years later by a huge Roman force under General Flavius Silva, who encircled the mountain and for months tried in vain to storm the fortress. The besieging army numbered some 10,000 legionaries and about 15,000 auxiliaries and slaves, accommodated in eight camps in the valley, the sites of which are still visible. Finally the Romans built an earthen rampart on the west side that reached almost to the top of Masada, mounted battering rams, and managed to breach the wall. After the breach the Zealots improvised a wooden wall, which the Romans set on fire. A wind carried the flames all along the wall. "The Romans," Josephus writes in *Wars of the Jews*, "returned to their camp with joy, and resolved to attack their enemies the very next day."

That night, when the inner wall caught fire, Eliezer gathered his people together and told them that the end was near. In a moving speech to the gathering, lit by the flickering flames, he reminded them of their resolution "never to be servants to the Romans, nor to any other than to God Himself." Rather than fall into the hands of the Romans, they decided to kill themselves.

> They then chose ten men by lot out of them, to slay all the rest, every one of whom lay himself down by his wife and children on the ground, and threw his arms about them, and they offered their necks to the stroke of those who by lot executed that melancholy office; and when

those ten had without fear, slain them all, they made the same rule of casting lots for themselves, that he whose lot it was should first kill the other nine, and after all, should kill himself.

The next day the Romans, coming in full armor to the attack, "were met with a terrible solitude on every side . . . as well as a perfect silence." Two women and five children who had hidden in a cave came out and "informed the Romans what had been done as it was done." Josephus adds that the Romans could only "wonder at the courage of their resolution and the immovable concept of death, which so great a number of them had shown, when they went through such an action as that was."

Masada had until recently been almost untouched by the spade of the archaeologist, but in the winter of 1963 and again in 1964, Professor Yigael Yadin launched a full-scale excavation with the help of the Israel Defense Forces and teams of volunteer amateur "diggers" who came not only from Israel but from many countries. In the debris of Herod's villa they found gruesome substantiation of the fate of the Jewish defenders as described by Josephus—the remains of skeletons of a man, a woman and a young boy who had chosen death rather than surrender to the Romans. Dark-brown plaits were still attached to the woman's scalp, and nearby were her sandals. In the ashes they also found coins of the Jewish revolt, a letter in Aramaic, arrows and silvered scales of armor. The walls of this palace-villa had been plastered in color, some of which still remains—green striped with red and bordered in red and black.

The buildings now being reconstructed on the top are the main palace building, extensive storehouses, a large Roman bathhouse and a Jewish ritual bath. One room in the casemate wall was oriented towards Jerusalem and contained tiered benches, leading Yadin to the conclusion that it was probably a synagogue. In an adjoining room were found fragments of scrolls, Biblical documents earlier in date than A.D. 73. One fragment has a text identical with that of a scroll found at Qumran. According to Professor Yadin, this suggests that some of the Essenes fought here together with the Zealots. Other fragments were a first-century copy of the apocryphal Book of Ecclesiasticus written by Ben Sirah (not to be confused with Ecclesiastes). This discovery has caused a stir in the world of scroll researchers, for it proves finally that the Cairo Genizah version was a copy of the Hebrew original and not a later retranslation from the Greek.

More than 2,000 coins were collected, including twenty silver shekels, the only ones ever found in an archaeological excavation. Three of them were dated the fifth year of the Jewish Revolt—the year of the destruction of the Temple.

There is a youth hostel at the foot of the mountain, and arrangements can be made for the energetic to climb to the top along the same serpentine path on the eastern slope that the Jews used nearly 2,000 years ago and down which the Romans were flung back. For the less energetic, there is a road from Arad that approaches Masada from the west, where the Israel army has built a path and staircase that winds past the ramp of wood and earth the Romans constructed and by which the Jews were conquered. From Arad there are daily command-car tours to Masada for which seats can be booked. One of the dreams of the Government Tourist Corporation is to run a regular helicopter service to the top of Masada, or to erect a funicular railway.

Ein Gedi

Ten miles north of Masada is the seashore settlement of Ein Gedi, the Biblical En-gedi (Spring of the Kid). This is an oasis in the wilderness formed by a stream of pure water that emerges from underground springs in the mountainside and comes down a deep wadi, forming glorious clear pools at the foot of waterfalls.

This oasis has been inhabited since very early times. Recent excavations have revealed the ruins of an early Canaanite temple as well as relics from the time of the Judean kings and later strata from the period of Ezra and Nehemiah, in the fifth century B.C. There is also evidence of the Roman occupation.

It was here at Ein Gedi that young David hid in a cave from the wrath of King Saul. When the King entered that very cave to rest, David cut a piece from his robe in the dark and when Saul left, David followed him, crying out:

> For in that I cut off the skirt of thy robe, and killed thee not, know thou and see that there is neither evil nor transgression in my hand . . . and Saul lifted up his voice, and wept.
> —I Samuel 24:11, 16

Saul told him that he now knew that David would surely become King of Israel.

The Song of Songs, attributed to King Solomon, says,

> My beloved is unto me as a cluster of camphire in the vineyards of En-gedi.
> —1:14

Camphire, or henna shrub, has been used since antiquity for making henna, a hair dye. Ein Gedi also produced balsam, a much-prized perfume and anointing balm made from the gum of the balsam tree. Vessels, tools and measures were found in the excavations. The Roman historian Pliny in the first century A.D. lamented the vanished fertility of this spot: "Its groves of palm trees are now like Jerusalem, a heap of ashes."

Nineteen centuries were to pass before its fruitfulness was to be revived. A group of young Israeli pioneers settled at Ein Gedi in 1956, planting vegetables and flowers, grapes and cotton, which they were able to get to market earlier than other places because of the warm climate and low altitude. The settlement has built permanent homes on a hilltop; the octagonal dining hall is perched on the edge of the escarpment, giving a fine sweep of view. Just below the kibbutz you can loll in the lukewarm water of the Dead Sea, and then wash off the salt under fresh-water open-air showers a few yards from the edge. On the next ridge is a center for field studies where groups of high school children spend a week or two learning about the local flora and fauna. From here the road is being pushed through northward along the edge of the Dead Sea to Ain Feshka and Qumran.

At places on the seashore between Sdom and Ein Gedi there are hot sulphur springs which are visited by sufferers from rheumatism, foreshadowing the development of spa resorts, such as the one which until 1948 existed at the northern end of the Dead Sea. Two air-conditioned bungalow-type hotels have been built on this strip of shore, at Ein Zohar and at Ein Bokek; the latter has a bathing beach, and a restaurant right on the sea called Bar Kochba Inn. A larger and more luxurious spa with indoor sulphur baths, called Galei Zohar, has just been opened.

Qumran

The ruined monastery of Qumran, which is near the caves in which the Dead Sea Scrolls were discovered in 1947, is thirteen miles to the north of Ein Gedi. The frontier with Jordan, which used to separate the two, was wiped out in the June, 1967 war. There are indications that a group of the Essenes, the sect associated with Qumran about the time of Jesus, maintained an agricultural settlement at Ein Gedi as well, and Josephus mentions this. In 1960 the Israel government and the Hebrew University jointly organized a large expedition to comb the caves in the vicinity of Ein Gedi in the hope of finding more scrolls. They discovered instead fragments of Biblical manuscripts and bundles of documents relating to the Bar Kochba revolt against Rome, including written orders to two local commanders. One unique find was a matchless collection of metal artifacts, probably cult objects, dating back to the Chalcolithic period.

BEERSHEBA TO EILAT

Before the opening of the central Negev highway from Beersheba to Eilat, the only route to Eilat lay down the Wadi Araba; it was a spine-jolting and dusty trip which took ten to twelve hours. In 1964 a new highway was completed down the Wadi, linking up with the central Negev highway near the Neve ha-Midbar (Desert Abode) restaurant and petrol station some twenty-five miles north of Eilat.

It now takes less than three hours to drive from Sdom to

THE NEGEV AND THE SINAI DESERT

Eilat; and as might be expected, the main traffic is largely the great potash trucks from the Dead Sea that come rolling down for their rendezvous with the ships that will sail out through the Gulf of Aqaba to markets in Africa and Asia. It is a comfortable and level run along the floor of the Wadi but as yet a lonely one. Apart from the road traffic and the grazing camels that wander across the nearby Jordanian border, not much stirs in the ancient trough between the Mountains of Moab and the Negev plateau. In the hundred-mile trip one passes a few Israel settlements, such as Ein Hussub and Ein Yahav. They are inhabited by young folk from Nahal or by older *moshavim*, who look upon the highway with mixed feelings. They are less cut off now and it is easier to get their produce to market, but the trucks, the occasional buses and the tourist taxis that pass their doors spoil for them the feeling that they are pioneering the wilderness.

The central highway opened in 1956 from Beersheba to Eilat runs for a straight 155 miles down the center of the Negev. It is a comfortable four-hour trip by car or bus. Many tourists travel overland one way and by air the other, on one of the scheduled Arkia flights between Eilat and Tel Aviv, and Eilat and Jerusalem.

From Beersheba the road heads southward into the Wilderness of Zin, so desolate that your heart goes out to the ancient Israelites who, wandering from Egypt to the Promised Land more than 3,000 years ago, cried out in protest:

> Then came the children of Israel . . . into the desert of Zin in the first month. . . . And there was no water for the congregation: and they gathered themselves together against Moses and against Aaron. . . . Why

• 195

FROM DAN TO EILAT

> have ye brought up the congregation of the Lord into this wilderness, that we and our cattle should die there? And wherefore have ye made us to come up out of Egypt, to bring us in unto this evil place? it is no place of seed, or of figs, or of vines, or of pomegranates; neither is there any water to drink.
> —Numbers 20:1-5

Nearly halfway to Eilat, just beyond the Mitzpe Ramon lookout point, the highway plunges dramatically down a thousand-foot escarpment into a vast depression known as the Maktesh Ramon (Ramon Crater), and then runs for ten miles across its floor. It has been suggested that the name Ramon may be a corruption of the Hebrew word *rimmon* (pomegranate), and that this was the Rimmon-parez mentioned in the Bible as one of the places where the Children of Israel halted in their wanderings.

The depression starts at the foot of Har Ramon (Mount Ramon), a 3,395-foot peak which can be seen to the southwest near the old Sinai border, and runs northeast for thirty-five miles. Like the Hamaktesh Hagadol (Big Crater) and the Hamaktesh Hakatan (Small Crater) which lie to the northeast, towards the Dead Sea, this strange depression was formed by a subsiding of the geological strata and then scoured out by sandstorms and winter torrents. In its bed have been found rare fossils, including those of giant lizards that have been extinct for nearly 200 million years. Gypsum is quarried in the Maktesh for cement making, and oil exploration is taking place there.

The road continues over the ridges and plains of the southern Negev, crossing the large dry watercourse known as the Brook of Paran, its bed dotted with the tamarisks and acacias which are the typical Negev trees. It then descends

THE NEGEV AND THE SINAI DESERT

into the Wadi Araba and runs for forty miles along the floor of the valley parallel to the Jordanian border, with the Mountains of Edom rising up on the left and the Negev highlands on the right. After passing Yotvata, Timna, Be'er Ora, Grofit and the new settlement of Eilot, you coast at last down into Eilat, with the brilliant blue waters of the Gulf of Aqaba stretching ahead.

The following are the main places of interest on the Beersheba-Eilat run:

Shivta

Twelve miles south of Beersheba, the road forks. The right-hand branch is the old military highway which reached the Sinai border just beyond Nitzana, thirty-four miles away, and then crossed the desert to Ismailiya on the Suez Canal. This was one of the main axes of the Israel advance into Sinai in 1956 and again in 1967. Halfway to Nitzana a turnoff onto a tarmac road leads to the ruins of the Nabataean and Byzantine city of Shivta (Subeita).

Shivta stands empty on its ridge with its restored houses, shops, churches and streets almost as they were 1,500 years ago. The key to its existence then was water, which is still the key to living in the Negev today.

Although the present remains are almost all Byzantine (fourth to sixth century A.D.), it is clear from *ostraca* (inscribed potsherds) found on the site that the Byzantines took over the ingenious methods devised by the earlier Nabataeans for conserving every available drop of moisture. About 500 yards to the northeast of the town are hills and wadis threaded with an intricate system of dams, channels and terraces to catch the water from the winter rains, with their accompanying flash floods, and store it for summer use. There seems to have also been a method of making small heaps of stones in the fields to catch the heavy dew at night at certain times of the year. These techniques were successful, for in the town one can still see wine presses used for grapes grown on the surrounding terraces and the oven in which bread made from local wheat and barley was baked.

For obtaining domestic water, each house had a flat roof sloped to a channel in one corner that carried the rainfall down to a rock cistern in the basement. The walls were thick and the windows narrow to keep out the sun. The streets were also slanted and channeled to the public reservoirs. These, during the Nabataean period, were kept in good condition by the local citizens, who taxed themselves a day's work each to clean them out. One *ostracon* that was found is a receipt made out to "Flavius Gormos, son of Zachariah: You have completed one corvée for the reservoir. Written on the 25th Dies in the 9th Indiction."

There are three churches in Shivta. The largest one, near the reservoir at the southern end, was built in the fifth century A.D. and has two rows of columns leading to a raised altar. A smaller church stands in the center of the town, and another, larger one at the northern end. This was built later, and there seems to have been some attempt at organized planning in that part of the town, probably because it held the commercial center. The adjoining chapel has an interesting mosaic floor in which the name and date of the donor are worked. It was laid down in the sixth century "in the Episcopate of Thomas and under the Governorship of John."

Unlike the other Nabataean cities in the Negev, Shivta is

not situated at a strategic crossroad and has no protecting wall; it is presumed that its main task was to supply other Negev towns with food.

This site and that of the Nabataean city of Avdat (Abde) have been restored by the Commission of Landscaping and Preservation of Antiquities (National Parks Authority).

Sde Boker

Sde Boker (Field of the Rancher) is on the main road about thirty miles from Beersheba. It was established in 1952 by a group of sixteen young men and three young women. It was a daring pioneering project for these Negev plains, on which they hoped to raise sheep and cattle; they had no roads, no water and no neighbors. In their first year one of the girls, a university graduate from Jerusalem, was murdered by Arab marauders while out with the sheep. But the group persevered and in 1954, when David Ben-Gurion retired from public office for a while, he joined them in their Negev outpost and became a member of the kibbutz. He and his wife Paula (who died in January, 1968) made it their permanent home. Today he divides his time between his books and writing, the Knesset, and the promotion of the Sde Boker Institute of Negev Studies, on high ground a mile and a half south of the kibbutz. Here research is carried on and courses conducted on the problems of arid zones. The complex of buildings includes a teachers' training college to serve the Negev development towns, a regional high school, dormitories for the students and a field school for youth groups.

Although this desert kibbutz is less than twenty years old,

the fruit trees and vineyards have been so successful that in the summer season a stall is opened on the main road, where fresh grapes and plums, apples and peaches, neatly packed in plastic bags, are sold to grateful travelers.

Avdat

Eight miles south of Sde Boker, you see on your left what looks like a small acropolis; columns rise in the clear air on the top of a hill and there seem to be houses tumbling down the side. At the bottom of the hill you may see a startling patch of green, cupped in striated rocky hillsides. These are the fields, long arid and now restored to cultivation, of the Nabataean city of Avdat (Abde in Arabic), founded in the third century B.C.

The residents made their homes in large caves cut into the rock near the top of the hill, giving them a wide view of the surrounding landscape and thus ample warning of attacks. But their chief problem was water. As in Shivta, their methods were to conserve the rain water by a system of dams in the wadis, cisterns near the houses and channels cut in the hillsides to direct the run-off water into their fields. Here they grew enough food to be self-sufficient.

Nabataean rule of the Negev came to an end in A.D. 106, when the Nabataean kingdom was annexed by the Romans, who built a road linking Eilat with Damascus and bypassed Avdat, which began to decline. Then, in the third century, the Emperor Diocletian renewed the defenses of the Roman territory and built a series of forts linking the valley of the Dead Sea with the northern Negev. Avdat was one of the positions chosen. From inscriptions, coins and pottery found on the site, archaeologists date the watchtower and colonnaded terrace and a camp northeast of the town to this period. Avdat continued to flourish and reached its peak under Byzantine rule in the sixth century. It was then that the fortress at the top of the hill was built, as were two churches, the monastery, the baptistry, additions to the hilltop terrace, the houses and some more cave homes.

The Moslem conquest of the Negev in A.D. 634 brought about the second decline of Avdat, which seems to have fallen without offering resistance. The new rulers were less concerned than their predecessors with protecting their caravan routes, so Avdat became just a stopping place, with a bathhouse at the foot of the hill at the disposal of travelers. In the tenth century the site seems to have been abandoned, and left to the desert for a thousand years.

The large-scale restoration project begun in 1959 has now been completed, while Professor Michael Even-Ari of the Hebrew University has succeeded in growing barley and other crops by reviving the water run-off system used by the Nabataeans. Near the café at the roadside is a small museum that displays statuettes, pottery and inscriptions of the people who created a desert way of living for themselves 2,000 years ago.

Yotvata

Twenty-five miles north of Eilat is a small settlement (to the right of the road) called Yotvata, after the Israelites' Jotbathah, "a land of rivers of water" (Numbers 33:33 and Deuteronomy 10:7). It is from the wells here that Eilat is supplied with fresh water by a pipeline. (The other pipeline you now see carries oil from Eilat to Haifa.) The surrounding wadi is planted with palm trees and vegetable fields. Besides having to maintain permanent watch for marauders at all times, these desert farmers face another hazard—the birds, which gather here for water and devour their precious crops.

About fifteen miles south, Be'er Ora, too, has a bird problem. Here the vegetable fields are protected by all kinds of ingenious devices designed to scare the birds, who come from miles around, drawn by the startling emerald-green patches. Be'er Ora boasts a swimming pool, fed by underground springs, which cools the settlers and then irrigates the fields lower down.

Timna

Here are the copper mines of the south. The red-black rock of the wadi here has been chiseled by wind and sand into strange shapes of castles and spires, animal heads and human forms. Like some ancient gods, these seem to keep watch over the modern Israelis who have built a large smelting plant and are mining copper ore in the surrounding area. The dust and the roar of the project billow and echo through the hills. Less than two miles from here were King Solomon's famous copper mines 3,000 years ago, but all that is left of that venture is the black and shiny slag heaps where his slaves, with primitive tools, hacked the green gold out of these same hills and utilized the perpetual wind that blows through the wadi to keep the smelting flames at full blast. Also worth visiting is a strange rock formation nearby known as the Pillars of Solomon. Here erosion has cut the cliff face into five giant half-columns that remind the visitor of the entrance to Petra in Jordan, the "rose-red city, half as

THE NEGEV AND THE SINAI DESERT

old as time" that was the capital of the Nabataeans. It is easy to imagine altars being built at the base of these columns and sacrifices offered to the gods who shaped them.

EILAT

Eilat grew rapidly after the Gulf of Aqaba was opened to Israel shipping by the Sinai Campaign of 1956. The closing of this gulf again by Egypt in 1967 was one of the factors leading to the Six-Day War. Israel troops landed at Sharm-el-Sheikh at much the same time as the navy arrived there, to find the Egyptians had fled.

Today Eilat is an active city of more than 15,000 inhabitants. Its port handles cargo vessels which load phosphates, potash, salt, cement and copper cement at its covered jetties, and oil tankers which discharge further south, at the terminal of the oil pipeline.

The development of this port traffic still faces quite tough obstacles. Because there is no well-populated area close by, the haulage up and down the Negev is costly, and it is not easy to find cargoes for the vessels returning to Eilat from African or Asian ports. All the same, the possession of this six-mile strip at the head of the Gulf of A'qaba makes Israel a two-ocean state, with a back-door outlet to the Red Sea and the Indian Ocean as well as a Mediterranean coastline. This geographical fact is of great strategic importance for Israel's future, and especially so when its land communications are blocked by hostile borders and the Suez Canal remains closed. As the Negev has become more settled and as more Indian Ocean and Pacific markets develop for Israel's exports, Eilat continues to grow in size. As the city expands, the need to find new fresh-water sources increases.

A 60,000-kilowatt power station has been built, with a seawater distillation plant harnessed to the exhaust steam.

As with so much else in Israel, here too the Biblical past echoes through the busy present. The name of the port first occurs in the Old Testament in the First Book of Kings:

> And King Solomon made a navy of ships in Ezion-geber, which is beside Eloth, on the shore of the Red sea, in the land of Edom.
>
> —I Kings 9:26

It was from here that the galleys built for Solomon by Hiram, King of Tyre, carried away copper and probably salt, and brought in gold and spices from the land of Ophir in Africa. The Queen of Sheba must have landed here and gone swaying on camelback up the caravan trail to Jerusalem. Later this sea outlet must have been abandoned, for it is related that King Azariah "built Elath, and restored it to Judah"—II Kings 14:22. By modern times whatever port there may have been was engulfed again by sand. Just beyond the coils of barbed wire which separate Eilat from the Jordanian port of Aqaba there is a mound which may have been the site of Ezion-geber. An ancient copper smelting and refining plant has been uncovered there.

Eilat still has a town-in-the-making feeling. The shopping center is thronged with immigrant settlers, sailors off the ships, fishermen, soldiers and dock workers, and beatniks (Eilat has a small colony). Tourists arriving by plane from Jerusalem and Tel Aviv (the trip takes less than an hour) and by air-conditioned bus (four hours from Beersheba) fill the hotels and motels (several of which are right on the beach), stretch out in their swimsuits along the sea's edge or beside the hotel swimming pools. Two arms of stone stretch out into the sea, giving good swimmers a perfectly

THE NEGEV AND THE SINAI DESERT

safe area free of the water skiers who glide across the surface behind speedboats hired by the hour.

For the more venturesome, Eilat offers some of the finest skin diving in the world. Lessons can be had and the latest equipment rented at the Coral Beach, which is about two miles south of the town. Here, too, you can take a glass-bottomed excursion boat to view the fantastic coral reefs, through which gay-colored tropical fish glide in shoals. Since the Six-Day War, the excursions, which start at 8:30 A.M. and 2:30 P.M., include a visit to an island about eight miles south of Eilat where the Crusaders erected a castle on whose foundations the Moslems later built a fortress to guard the old pilgrims' route to Mecca from Egypt. Still farther south you will visit a fjord which cuts into the coastline for about half a mile, with steep cliffs on either side. This is a fisherman's paradise, as almost every species of Red Sea fish can be found here. If you have taken the afternoon trip you will come back to Eilat in a sunset glow that slowly turns the mountains of Saudi Arabia a brilliant purple.

Places to visit in Eilat are the Philip Murray Cultural Center (named after the American labor leader), with its concert hall, library and restaurant; the Histadrut House; the small Maritime Museum, which is planning to build a modern aquarium; and the Ben-Gurion Garden, which has an open-air amphitheater and a number of experimental plantings of trees, shrubs and other plants struggling against the climate. There are several restaurants in Eilat that specialize in seafood; The Blue Fish and The Dolphin are good. For after dinner, there is a night club, beatnik style, called End of the World Club.

Between Eilat and the border on the Jordanian side is an

area of salt flats with scattered, wind-bent palms. This area has been turned into a series of lagoons fed by sea water, and there is an ambitious plan afoot to build rows of hotels with private beaches and fishing bays, to extend the "coastline." In midsummer the temperature at Eilat may rise to 120° F, but the air is so dry that the heat is not oppressive; and in winter the climate is superb—constant sunshine and blue skies and warm enough for swimming, sunbathing and skin diving in the spectacular setting of stark mountains and dazzling blue water.

Wonderful drives are now available to tourists. You can take a jeep ride southward from the harbor area, past the water distillation plant, the black-granite quarry, the Coral Beach (with bathing shelters and a café), the oil terminal with its storage tanks, and the lonely house at the entrance to a wadi that was built and occupied long before the State by an eccentric English explorer, Captain Williams. From here a rough track leads inland through the mountains and into a valley, where scratched on the rock are hundreds of messages from pilgrims who camped there on the way to Mecca.

The ancient caravan road from Egypt around the head of the Gulf to Jordan and Arabia comes through the mountains some ten miles to the northwest of Eilat, at strategic Ras-en-Nakeb (Head of the Pass); then drops 2,000 feet to Eilat, with a spectacular view over the whole region. One of the most exciting trips from Eilat is a day's jeep ride into the mountains and along this track. Most of the way you ride along the old Sinai border, climbing through the stark mountains that gleam black and dark red. The remains of the old Roman road is still in use, and if you are lucky you will spot a herd of ibex (mountain goats) whose forebears roamed these same mountains thousands of years ago and which cross borders with impunity. You can watch many kinds of game birds drinking from a trough at the bottom of a wadi kept filled by the only spring for miles around. Your guide will take you through the Red Canyon, a narrow defile between rose-colored rocks.

With the growth of modern air-conditioned hotels at Eilat and the improved land and air links, this city is playing a key part in developing Israel as a country of winter tourism.

THE SINAI DESERT

The Sinai Peninsula (probably named after the Akkadian moon god Sin) is the area bounded by the Gulf of Suez and the Suez Canal to the west, the Gulf of Aqaba and the former Palestine frontier to the east, and the Mediterranean Sea to the north. It is a desolate and nearly empty land, three times the size of the State of Israel within its pre-June, 1967, borders.

From the dawn of history, the coastal belt of Sinai has been a through route for armies and trading caravans passing between Egypt and the Land of Canaan and the lands beyond. It is a region of low scrub, date-palm groves and small sunken fields interspersed with salt marshes and stretches of sand dunes that can rise to 300 feet. After 1948, the coastal road and the railway line stopped short at the border of the Egyptian-held Gaza Strip, but since the Six-Day War they have been linked up again with Israel. Ironically, the first task of the railway was to haul into Israel the vast quantities of military equipment, ammunition and supplies abandoned by the Egyptian army.

FROM DAN TO EILAT

The only town on the coast is El Arish, now with 33,000 inhabitants. The local Arishia are a sturdy folk, neither Palestinians nor Egyptians, who speak their own dialect of Arabic. They have long lived in poverty, maintaining themselves mainly by fishing, smuggling and their date crop. After generations of neglect and corruption under the Turks and Egyptians, the Israel authorities are improving their farming methods and social services.

The Central Sinai is a gravel plain broken by limestone ridges and spanned by a few strategic roads that were the axes of advance and retreat in the Israel-Egyptian desert battles of 1956 and 1967. The main east-west highway is from Ismailiya, halfway along the Suez Canal, through Abu Aweigila, which was the main Egyptian fortified base near the Israel border. A parallel road a little farther south crosses the desert to the port of Suez through the key Mitla Pass. In the Sinai Campaign of 1956 the road was seized and held by Israel paratroopers dropped behind the enemy lines more than 100 miles ahead of the ground forces. In the Six-Day War the retreating Egyptians were cut off at the Mitla Pass and their tanks and guns destroyed largely from the air. Hundreds of burnt-out tanks and vehicles stretched for many miles along the road.

The southern third of the Sinai Peninsula becomes more rugged. In the center of this area a cluster of gaunt red granite peaks rises to a height of 8,000 feet. By Christian tradition this is where Moses received the Ten Commandments on Mount Sinai, although scholarly opinion is skeptical. From the second century A.D., the connection with Moses and the Children of Israel, and the presence of springs of water and oases, attracted Christian hermits to this wild and isolated region. A little to the northwest some

THE NEGEV AND THE SINAI DESERT

5,000 monks and hermits lived during the fifth and sixth centuries in the oasis of Feiran (Pharan), a narrow strip of lush vegetation drawn for three miles across the wilderness and shut in by lofty mountains.

One of the group of peaks in the southern Sinai became identified with the Biblical Mount Sinai; it is called Jebel Musa (Moses' Mountain). On the lower slope of an adjacent peak, Jebel Catherina, stands the Monastery of St. Catherine. St. Catherine was a young and vocal virgin in fourth-century Alexandria who protested the persecution of Christians. She was tortured on the wheel and had her head cut off. For some undisclosed reason, the head reappeared at the monastery in Sinai and is preserved there as a relic—hence the name. The manner of her death also made her the patron saint of wheelwrights. St. Catherine's monastery was founded in A.D. 327 by the Empress Helena (the mother of Constantine) on the spot where it is claimed God spoke to Moses from the burning bush. In A.D. 530 the Emperor Justinian built around the monastery the fort-like wall of gray granite to protect the monks from robbers.

The monastery and the church within have been in continuous use since the sixth century. There is also a small mosque, built in the eleventh century by the Sultan Hakim to appease the advancing Moslem troops of the Sultan Hakim, and to persuade them that the Prophet Mohammed had extended his protection to the monastery.

It is a storehouse of historic and religious treasures. Its collection of ancient Christian manuscripts is second only to that of the Vatican. It includes the Codex Syriacus, a Syriac text of the Gospels written about A.D. 400. Until 1859 the monks also owned a still older Biblical manuscript, the Codex Sinaiticus, a Greek translation of the Old Testament from the original Hebrew and one of the oldest known texts of the New Testament, dated about A.D. 340. It was discovered and removed by a German scholar, Von Tischendorf, was acquired by the Czar, and in 1933 was sold by the Soviet government to the British Museum for £100,000.

The monastery also owns the world's greatest collection of icons (paintings or mosaics of sacred personages which are used in the Eastern churches). There are about 2,000 of them in the collection. The monastery also contains a famous ossuary, a charnel house of the bones and skulls of all the monks who have died there in thirteen centuries. They are guarded by the skeleton of the monk Stephen, dressed in ornate vestments and preserved in a glass case. He died in A.D. 580.

Today there are seven monks under the Archimandrite Dionysius. They maintain a pilgrim hostel with 150 beds, much used since the Six-Day War. Energetic guests can rise at 2 A.M. and climb the Jebel Catherina in one day—a nine-hour trip. The monastery and hostel are served by twenty-four families of the small Jebeliyah Bedouin tribe, said to be descended from Bosnian and Wallachian serfs sent from the Balkans by Emperor Justinian to guard the monks; these tribesmen are despised and shunned by the other Bedouin in the southern Sinai. The monks have always fed them, and the Israel government now supplies the food.

Near the southern tip of the Sinai Peninsula are the Straits of Tiran, the entrance to the Gulf of Aqaba from the Red Sea. Guarding the Straits is the military camp and landing field of Sharm-el-Sheikh. It made world headlines when captured by the Israelis during the Six-Day War, thus wiping out the Egyptian blockade of the Gulf. Sharm-el-

THE NEGEV AND THE SINAI DESERT

Sheikh is a lonely desert outpost painted in technicolor, the shore in pink and the water in vivid purples and greens.

One way to see the Sinai is from the air, by way of the day tours run by Arkia Inland Airlines. For those who have the time and the spirit of adventure, there are organized five-day overland trips in command cars and buses.

The route is usually from Beersheba by way of Abu Aweigila, the Mitla Pass, the manganese mines at Umm Bogma near the Gulf of Suez and St. Catherine's Monastery to Sharm-el-Sheikh, with the return route along the Gulf of Aqaba to Eilat. By day one can travel for hours without seeing a living creature except an occasional ibex, gazelle or jackal, black-and-gray desert crows, or a falcon wheeling against the intense sky. At night one stretches out on the ground in a sleeping bag near a campfire, under the moon or coruscating stars. Time in the Sinai wilderness has stood still since the wandering Israelites encamped here on their way from bondage to the Promised Land.

CHAPTER 9

Tel Aviv-Jaffa

I will build thee, and thou shall be built.
—*Jeremiah* 31:4

TEL AVIV

As the plane approaches the coast of Israel and circles into Lod airport, Tel Aviv appears as a huge expanse of gray-white cubes, as if constructed by children out of beach sand and patted into shape by their wooden spades. Its flat look is broken only by a scattering of tall modern buildings and by the vertical notes of spire and minaret in Jaffa, adjoining it to the south. Beyond the city is a sea of glossy green orange groves and, twenty miles to the east, the plain is contained by the low rampart of the Judean Hills, blue and soft in the clear air.

TEL AVIV-JAFFA

Jerusalem is a stone city set in its stony hills, its inward ear tuned to the vibration of the centuries. Haifa lies proudly in the great amphitheater rising from the blue sweep of its bay to the top of Mount Carmel. Tel Aviv is without ancient memory or striking scenery, but does not give a damn. It is young and brash, the biggest city in Israel and the liveliest. Tel Avivians may be fiercely critical of their city's shortcomings, but they would not live anywhere else. Why should they? This is the real heart of modern Israel, the center of its commerce and its culture, the stronghold of its struggle for nationhood—a self-made city, built in two generations by Jews, for Jews, out of nothing but their energies and their needs.

The saga of Tel Aviv began before World War I in a Turkish Palestine which to the *sabras* of today seems like "dim far-off forgotten things and battles long ago." Yet that time is within the memories of some of Israel's older citizens. The Jewish population of the country in 1909 was about 80,000. This included 25,000 Jews in Jaffa, the country's chief port city at that time, where they earned a livelihood as storekeepers, shipping and banking agents and artisans. Tired of the cramped and noisome Arab quarters in which they lived, a group of these Jewish residents bought thirty-two acres of bare sand dunes to the north of the railway line and the old road from Jaffa to Nablus, along which plodded the camel trains. On the great day in 1909, sixty families marched out to the site, conscious enough of history to wear their best clothes and to take along a cameraman. The fading photographs can still be seen, including one which shows their leader, Meir Dizengoff, in white trousers and tight double-breasted black jacket, addressing

• 213

the group in what appears to be the middle of the Western Desert. In a fine flight of rhetoric, he is prophesying a city of 25,000 people.

Lots were drawn for the building plots flanking the single street, which was named after Dr. Herzl. The new suburbanites set to work under the hot sun with shovels and a single wheelbarrow, clearing the sand for the little cottages and gardens which were the germ of the first all-Jewish city of modern times, called Ahuzat Bayit.

The breadwinners commuted daily to Jaffa, on foot or in *droshkies* (horse cabs), while the housewives shopped at the stores and booths that crept into the fringe area between the Nablus road and the railroad. At night, by the light of oil lamps and candles, there was much vigorous discussion about the old life and the new, and much flowing of tea from the Russian samovars while the jackals howled in the darkness outside. The village was guarded against marauders by a force of four watchmen: a Russian Jew, a Yemenite, a *sabra* and a Circassian. On Shabbat (the Sabbath) the suburb symbolically cut itself off from the outside world with a heavy chain slung across the roadway which led from the railway crossing into Herzl Street.

After a little while they felt the need for a fancier name than Ahuzat Bayit, and called their garden suburb Tel Aviv (Hill of Spring) after the Hebrew title of Herzl's book *Altneuland*, echoing the place name in the Babylonian exile referred to by Ezekiel:

> Then I came to them of the captivity at Tel-abib . . . and I sat where they sat, and remained there astonished among them seven days.
> —Ezekiel 3:15

CITY OF TEL AVIV - JAFFA

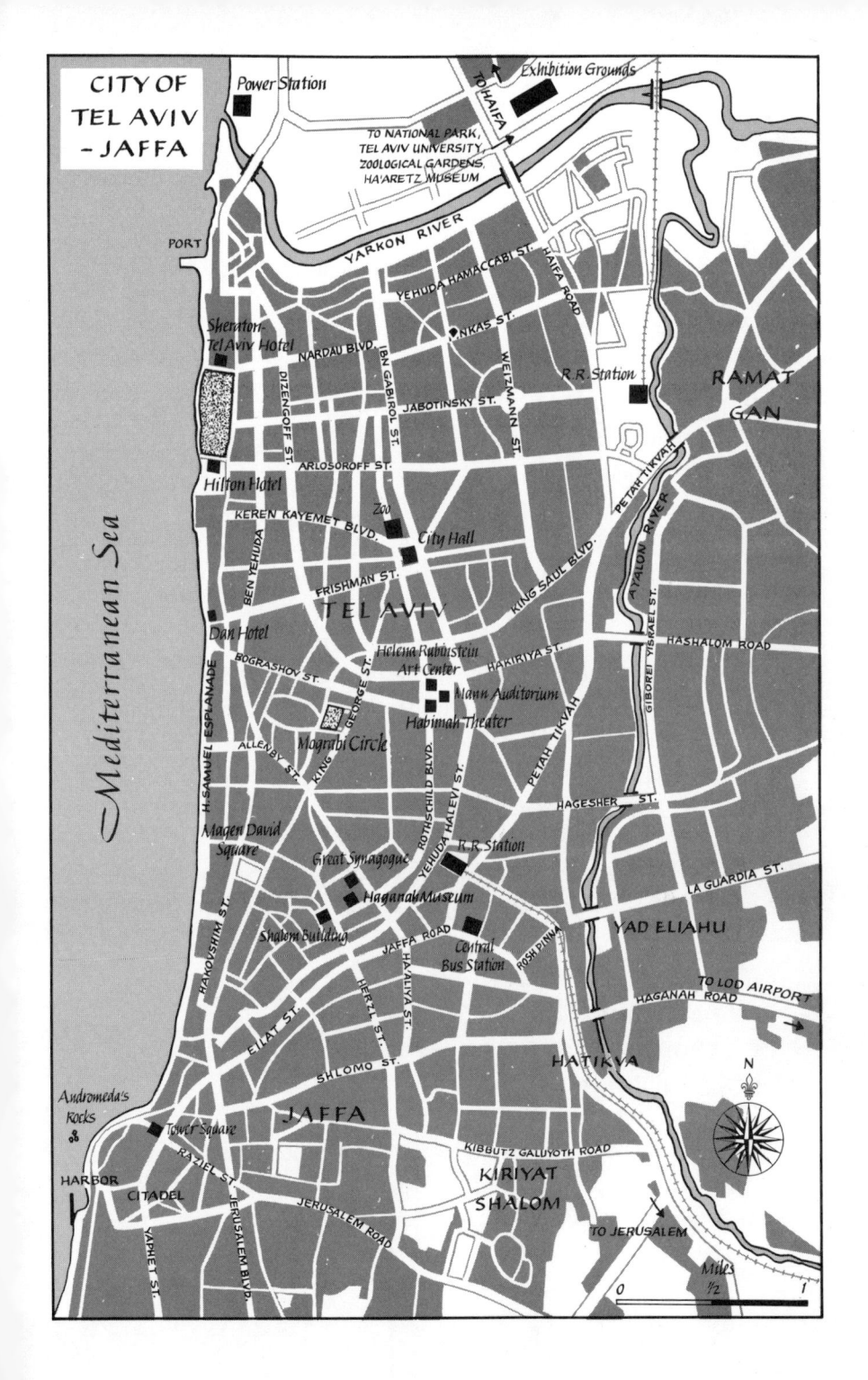

A steady stream of immigrant Jews from Russia moved in, and by the time World War I broke out, Tel Aviv was already a busy townlet of 3,000 inhabitants, with a number of criss-crossing streets and a commercial center. Like the rest of the country, it suffered a decline during the war years. One black Thursday in the spring of 1917, its inhabitants were rounded up and moved elsewhere by order of the Turkish governor, Jemal Pasha. But they came back as soon as General Allenby's advancing forces occupied Jaffa in November of that year.

The beginning of postwar British rule launched a fresh wave of Jewish immigration. Tel Aviv swelled with newcomers and pushed out steadily into the dunes and fields. In 1921, following Arab anti-Jewish riots, it split off from Jaffa and obtained a separate municipal charter. Its population was by then 15,000. Dizengoff became the first mayor and his paternal rule lasted until his death fifteen years later.

The town also took unto itself a fine coat of arms, which presented it both as a beacon of light for the Jewish Diaspora and a gateway for the Return to Zion. A large number of the returnees did not get beyond the gateway!

At the outbreak of World War II in 1939, the town had grown to more than 100,000. By 1949 Tel Aviv had swallowed up Jaffa, and within the boundaries of the new municipal area there lived by 1967 a dense population of 400,000. Today, Tel Aviv, together with the adjacent satellite towns, forms a continuous built-up area holding a fifth of the country's total population.

In keeping with its buoyant nature, Tel Aviv became stronger each time the Arabs made trouble for it. It was born as a reaction to the difficulties of Jewish minority life in Jaffa. It obtained an independent municipal status out of

TEL AVIV-JAFFA

the 1921 riots. The Arab general strike of 1936, which tied up shipping in Jaffa, again pushed Tel Aviv forward by giving it a jetty of its own. Until 1965 the port handled an impressive volume of citrus and general cargo, but owing to planning problems at Tel Aviv and the need to stimulate Negev development, the government decided that the country's second major deep-water harbor (after Haifa) constructed farther south, at Ashdod, would handle the bulk of the cargo. Tel Aviv port will be developed as a marina and fishing harbor.

In July, 1946, when the Attlee government was trying to suppress Jewish resistance in the country, one of its measures, called "Operation Hippo," was to throw an army cordon completely round Tel Aviv. For the next four days the city was cut off from the rest of the country and all the citizens were placed under house detention. About 22,000 troops were engaged in a house-to-house search. Out of 102,000 people screened, two young men were finally detained as terrorists. Tel Aviv thereupon resumed its busy life exactly as if this interlude of being "enemy-occupied territory" had never happened.

This unshakable quality was again evident a year later during the months preceding independence. At this time the streets at the southern end of Tel Aviv were being sprayed by bullets from the rooftops of Arab Jaffa, and both sides were making forays across a narrow no man's land between the two adjoining cities. One special nuisance was a sniper's post in the minaret of the nearby mosque of Hassan Bek, from which pot shots could be taken at strollers on the Tel Aviv esplanade and at shoppers in the streets below. Finally the Jews erected high concrete walls across the ends of the streets to protect the pedestrians.

FROM DAN TO EILAT

The border warfare that had developed between Tel Aviv and Jaffa in the period before the end of the Mandate came to a climax on May 11, forty-eight hours before the proclamation of the State. The resistance of the Jaffa Arabs was broken after much of the border quarter of Manshieh had been blown up by Jewish saboteur squads and the town penetrated by fierce street fighting. The British authorities intervened and with their help, nearly all the 70,000 Jaffa Arabs were evacuated to Arab-controlled areas.

The municipal authorities of Tel Aviv had mixed feelings at suddenly acquiring Jaffa, most of it untidy, unhygienic and empty. Even without this extra burden, Tel Aviv proper was already paying a heavy price for its own hectic growth. In the early stages, any effort at rational and far-sighted city planning had not been strong enough to curb immediate pressures and booming land values. The older parts of Tel Aviv are cramped, often shoddy, and full of traffic bottlenecks which produce a great volume of exuberant honking and yelling.

But the more recent housing areas reflect careful planning supported by rising prosperity. There are wide boulevards with tropical trees or flowering shrubs down the center, lined with handsome four-story apartment buildings in modern functional style. Each apartment has a balcony, on which the family usually eats and takes its ease on summer evenings. On the eastern edges of the city are big housing projects, the apartment buildings being laid out at right angles to the road, with gardens between them. It has become common for new buildings to be built on stilts, providing a free space underneath for air circulation, parking, children's bicycles and baby carriages. Other welcome features of recent buildings are the panels of gay color on the outer walls, the vertically slanted louvers which provide both shade and air, and the perforated balcony screens which echo a Moorish theme. In these ways, Tel Aviv is breaking away from the square-cut monotony, the ugliness and the jerry-built look of its earlier building boom and endowing its cube-shaped structures with a new grace and solidity.

Among the new civic buildings are the tall City Hall and the Law Courts.

As in New York and other large cities, the detached town house is a vanishing breed in Tel Aviv, and the business or professional man who hankers for his own home and garden is migrating into suburbia and becoming a commuter. Ramat Gan (Garden Hill), ten minutes to the north, remains a preserve of villas (as private homes are invariably known locally) and a number of the choice ones are rented to foreign diplomats. Within a twenty-minute radius of Tel Aviv are several more peri-urban garden townships, such as Herzliya and Kfar Shmaryahu to the north, and Savyon to the southeast. The latter, established by a South African group, boasts a fine sports club with tennis courts, swimming pool and bowling green, and some of the best gardens in the country.

One of the fruits of uncontrolled early expansion is the lack of parks within the city itself. Fortunately it has a great open lung in its foreshore. The broad concrete "boardwalk," the Herbert Samuel Esplanade, runs north from the foot of Allenby Road to the Dan Hotel. It is being continued, to run past the Hilton Hotel, the Independence Garden and the Sheraton Hotel. On a Shabbat in the summer (which lasts most of the year), Tel Aviv relaxes here in its own cheerful, uninhibited way. Tens of thousands of people crowd into the space between the glittering blue sea and Hayarkon Street. The hotels and cafés are filled to overflowing; on the boardwalk, armadas of fancy white baby carriages thread through the ambling crowd; while the sand below looks like Coney Island or Blackpool on a bank holiday—a scene of gay and colorful humanity, tanning a rich brown in the hot sun, sprawled at ease in striped deck chairs, splashing in the warm water under the watchful eye of the lifeguards, riding over it on floats (*hassikas*) and pedal-machines, and eating picnic lunches. The air is filled with the mingled cries of children, anxious mothers, frolicking teenagers and the vendors of ice cream, corn on the cob, pink spun sugar, *felafel*, and *sum-sum* (sweetmeats made of sesame seeds). Some of the bathers congregate at the large municipal swimming pool a little farther up the beach.

The esplanade has plenty of strollers in the evening too, but now the crowds converge on the brightly lit streets further inland which hold the theaters, movie houses and popular cafés.

The open square at the end of Rothschild Boulevard is the nearest thing in Israel to an artistic Parnassus, since it holds the porticoed home of Habimah (the Israel National Theater), the Helena Rubinstein Art Center and the functional building of the Mann Auditorium, where the Israel Philharmonic Orchestra performs.

The orchestra enjoys international renown. It was founded in 1936 by Bronislav Huberman, the violinist, using mainly refugee musicians from leading European orchestras; it was licked into shape by Maestro Arturo Toscanini himself. Israel is so full of music lovers that although the Mann Auditorium has 3,000 seats, each subscription concert has to be repeated eight times. When the orchestra

TEL AVIV-JAFFA

visits Jerusalem, every one of the 3,600 seats in the Convention Center hall is occupied. With other appearances in Haifa, Ein Gev and elsewhere, the concerts add up to 200 a year for the ensemble of 100 men and women. The orchestra has performed under the batons of many illustrious conductors who, apart from Toscanini, have included Serge Koussevitzky, Leonard Bernstein, Paul Paray, Jean Martinon, Jan Kubelik and Sir John Barbirolli; and it counts among its visiting soloists such giants as Jascha Heifetz, Issac Stern, Yehudi Menuhin, Artur Rubinstein, Claudio Arrau and Gregor Piatagorsky. In the 1960's the orchestra successfully toured Europe, the United States, Canada, Mexico, Japan and India.

With all its luster, the orchestra has not lost the simplicity of Israel life, and its concerts are not "dress affairs." It is uniquely organized as a cooperative of its own players, who pay themselves modest salaries based on the size of their families rather than on their importance; and it is not above leaving its fine hall to perform in some kibbutz dining room or under the open sky in a pioneer town like Eilat. In the 1948 War of Independence the orchestra, led by Leonard Bernstein, piled into trucks which lurched and jolted up to Jerusalem along the "Burma Road," a rough track which had just been hacked through the mountains to relieve the besieged city; and later, when Beersheba was captured in the Negev fighting against the Egyptian army, the orchestra arrived again (clutching their instruments in their arms to save them from being smashed along the way) and gave a memorable sunset concert to an audience of tired, dusty Israel soldiers sprawled among the ruins, with the rumbling guns providing an offstage accompaniment.

Tel Aviv has many professional theater companies (three

of them straight repertory), a national opera, and several small revue groups. The most famous theater company is the Habimah, which in 1958 was recognized as the National Theater on the tenth anniversary of the State and awarded an annual government subvention of IL 100,000. Habimah has had a romantic history. It was founded in Russia in 1918, just after the Bolshevik Revolution, and trained in the stylized manner of the great Stanislavsky. In 1928 it moved to Palestine. Its leading players, such as Rovina and Meskin, soon became national figures in the *Yishuv* (the Jewish community), and its remarkable repertoire introduced to a small poioneering community, in the revived Hebrew tongue, the great masterpieces of Shakespeare, Molière, Shaw and O'Neill, as well as current hits translated from various languages and original plays depicting Israel life. Its favorites remained, however, two plays of Jewish life in Eastern Europe—*The Golem* and *The Dybbuk*. It has done the latter some 3,000 times, including performances before packed houses in New York, London and elsewhere on the company's tours abroad; and it was by general demand that on the evening Habimah was made the State Theater, the program included a scene from *The Dybbuk* and a scene from *The Golem*. Habimah, too, is run as an actors' cooperative, with little disparity in salary between the leading lady and a bit-part player, and it has its own housing project for its members. It sometimes brings in well-known outside directors, such as Tyrone Guthrie, who directed a polished performance of *A Midsummer Night's Dream* in Hebrew, without knowing a word of that language.

Habimah's younger rival is the Cameri (Chamber Theater), which also has a permanent building in Tel Aviv. This

TEL AVIV-JAFFA

group has a flair for plays in lighter vein, ranging from Shaw's *Pygmalion* (which it performed 200 times) to *Born Yesterday*, the comedy of Washington politics. The Cameri is a valuable outlet for original Israel plays, the best known of which is Moshe Shamir's *He Walked in the Fields*.

The Ohel (Tent) Theater began as a workers' theater, founded in 1925 by the Labor Federation (Histadrut) and it is now an independent company, performing mostly in Tel Aviv.

These three repertory companies have an aggregate attendance of well over a million a year, which is fantastic in a country of some two and a half million souls.

Among newer groups worth mentioning are the Zavit and the Players' Theater. There are ten Little Theater groups in the country, including an Arab one in Nazareth.

A favorite showcase is the Alhambra Theater in Jaffa, where producer Giora Godik presents American musicals translated into Hebrew. He began in 1964 with a highly successful and lavish performance of *My Fair Lady*, complete with Cecil Beaton costuming, which traveled all over Israel, playing more than 300 times. He followed it with *Barefoot in the Park*, *The King and I*, and *Fiddler on the Roof*—also a smash hit. He has also begun to put on local musicals.

There are also about half a dozen theatrical groups that play in Jewish and that appear in the main cities. As yet, they have no permanent theater of their own.

There is a small but growing movie industry which is turning out full-length feature films on local themes. The most popular have been *Salah Shabati*—the struggles of an immigrant Yemenite family; and *I Like Mike*, about an American tourist in Israel.

Several full-length foreign movies have recently been made in Israel, such as *Exodus*; *Judith*, with Sophia Loren; a modern version of *She*, with Ursula Andress, mostly shot in and around Eilat; a co-production of *Never on Saturday*; and *Cast a Giant Shadow*, the stars of which included Kirk Douglas, Yul Brynner and Frank Sinatra.

The Israel National Opera is the creation of Edis de Philippe, from Brooklyn, and Mordechai Galinkin, from Petrograd. It made its debut with *Thaïs* (sung in Hebrew) on April 15, 1948, exactly one month before the independence of the State. The opening performance was attended by a number of leading figures, including David Ben-Gurion, and noisy accompaniment was supplied by gunfire from nearby skirmishes between Tel Aviv and Jaffa. After years of struggle, without funds for a permanent home, the opera made a fresh start in 1958 when it acquired and adapted the old building on the esplanade in which the first meetings of the Knesset had been held. It now has a company of 225 performers, musicians and stagehands, and an extensive repertoire of operas, all performed in Hebrew. They are about to move to permanent quarters in northern Tel Aviv.

The social and intellectual ferment of Tel Aviv (as in Paris or Rome) finds a happy outlet in its pavement cafés, especially along the tree-shaded sidewalks of Dizengoff Street, which on Friday and Saturday nights is the Tel Avivians' Times Square and Paccadilly Circus rolled into one. The favored haunt of the actors, artists and writers is Kassit, a sidewalk café which is specially licensed to remain open into the small hours and where there is endless enjoyable wrangling over ideas and endless downing of glasses of sweet lemon tea. Next door, at Rowal, the more fashionable set enjoys the best iced coffee and pastry in town. The many

TEL AVIV-JAFFA

other eating places and cafés that have sprung up near the movie houses in this area include cosmopolitan newcomers such as ice cream parlors, a hamburger heaven and a pizza-pie palace. The latest craze is *schwama*, thin slices of mutton grilled on a spit and served in a portion of *pitta* (bread) with a hot Oriental sauce. Many of the oldtimers shake their heads over such sophistication. For the tourist, however, it is fun to sit at a café table on a warm summer evening and watch a shirt-sleeved Mr. Israel with his wife and children, parading in high spirits past the brightly lit store windows, or surging in and out of the movies. Beer and wine are sold in the cafés without restriction, but drunkenness is unknown in Israel, and even the soldiers on leave prefer Tempo (lemonade) and *gazoz* (soda pop).

Tel Aviv's main business thoroughfare is Allenby Street, which comes up from the sea front to Mograbi Circle and then turns southeast. Together with the modern stores, office buildings, banks and cafés which line Allenby and adjacent streets, there are some picturesque survivals from an earlier generation. Off Magen David Square (a six-street intersection designed with more regard for history than traffic) there is the Carmel Shuk, an open-air market of little one-man stores and booths where noisy haggling over fruit, vegetables, flowers, eggs and chickens takes place in the good old-fashioned Oriental way, with a truly Oriental disrespect for hygiene. It is a congested, picturesque scene on Thursday and Friday, when supplies are being laid in for the Sabbath.

Farther down Allenby Street is the Wizo shop in which the tourist can see and buy some of the finest examples of Israel handicrafts. Wizo, the Women's International Zionist Organization, has branches in fifty countries.

Halfway down Allenby Street is the Great Synagogue (the largest in Israel), around which traffic is diverted on the Sabbath and Holy Days. Along its side are more sidewalk vendors, selling prayer shawls, skullcaps and other requirements of the worshipers. Before Succoth a brisk pavement trade develops here in green branches for the tabernacles of private householders, and the fragrant citrons, twigs of myrtle and palm shoots for ceremonial use on this festival.

Allenby Street is one of only three named after soldiers; the other two honor General Monash and Brigadier Kisch. On the other hand, Tel Aviv must have a larger proportion of streets named for writers than any other town in the world. Among the Jews, the list includes Bialik, Ahad Ha'am, Zangwill, Sholem Aleichem, Yehuda Halevi, Peretz, Rambam, Lessing, Mendele Mocher Sefarim and a host of others. There are also streets named for such non-Jews as Émile Zola and George Eliot, who championed Jewish causes. As for Biblical characters in the street names, the prophets too outnumber the warriors, with Amos, Deborah, Ezekiel, Hosea, Isaiah, Jeremiah and Jonah, though the military sector would be entitled to claim Joshua and Bar Kochba. This writer's two favorite names—ringing declarations of faith rather than mere street labels—are Rehov Am Yisrael Chai, which means "The-People-of-Israel-Lives Street," and Rehov Kol Yisrael Chaverim, which means "All-Jews-Are-Brothers Street."

Tel Aviv's biggest crowd of the year (half a million in 1968) turns out for the *Adloyada*, the great carnival procession marking the Feast of Purim at the beginning of spring. In early days the procession used to be headed by Mayor Dizengoff riding on a white horse. It features scores of elab-

TEL AVIV-JAFFA

orate floats on topical or Biblical themes. Every rooftop and balcony along the route is packed with a dense and colorful mass of people. Purim has become Israel's Mardi Gras and is in a special sense the children's festival. They swarm everywhere in gay fancy dress.

On the northern edge of Tel Aviv, the Yarkon River, fourteen miles long, flows sluggishly between two rows of eucalyptus trees until it enters the sea between the port and the great, squat bulk of the Reading Power Station. The river has always been popular for Sabbath boating and family picnics on the banks, but it has now been sadly depleted by the diversion of much of its flow to the Negev through a huge 66-inch pipeline. Near its mouth, next to the port, is the big enclosure where the Levant Fair was held in 1936. This has now been converted into the small Dov Hos domestic air terminal.

The *Maccabiah*, an "Olympic Games" for Jewish athletes from all over the world, held every four years, takes place in the huge Ramat Gan Sports Stadium a little north of the river, which seats more than 30,000 spectators. The "Maccabiah village" has been built nearby to house the sportsmen. It is in this arena that Israel's soccer team plays visiting foreign teams while the whole country is glued to its radio sets.

What has been a nearly empty area of dunes and fields north of the Yarkon River, towards Herzliya and Ramat Gan, is now filling up—partly with new residential suburbs, but also with civic amenities and institutions. An area of 4,000 *dunams* (1,000 acres) has been turned into a national park. On the edge of it is the campus of Tel Aviv University, a lusty infant which already has seven separate faculties, 8,000 students and an academic staff of more than 1,000. It also has Israel's second medical school.

The national park will be the home of the new Tel Aviv Zoo, which has been planned by the designer of the famous San Diego Zoo in California.

Just beyond the bridge over the Yarkon River on the Herzliya main road is a small mound, the Tel Kassile archaeological dig. The first people to settle here were the Philistines in the twelfth century B.C. The settlement was probably destroyed by King David in the tenth century B.C., and an Israelite city built on its ruins. Oil and wine presses dating from the eighth century B.C. have been found, as have *ostraca* (inscribed potsherds) recording the amount of oil and wine shipped from this Israel city to a Mediterranean port. It was rebuilt during the Persian period by the Jews returning from their Babylonian exile. There are also Hellenistic, Roman and Byzantine remains to be seen, and the primitive buildings of the early Arab period. Next to the dig is the growing Ha'aretz Museum complex, with separate small pavilions devoted to ancient glass, coins and ceramics, to science and technology, and to ethnology; there is also a planetarium. The gem of the collection is the circular green building on the crown of the hill, housing one of the finest collections of ancient glass in the world, left to the municipality by Dr. Walter Moses.

The foreshore area to the north of the Reading Power Station has been opened to development by a new bridge across the Yarkon and a strip of highway close to the sea. A feature of this area will be a sports city, and the Tel Aviv Country Club is already functioning here as a sports center.

JAFFA

The name Jaffa (Yafo, Joppa) means "beautiful" in Hebrew, Arabic or ancient Greek—but the visitor today would find this adjective inappropriate. The harbor and the citadel above it still have a theatrical air, and when the promontory dreams in a summer haze, or is gilded by the setting sun or lashed by a winter storm, the old legends come alive; but behind it, the town is mostly a mass of peeling buildings and narrow alleys, and the border quarter between it and Tel Aviv resembles a cleared bomb site left from the London blitz. The presentable thoroughfares are Jerusalem Boulevard (the former King George Street), which is lined with tall palms transplanted from Tel Aviv's Rothschild Boulevard when that town was evacuated in World War I; and Raziel Street, leading into Tower Square, containing the square-cut Abdul Hamid Jubilee Clock Tower, the stone-walled jail, and the Great Mosque, built in 1810.

The founding of Jaffa, like that of Jerusalem, goes back before recorded time. It is mentioned as a Canaanite city in the tribute lists of Pharaoh Thutmose III in the fifteenth century B.C. and in the Tel-el-Amarna Letters of the fourteenth century B.C., before Joshua fought the battle of Jericho. Later it formed the northern end of the string of Philistine cities which stretched up the coastal plain from Gaza and Ashkelon. Ancient Jaffa seems to have produced some whopping fish stories. There was Jonah, that hapless traveler, who took a ship from this little harbor, was flung into the sea to save the vessel from a storm, and then swallowed up by "a great fish," spending three days and three nights in its belly. "And the Lord spake unto the fish, and it vomited out Jonah upon the dry land"—Jonah 2:10. Then later there is the Greek legend of the virgin maiden Andromeda, who was chained to the rock that juts out into the water beyond Jaffa harbor as a sacrifice to a terrible sea monster; but Perseus dashed up, flying swiftly on his winged shoes, slew the monster and freed the maiden, with whom he presumably lived happily ever after. This legend blended afterwards with that of St. George and the Dragon, associated with Lydda, farther inland.

It was at Jaffa that the Phoenician King Hiram of Tyre offloaded cedar logs for King Solomon's Temple; and it was to Jaffa that the Romans brought their wheat ships a thousand years later. Simon the Maccabee captured it about 140 B.C., making it a Jewish city, and Vespasian sacked it in A.D. 68 when crushing the Jewish revolt. In the Christian era, Jaffa became the seat of a Byzantine bishopric in the sixth century and of Crusader counts from Venice in the twelfth century. It was destroyed by the Mamelukes in 1291; captured by Napoleon in 1799, and again by Allenby in 1917.

But hardly anything of this rich and stormy history remains visible. In the area of the Citadel, the high mount overlooking the harbor, there is an ancient lighthouse. Near it are a Franciscan church built in 1654 and a small ruined mosque alleged to be on the site of the house of Simon the Tanner, where St. Peter stayed for some time and heard the voice of God telling him to receive Gentiles as well as Jews into the Church: "God is no respecter of persons," said Peter (Acts 10:34). The small archaeological museum of Jaffa is beyond the church. The southern slopes of the Citadel hill have been taken over by local artists. The municipality and the Israel government have cleaned and restored

TEL AVIV-JAFFA

the winding lanes and haphazard staircases, and there are numbers of artists' studios, galleries, and restaurants that look out onto the sparkling Mediterranean.

The real interest of Jaffa lies not so much in its history or its buildings as in its present inhabitants. When 65,000 Arabs departed in April, 1948, 5,000 stayed behind and still occupy one part of the town. In all the rest, the empty houses rapidly filled up with assorted Jewish immigrants from all over the world. It now has 100,000 Jews, none of whom was in the country before the State. Here is *Kibbutz Galuyot* (Ingathering), taken neat. In Jaffa the most ardent tourist need not worry about remains of the past, but can simply relax and enjoy the cosmopolitan human scenery of the present. An extraordinary medley of languages bubbles up from the sidewalks or is scrawled on the stores, and just as extraordinary a variety of national dishes can be sampled in the little neon-lighted cafés and eating places. In a single swift leap, the young children have become Israelis. To their parents, they talk the tongue of the country from which the family came, whether it is Yiddish, French, Bulgarian, Arabic or what you will; but in their street games, they scream at each other in Hebrew.

Jaffa is well worth an "evening on the town." The shops are all open, there are several excellent fish restaurants near the harbor—among them The Ariadne and Jeannette's— and a night club called Omar Khayam, with at least as much atmosphere as a stage setting at the Paris Opera. You get to it through the narrowest of cobbled alleys, and inside you sit on reed-topped Arab stools, under fishing nets suspended from the medieval stone walls. It is gay, noisy, informal and friendly, the floor show is fun, and you can even dance on a minute floor.

FROM DAN TO EILAT

From having been the stepmother of Tel Aviv, Jaffa has now become its stepchild. Since the two towns were merged in 1949, a great deal has been done to clean it up and provide it with electric light, piped water and sanitation.

One of the most ambitious projects anywhere for the creation of a new urban center has been planned for the rubble-strewn area of the Manshieh quarter of Jaffa, which bordered on Tel Aviv and which was largely destroyed in the 1948 fighting. It occupies the stretch of foreshore between the foot of Allenby Street and the Jaffa harbor.

CHAPTER 10

The Sharon Plain

If you were to fly north from Tel Aviv to Haifa, a distance of sixty miles, the Sharon Plain would look like an emerald-green belt lying between the sea and the dusty hills of Samaria. This is the narrow waist of Israel, and also the most densely settled area. The Sharon was a beautiful, cultivated valley in Biblical times. But when the first Jewish pioneers started to reclaim it at the end of the nineteenth century, much of this coastal plain was a swampy wasteland, with sand dunes blown in upon it by the perpetual sea breezes. The sand dunes had to be pushed back and the swamps drained. As one drives through this rolling, soft country, with its vistas of red soil and glossy orange groves, its cheerful market towns and farm villages, it is difficult to believe the whole scene is only about fifty years old.

But the reclamation battle is not over; from the air you

see thousands of dunams of sand hills that still have to be curbed and eventually used as sites for housing or industry.

There are two roads up the coastal plain: the old main road through Petah Tikvah, and the new coastal road through Herzliya. They join at Hadera, halfway to Haifa.

THE OLD MAIN ROAD

The old main Tel Aviv-Haifa road runs inland for miles through a series of satellite towns which are becoming an unbroken built-up extension of Tel Aviv, in the way cities are spreading everywhere in the world. One of these is Ramat Gan, on the high ground just to the north. It is part industrial zone and part garden suburb, and has happily clung to planned streets and green belts. It has one of the biggest parks in Israel, which contains an open-air stadium, an artificial lake, picnic areas and forests. Beyond it is *Bnei Brak*, an Orthodox citadel, where synagogues and *yeshivot* (Talmudic colleges) mingle with small factories and workshops. Nearby is the Bar-Ilan University, a small "modern Orthodox" university founded by the Mizrachi Movement (Religious Zionists). It has nearly 3,000 students who receive academic training in Judaica, languages and literature, the social sciences, the natural sciences and mathematics, and Middle Eastern and African Studies.

Petah Tikvah (Gateway of Hope), three miles farther on, is a sprawling town today, but its special place in Israel's history is as "Mother of the Colonies," having been founded in 1878 as the first Jewish agricultural settlement in modern Palestine. The malarial marsh here was drained after much hardship, and citrus growing developed. In the main street is a fine stone arch in memory of Baron Ed-

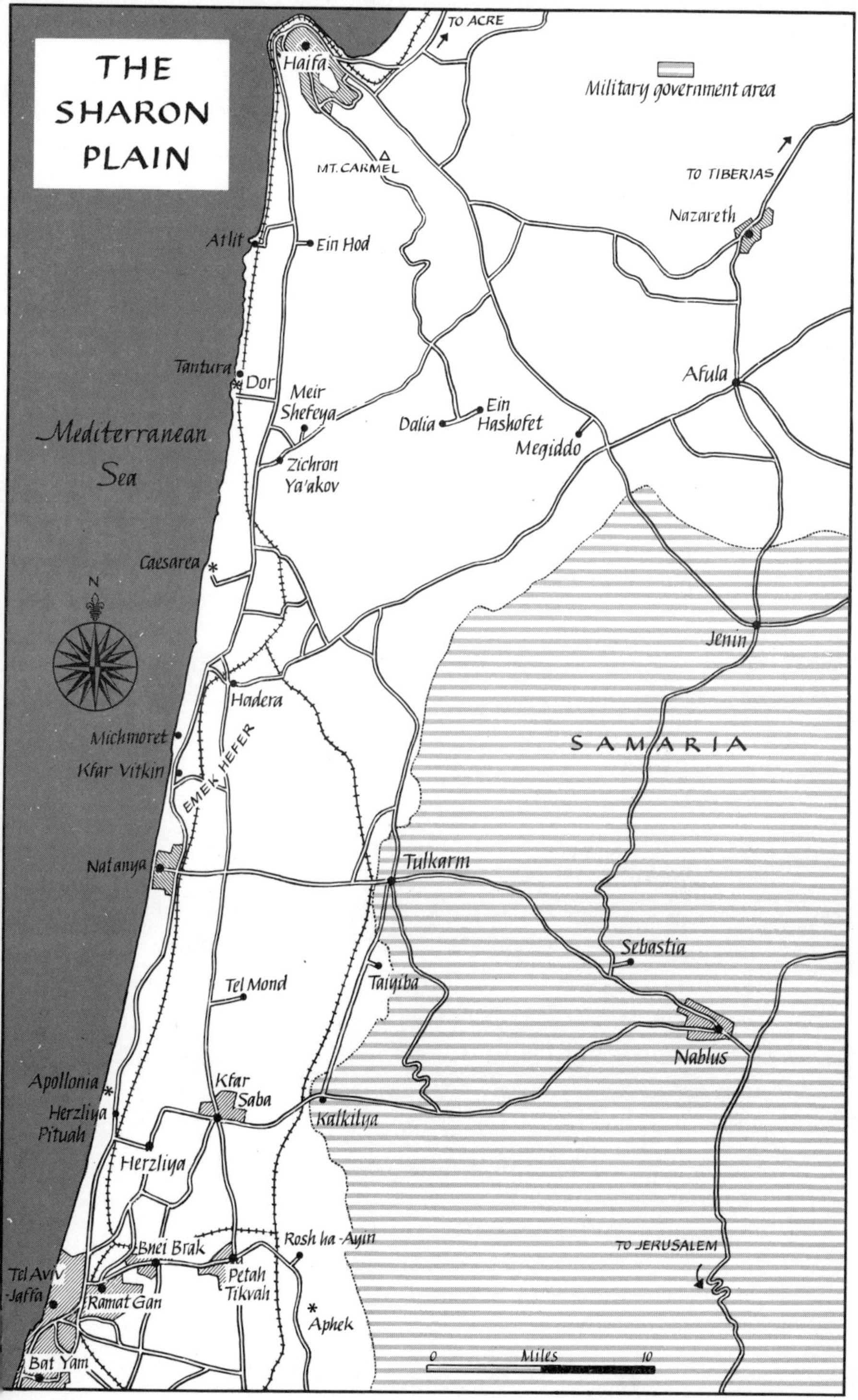
THE SHARON PLAIN
Military government area
TO ACRE
Haifa
MT. CARMEL
TO TIBERIAS
Nazareth
Atlit
Ein Hod
Tantura
Dor
Meir Shefeya
Dalia
Ein Hashofet
Afula
Megiddo
Mediterranean Sea
Zichron Ya'akov
Caesarea
N
Hadera
Jenin
Michmoret
Kfar Vitkin
EMEK HEFER
SAMARIA
Natanya
Tulkarm
Sebastia
Tel Mond
Taiyiba
Nablus
Apollonia
Kfar Saba
Herzliya Pituah
Kalkilya
Herzliya
Rosh ha-Ayin
TO JERUSALEM
Bnei Brak
Tel Aviv -Jaffa
Ramat Gan
Petah Tikvah
Aphek
0
Miles
10
Bat Yam

mond de Rothschild, who gave the early settlers much-needed help.

A few minutes' drive to the northeast is a grass mound crowned by crumbling masonry. This has been identified as the *tel* under which lies the Biblical city of Aphek that once guarded the main highway to Jerusalem before it entered the hills. It was here that the Hebrews were severely defeated by the Philistines in the days of the Judges:

> Now Israel went out against the Philistines to battle . . . and the Philistines pitched in Aphek. . . .
> Israel was smitten, and they fled every man into his tent: and there was a very great slaughter. . . .
> . . . and the Ark of God was taken.
> —I Samuel 4:1, 10, 11

A thousand years later, Herod built a square fortress here and named it Antipatris in memory of his father. The remains now visible are Crusader fortifications.

Near the foot of the hill is Rosh ha-Ayin, in a low-lying area overgrown with vegetation and full of fresh-water springs that are the sources of the Yarkon River. From here a big pumping station sends water flowing southward to the Negev through sixty-five miles of giant pipeline. The water in this pipe is now supplemented by water pumped from the Sea of Galilee and increases threefold the amount going to the Negev. An abandoned British Army barracks at Rosh ha-Ayin was converted in 1951 into the main reception camp for the Yemenite Jews brought to Israel by the airborne operation known as "Magic Carpet." A number of them have settled down here as farmers, dwelling in a curving sweep of small cottages.

From Petah Tikvah to Hadera, via the small market town of Kfar Saba, the road goes through a busy farm belt of or-

THE SHARON PLAIN

ange groves (protected by windbreaks of tall cypress trees), dairy herds, poultry runs, reddish ploughland and irrigated fields of melons, alfalfa and flowers in which the overhead water sprinklers twirl like ballet dancers. Near Tel Mond there is the charming Youth Aliyah children's village of Hadassim, with its own farm, school, workshops and amphitheater.

THE COASTAL ROAD

Herzliya (named after Theodor Herzl) lies about eight miles north of Tel Aviv. The old village has not changed much, but its coastward development, Herzliya Pituah, has become a seashore resort, with some of the prettiest private villas in Israel, surrounded by lawns and gardens. Most of the residents commute daily to Tel Aviv. Three good modern hotels, the Sharon, the Ring Apollonia and the Accadia, standing less than a mile apart, overlook a wonderful stretch of golden sand. To the north of the Sharon Hotel stands the abandoned Mosque of Sidna Ali, with its tall minaret. Beyond it, crumbling blocks of masonry built into the rim of the cliff or lying in the clear water are all that is left of the small port city of Apollonia, whose history goes back thousands of years. It was built on the site of the Canaanite city of Rishpon, dedicated to their god Reshef, a statue of whom was found farther up the coast, at Atlit. The Greek city of Apollonia was named after the god Apollo. It was near here that Richard the Lion-Heart held his own against the Moslem leader Saladin; in 1265, the city was captured and destroyed by the Moslems, and since then the sea and the sand have had their will.

• 237

FROM DAN TO EILAT

From Herzliya the road runs northward parallel to the sea, through sand dunes arrested by the planting of Port Jackson willow trees. To the left a modern square building dominates the landscape—the Wingate Institute, a school of physical culture, named after Orde Wingate, the bearded, unorthodox, Bible-loving British general who was killed during World War II while directing jungle warfare against the Japanese in Burma. During the Arab Rebellion of 1936–39, Wingate was a captain with the British forces in Palestine. He obtained permission to organize picked members of the Haganah (Jewish self-defense force) into what became known as "special night squads," which operated successfully against the Arab guerrilla bands on the northern frontier. Wingate himself was sent back to England, being regarded as too sympathetic to the Jewish cause in Palestine. But his night squads developed into the Palmach, the elite corps of the Haganah, and he has remained one of Israel's heroes. His name is also commemorated in a Youth Aliyah children's village called Yemin Orde, in the Carmel Hills.

Natanya (also spelled Netanya and Nathania), established in 1928, is a bright town with wide streets, a pleasant beach and a beautiful outdoor amphitheater in the midst of public gardens overlooking the sea. Worth visiting here are the Goldmunz Art Museum and the training institute for blind girls at the Beit Haluzot, whose Braille library serves the whole country. Natanya has a thriving industrial zone near the railroad and is the center for the diamond cutting and polishing industry started by Belgian refugees in World War II. Today the export of polished diamonds grosses over $150 million a year. To the north of Natanya is *Kiryat Zans*, the new home of the Chasidic Rabbi Klausenberg and his followers, who came here from Williamsburg, in New York City, and built homes, a synagogue, a hotel and a yeshiva.

After Natanya the road runs through the Emek Hefer, mentioned in the Bible as one of the twelve regions appointed by King Solomon, each to provide his household with farm produce one month a year (I Kings 4:10). In 1929, a marshy 3,000-acre tract of this land was purchased with money raised by the Canadian Zionists; today it contains more than twenty settlements, the largest of which is Kfar Vitkin. Two of these settlements, Beitan Aharon and Havatzelet, are named after A. J. Freiman (president of the Canadian Zionist Organization at the time of the purchase) and his wife.

Just before the coastal road reaches Hadera, it crosses the little Alexander River and to the left is the fishing settlement of Michmoret. It contains a Government Fishing School, in which hundreds of Israel boys have been trained in the latest techniques of coastal and deep-sea fishing. The school was founded and long directed by Rafael Ruppin. Michmoret has a wonderful beach, and there is a bungalow-type hotel called Miramar within a few yards of the sea.

A few miles away, on the old highway, is Mossad Ruppin, the Agricultural Institute of the Histadrut, named after Rafael's father, Dr. Arthur Ruppin, who established the first Zionist farm colonization office in Palestine in 1907.

HADERA TO HAIFA

Hadera, where the coastal road joins the main highway again, was founded in 1890 by the pioneers of the First Aliyah, and the local cemetery bears silent witness to the decimation of its early settlers by malaria. (Hadera, the Arabic for "green," referred to a weed that grew all over the marshes.) The fertility of the area today is self-evident as Jewish and Arab farmers come to town to sell their produce at the Thursday market. Just north of the town, where the coastal road joins the old highway, is an industrial area dominated by two huge plants, the Israel-American Paper Mill and the Alliance Tire Factory.

Caesarea

North of Hadera is Caesarea. Until recently it was Israel's most neglected beauty spot, in spite of its rich history and its closeness to the country's main motor artery. Only a few years ago, the occasional visitor could turn off the highway onto a sandy track, pass the banana groves of the nearby kibbutz, park next to some Arab fishermen's crumbling houses, and walk on the seawall with its marble columns jutting out from the storm-battered blocks of masonry; or stretch out in the soft sand, with the silence of buried cities all around and only the gulls moving in the solitude of sea and sky. Now this enchanting spot is coming into its own, and new life is springing up again where a busy and luxurious city once flourished.

King Herod the Great founded Caesarea about 22 B.C. on the site of a small Phoenician town called Strato's Tower. He took ten years to build it and named the city in honor of his patron, Augustus Caesar. Flavius Josephus, in his famous history *Antiquities of the Jews*, gives an account of the construction of the city and port:

> And when he observed there was a city by the seaside that was much decayed, but that the place, by the happiness of its situation, was capable of great improvements,

THE SHARON PLAIN

> he rebuilt it all with white stone, and adorned it with several most splendid palaces . . . for the case was this, that all the seashore between Dora and Joppa, in the middle between which this city is situated, had no good haven, insomuch that every one that sailed from Phoenicia for Egypt was obliged to lie in the stormy sea. . . . But the king overcame nature, and built a haven larger than was the Pyreeum [at Athens] . . . [with a] quay which ran round the entire haven, and was a most agreeable walk to such as had a mind to that exercise. . . . At the mouth of the haven were three great Colossi, supported by pillars. . . . He also built the other edifices, the amphitheatre, and theatre and market-place and appointed games every fifth year, and called them in like manner Caesar's Games.

In A.D. 4 the whole of Judea came under direct Roman rule, and for the next five hundred years Caesarea remained the Roman capital of the country as well as its biggest city and main port. The built-up area of the city covered several hundred acres.

In A.D. 66 the Jewish revolt in Palestine was sparked by a violent dispute in Caesarea between its Jewish and Syrian inhabitants. The Roman forces operating under Titus were based in Caesarea, and in its arena 2,500 Jewish captives were put to death after Jerusalem was sacked in A.D. 70. The Emperor Vespasian then made Caesarea a *colonia*, or semi-autonomous city, and populated it with a number of veterans from the legions.

Caesarea became one of the centers of the new Christian sect and the Acts of the Apostles mention it frequently. The Deacon Philip (St. Philip the Evangelist) preached the Gospel here; St. Peter baptized his first Gentile converts, the Roman centurion Cornelius and his family, at Caesarea;

St. Paul visited the city frequently, and it was here he was brought as a prisoner and demanded to be judged by Caesar, whereupon King Agrippa agreed to send him to Rome (Acts 25, 26).

Caesarea was the last Byzantine city in Palestine to surrender to the Moslem Arab invaders. It capitulated in A.D. 640 after a long siege. The Crusaders took it in 1101, but did not try to revive the whole area of the former city, occupying only a smaller enclosure, with a wall and sea-moat to protect the port area. Acre, to the north, was a much more important Crusader stronghold, and after it was taken by the Moslems in 1291, Caesarea was also destroyed.

William of Tyre, the historian of the First Crusade, records that when Baldwin I took the city, the most precious prize was a green crystal bowl, the Holy Grail, believed to be the vessel used at the Last Supper. The Genoese fleet that had taken part in the battle claimed it as their share of the booty and carried it off to Genoa, where it is known as the *Sacro Catino* and it can be seen in the Cathedral of St. Lorenzo. (The search for this legendary Holy Grail figures prominently in the stories of King Arthur and the Knights of the Round Table.)

There has been a great deal of recent archaeological activity at Caesarea. An Italian expedition has unearthed the Roman theater built into the sea cliff to the south. This has now been restored, complete with Pontius Pilate's reserved area, and is used each year for the summer festival. During the dig a stone was found with the name Pontius Pilate cut into it. This is unique, as the name of Pontius Pilate, Roman Procurator at the time of the Crucifixion, was previously known only from the Gospels and the writings of Jo-

THE SHARON PLAIN

sephus. The stone is now in the Israel National Museum in Jerusalem.

An American expedition led by Edwin Link, the industrialist and engineer, has carried out a fascinating underwater exploration of Herod's submerged harbor, the plan and dimensions of which have now been clarified.

The Israeli authorities have dug out the whole of the city's moat, which is intact: it is thirty feet wide and about forty feet high. It was built in the thirteenth century by Louis IX of France, as was the main gate and bridge supported on four pointed arches. Inside the city is a Crusader street, paved with large blocks of marble taken from the original Roman buildings. Where the ground rises in the north are the three apses of a Byzantine cathedral that was never completed. Each period of settlement seems to have used the remains of earlier structures as building material, which accounts for the Roman columns used to fortify the walls or sliced up to serve as millstones and for the marble facing used as flooring in early Arab houses. But the bulk of the original Roman city, which was six times the area of the Crusader citadel, remains buried, though its outlines can partly be seen from the air—for instance, the great hippodrome, today almost covered by banana groves in which pieces of marble columns stick out at all angles among the trees. Along the beach to the north of the port, the sand has recently been pumped away from a segment of a beautiful second-century Roman aqueduct which brought water to the city from the hills to the north. The top of the rest of the aqueduct is visible just above an embankment of sand running northward parallel to the shore. Close by are the remains of fourth- to seventh-century synagogues, in one of

• 243

which was found a large hoard of coins, the latest dated A.D. 351 during the reign of Gallus Caesar. Closer to the sea, a fine circular stone building was uncovered and identified as the original location of Strato's Tower.

Just off the road, near the Crusader moat, are the remains of a fifth-century Byzantine forum, adorned with Roman columns and two huge headless seated statues with draped togas, one made of white marble and the other of red porphyry. At the foot of a broad flight of stairs a Greek inscription can be read in the mosaic floor:

> In the time of the Governor Flavius, the Mayor Flavius Stategius built the wall, the steps and the apse out of public funds, in the tenth indiction, in a good hour.

Caesarea is now being developed as an important tourist center. It has a first-class eighteen-hole golf course, the only one in Israel. The land was part of the holdings originally acquired by Baron Edmond de Rothschild nearly eighty years ago and recently donated for the golf club by the Rothschild family, who also built the spacious clubhouse. The course was opened in January, 1961, by the widow of James de Rothschild of London, the initiator of the scheme, and there are already more than 1,500 overseas members. Sets of golf clubs are available for hire to visitors, but one does not have to be a golfer to enjoy the sight of the brilliant green fairways, Israel's biggest expanse of grass lawn.

The 8,000-acre area belonging to the Caesarea Development Corporation includes a garden township in which most of the villas and apartments will be owned by people who live overseas, but spend part of the year in Israel. Their homes here are looked after by the corporation. There are

THE SHARON PLAIN

tennis courts and fishing facilities in front of the ancient aqueduct.

The kibbutz Sdot Yam to the south of Caesarea also has a fine beach with a fully equipped picnic site and guesthouse.

The attractive hill village of Zichron Ya'akov (Jacob's Memorial), in the Carmel foothills near Caesarea, was established by Baron Edmond de Rothschild in 1882 and named after his father. Like its sister village Rishon-le-Zion south of Tel Aviv, Zichron was developed as a wine-making center. It too has wonderful thick-walled cellars, where the grapes from the terraced vineyards all around are turned into red and white wine. There is also a brandy distillery. However, Zichron, unlike Rishon, has remained a farm village, peopled by the descendants of the original settlers. Israelis come here for quiet holidays or to celebrate the grape harvest at the end of the summer. It was here in this sunny spot that the bodies of "the Baron" and his wife Adelaide were reinterred in 1954, in a rock vault surrounded by a beautiful formal garden, with a sweep of view southward over the Sharon Plain and northward to Haifa Bay.

From Zichron the inland road winds through the hills, past the children's village of Meir Shefeya, to a group of kibbutzim in the Hills of Ephraim. One of them is Dalia, where the National Folk Dancing Festival is held every two years in a specially built amphitheater, attracting spectators from all over the country. Two neighboring settlements, Ein Hashofet (Spring of the Judge) and Ramat Hashofet

(Hill of the Judge), were founded by groups of American pioneers and named after Justice Louis D. Brandeis of the United States Supreme Court, who was an outstanding Zionist leader. During the Mandate this isolated hill district was used as a training area for the Palmach, the special unit of the Haganah.

The solitude that has fled Caesarea still lingers a few miles up the coast at Tantura, close to Kibbutz Nahsholim. There is a cove here, protected by a reef of rocks where the swimming is the best along this coastal stretch. Close by is the mound on which stood the Biblical city of Dor. King David captured it from the Philistines, and King Solomon made it a regional center. In Roman times the town was called Dora. Remains of the Roman period that are still visible include pieces of the marble columns that adorned the harbor and remnants of the theater.

In antiquity Dor was one of the centers for producing the dye known as Tyrian purple (from Tyre, the great Phoenician city, further to the north), or as royal purple, for it was so expensive that its use was confined to emperors and nobles. The color—actually a purplish red—was extracted from a tiny sac found in a mollusc called murex, which abounded along this coast; the smell of the decaying heaps of shellfish must have been unpleasant. It was only with the development of synthetic chemical dyes in the nineteenth century that the Tyrian purple could be matched. (It may be mentioned here that in Roman times the Jews of Palestine were famous for their skill in dyeing cloth, the three primary colors being blue from the indigo plant, yellow from the saffron crocus, and red from a small beetle. Even

THE SHARON PLAIN

in medieval Italy, the great center of sumptuous colors and fabrics, the master dyers were Jews.)

On a square-cut promontory between Dor and Haifa are the stark and imposing ruins of the Castle of Atlit (Athlit), which was one of the largest Crusader strongholds in the country. It was built at the end of the twelfth century by the Knights Templars, whose house in Jerusalem was on the site of Solomon's Temple, hence their name Knights of the Temple of Solomon. This religious-military order started with a small group of Crusader knights detailed to protect pilgrims traveling up to the Holy City from Jaffa; and it spread to Europe, where it grew into a powerful and exceedingly wealthy organization. The two knightly orders in Crusader Palestine, the Templars and the Knights Hospitalers (Order of the Hospital of St. John of Jerusalem) became so independent that their Masters (heads) did not owe allegiance to the King of Jerusalem but directly to the Pope. These two orders became responsible for the defense and policing of the whole country, and in the discharge of this function they built a network of powerful castles situated at strategic points—in much the same way as the British, during the Arab rebellion of 1936-39, tried to control the Palestinian countryside from some sixty police strongholds known as "Tegart's Forts." After Jerusalem fell, the German Crusaders set up a third small group, the Teutonic Order, or Teutonic Knights. This order constructed a chain of castles in western Galilee, the most important of which was Starkenberg (Montfort), which is today the best preserved Crusader castle in the country. The three orders came to own much of the land round their castles, and the

• 247

knights became, in effect, feudal lords with fiefs, serfs and private armies, in the pattern of medieval Europe. However worthy the original objectives of the orders may have been, riches and power corrupted them, and their arrogance and quarrels helped to bring about the defeat and collapse of the Latin (Crusader) Kingdom. Its doom was sealed at the Battle of the Horns of Hattin near Tiberias in 1187, when Saladin wiped out most of the knights and went on to capture Jerusalem, as well as the main coastal centers of Acre, Jaffa and Ashkelon. Acre was recaptured two years later by an expedition led jointly by the kings of France and England; and the coastline north and south of it remained in Crusader hands for another century. It was during this period that Atlit was the main base of the Knights Templars and the chief port of entry for Christian pilgrims, whose transit camp was in the walled area dominated by the huge castle. (It is a sardonic footnote to history that in the last years of the British Mandate, Atlit was the reception camp for a different kind of pilgrim, the "illegal" Jewish immigrants arrested by the authorities and kept behind barbed wire while awaiting deportation.)

Even after being battered by centuries of wind and wave and ravaged by an earthquake in 1837, what is left of Atlit castle is still monumental. On the landward side the Templars built a moat right across the neck of the promontory which could be flooded, thus isolating the castle from the coast. They then added an outer wall twenty feet thick and fifty feet high, strengthened by three nine-foot towers. Behind this wall yet another wall was built with two enormous turrets; the wall of one still stands at a height of 110 feet. Inside these defenses the Crusaders built their castle, most of which has crumbled or has been carried away by the

Arabs stone by stone to be used in Acre. The storage chambers near the tower are fairly well preserved, and the large hall with the vaulted roof is a fine example of Crusader architecture. Part of a hexagonal chapel stands near the original landing stage. This was one of three chapels attached to a large round church similar to the mother church of the Templars in Jerusalem. When the English Bishop Pococke visited the site in the eighteenth century, church and chapels, though ruined, were still standing, and in his travel account he wrote of the "fine lofty church of ten sides built in slightly Gothic taste."

Since Atlit is in a military security area, would-be visitors should first learn whether they may visit the ruins.

In the Carmel Hills overlooking the coast at Atlit is the abandoned Arab village of Ein Hod, now converted into a picturesque artists' colony, of which Marcel Janco, one of Israel's leading painters, is the founder. The municipality of Haifa has provided it with electricity and water, and the small stone house-studios have charming patches of flowers and patios and a view of the ocean. In the restaurant-café, gay with murals, the villagers and the visitors relax together. There is a gallery where the artists' pictures and ceramics are exhibited and sold.

From here Mount Carmel closes in on the sea, forming the headland behind which lies the curve of Haifa Bay.

CHAPTER 11

Haifa

In 1898, Dr. Theodor Herzl came sailing across the sparkling water of Haifa Bay, moved to tears at his first sight of the Holy Land. He was thirty-eight years old and already becoming a legend as the messianic prophet of an international Zionist movement.

At that time, coming to the small, still primitive town of Haifa with its few hundred Jews, its colony of German Templars and its Arabs riding on camels and donkeys, his soaring imagination converted it into a great modern metropolis, with the ships of many nations thronging its docks, thousands of white houses up the mountainside, and even a funicular railway mounting to the top of Mount Carmel. On his return to Vienna from Palestine he started work on his novel, *Altneuland* (Old New Land), which was completed in 1902 and described in detail his vision of the future port city in a future Jewish State.

HAIFA

Herzl's city of tomorrow is now a city of today—the second largest in Israel, draped in shining white between the pine forests at the top of the Carmel and the edge of the Mediterranean.

As a harborage, Haifa has no known Biblical past. Other coastal towns with easier land access developed to the south of the Carmel Range (Caesarea, Jaffa, Ashdod and Gaza) and to the north (Acre and the Phoenician ports of Tyre and Sidon). Recent excavations in a *tel* to the south of the city, called Shikmona, indicate that there was Jewish settlement here as far back as the time of the Romans. It was only in the last half-century of Turkish rule, prior to World War I, that the port and town started to grow, stimulated by the German Templar colony established in the 1860's and by the narrow-gauge railway line built by the Turks in 1905, with German help, to link up with the Hejaz railway from Damascus to Mecca.

It was the British who really developed Haifa as a modern seaport, oil-refining center and naval base after their capture of Palestine from the Turks in 1918. But the birth of Israel in 1948 cut Haifa off from the Arab hinterland. The Hejaz railway branch line was severed, and so was the oil pipeline from Iraq. Jordan's trade was diverted through Beirut, the refineries were shut down and the British Navy steamed away for good. There were at that time many who expected Haifa to wither like a sawed-off branch. The opposite has happened. As Israel's only modern deepwater harbor, Haifa had to go on developing rapidly to keep pace with the phenomenal economic growth of the new State. It has once again become an oil terminal and refining center served by a new pipeline from Eilat.

In an average year the port has been handling about

1,200 ocean-going vessels, carrying more than half of the goods entering or leaving Israel and more than 230,000 passengers.

Haifa's most important business is ships, and its most poignant moments in the struggle for independence were connected with ships of a special kind—the small and shabby vessels that tried to bring Jewish refugees to the forbidden shores of the Promised Land. But most of them were boarded from British naval vessels when they reached territorial waters and were towed into Haifa harbor, where their passengers were disembarked and dragged straight onto waiting prison ships with deck areas caged in by wire, in which they were shipped out again to the detention camps in Cyprus—or, in the case of the *Exodus*, all the way back to Germany, a story that made front-page news all over the world.

Haifa never got used to the anguish of these transshipments, or to the crowd of weeping relatives and friends pressing against the military barriers at the port. Then, suddenly, the Mandate was no more, and Haifa was the wide-open door to the Jewish State.

Through it came a great stream of displaced persons and immigrants. For them the excited moment of homecoming was when they packed the deck in the early morning to watch the rosy top of Mount Carmel rise out of the sea and hail the pilot's launch riding out to meet them ("A Jewish pilot," they told each other, "in a Jewish launch!").

As the country's one big seaport and the dominant city in the north, Haifa was a glittering prize in the fighting of 1948. Actually, its possession was dramatically settled in the strange period of the Arab-Jewish subwar, between the

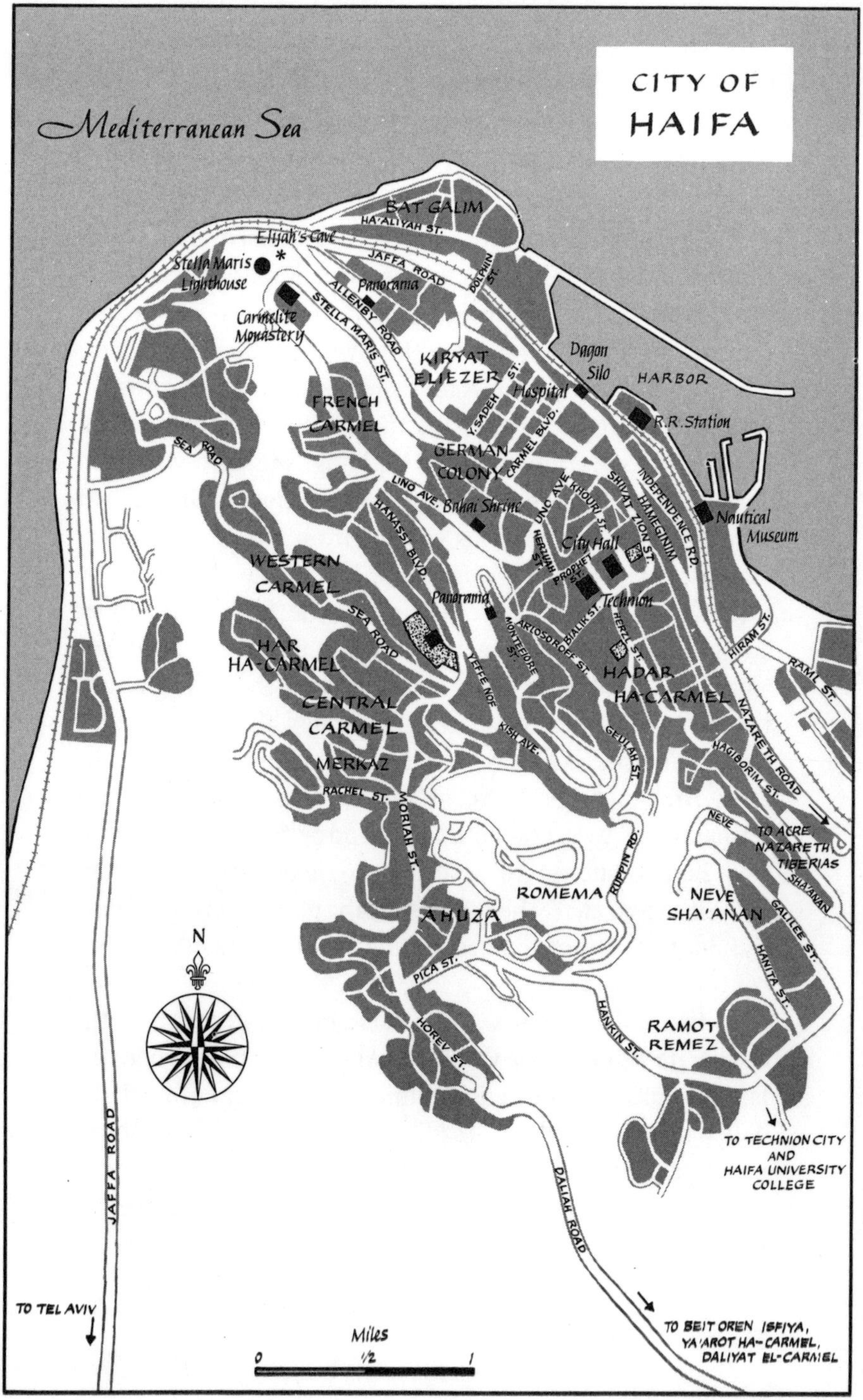
CITY OF HAIFA
Mediterranean Sea
BAT GALIM
HA'ALIYAH ST.
Elijah's Cave
Stella Maris Lighthouse
JAFFA ROAD
DOLPHIN ST.
Panorama
ALLENBY ROAD
STELLA MARIS ST.
Carmelite Monastery
KIRYAT ELIEZER
Dagon Silo
HARBOR
Hospital
R.R. Station
FRENCH CARMEL
Y. SADEH ST.
CARMEL BLVD.
GERMAN COLONY
SEA ROAD
LINO AVE.
Bahai Shrine
UNO AVE.
KHOURI ST.
SHIVAT ZION ST.
HAMEGINIM
INDEPENDENCE RD.
Nautical Museum
HANASSI BLVD.
HERZLIAH ST.
City Hall
PROPHET ST.
WESTERN CARMEL
Panorama
BIALIK ST.
Technion
SEA ROAD
MONTEFIORE ST.
ARLOSOROFF ST.
HERZL ST.
HIRAM ST.
HAR HA-CARMEL
YEFFE NOF
HADAR HA-CARMEL
RAML ST.
CENTRAL CARMEL
NAZARETH ROAD
KISH AVE.
GEULAH ST.
MERKAZ
HAGIBORIM ST.
RACHEL ST.
MORIAH ST.
RUPPIN RD.
NEVE
TO ACRE, NAZARETH, TIBERIAS
SHA'ANAN
ROMEMA
NEVE SHA'ANAN
AHUZA
GALILEE ST.
N
PICA ST.
HANITA ST.
HANKIN ST.
RAMOT REMEZ
HOREV ST.
JAFFA ROAD
TO TECHNION CITY AND HAIFA UNIVERSITY COLLEGE
DALIAH ROAD
TO TEL AVIV
Miles
0
1/2
1
TO BEIT OREN ISFIYA, YA'AROT HA-CARMEL, DALIYAT EL-CARMEL

United Nations' partition decision at the end of November, 1947, and the birth of Israel in the middle of May, 1948.

The turning point came on April 21, when the British commander-in-chief, General Stockwell, announced that his troops, getting ready to embark, had given up further responsibility for Haifa and withdrawn into the harbor area.

Under cover of darkness four small Haganah columns advanced towards key points in the city—the telephone exchange, the government office building, the railway station and the Arab headquarters. Fighting continued all the next morning, with tremendous crashes from the Jewish home-made mortars called "Davidkas" (little Davids), but the tide swung in favor of the Jews when the Arab commander and his aides fled. General Stockwell stepped in to arrange a truce, and the Jewish commander offered the Arab population full safety and equal rights, provided that they handed over their arms and all the foreigners fighting for them. The local Arab notables were at first willing to accept these terms, but after a few hours they sorrowfully declared that they had to submit to orders from their national leaders, who insisted that the whole Arab population of Haifa should leave rather than settle down peacefully in a Jewish-controlled city.

British police reports give a terse official account of the deliberate self-exile of the local Arabs at a time when the fighting was over in Haifa. Similar evacuations from Jaffa, Tiberias and elsewhere steadily swelled a refugee problem which remains unresolved to this day.

On June 30 the final British contingent embarked, the last remaining figure on the quayside being a brigadier-general who stood stiffly at the salute while the bugles rang out and the Union Jack was furled. Thus the final curtain rang down on British rule which had been so gallantly ushered in thirty years earlier when Allenby's army came marching in from the south. The Mandate had ended, to use T. S. Eliot's words, "not with a bang but a whimper."

THE CITY

In its human atmosphere as well as in its natural setting, Haifa is quite different from the ageless serenity of Jerusalem or the brash bustle of Tel Aviv. Haifa men pride themselves on being down-to-earth, civic-minded folk. During the most trying times, Arab and Jewish city councilors, merchants, professional men and workers managed to remain friends with each other and with the local British officials. This tolerant and progressive air has remained unchanged since the establishment of the State; the city is under the brisk rule of a Labor Party mayor, Abba Khoushy, who is apt to check on the street cleaners at dawn, forbids drivers to honk their horns, permits public transport on the Sabbath, and has planted pink oleanders down the center of the main approaches to the town.

THE LOWER TOWN

Haifa is built like a three-decker sandwich. The lower town contains the dock area and the business center; up the slopes is the Hadar ha-Carmel (Beauty of the Carmel); and at the top is Har ha-Carmel (Mount Carmel). The quickest way from "downtown" to the suburbs on top of the

Carmel is by the Carmelit, Haifa's tilted subway, which whirls you up at a preposterous angle in less than ten minutes.

The main business thoroughfare, running in the reclaimed area adjoining the harbor, used to be known as Kingsway, but has been renamed Independence Road. The street crowd is a colorful and amiable mixture of seamen, port officials and dock workers, young men and women in trim naval uniform, businessmen parleying over endless cups of Turkish coffee or glasses of lemon tea, tourists, Arabs and Druses in flowing robes, and khaki-clad kibbutzniks hurrying from the bus station with the inevitable ancient briefcases in their hands.

Two prominent buildings on the seaward side are the Dagon grain silo and the huge Government Hospital, to the south of which are the Bat Galim and Carmel bathing beaches. The silo is one of the tallest buildings in Israel and one of the most beautiful. It is worth visiting, both for the view from the top and for its small exhibition tracing the history of wheat and flour in the Holy Land from Biblical times.

From the railroad station, Carmel Boulevard sweeps up through the old German Colony, with its solidly built gabled houses, many of them still bearing inscriptions above their doors in old Gothic letters. Pross' restaurant, which dates back to the last century, still provides a good and substantial meal. The former residents of this quarter, descendants of the original German Templar settlers, a Protestant group from southern Germany that started to set up its own colonies in the Holy Land from 1868 onwards. They were deported by the British authorities as enemy aliens at the beginning of World War II and have never come back. (A number of them now live in Australia.)

Hadar ha-Carmel

Hadar ha-Carmel has rather steep and congested streets, but it is pleasant to stroll along Herzl Street and to have coffee and wonderful pastries at one of its pavement cafés, which have a Viennese air about them.

The handsome City Hall on Bialik Street houses in one wing a gallery of modern art and an archaeological museum, which should be visited for its Roman and Byzantine exhibition, mainly from Caesarea, and for a noteworthy collection of ancient local coins. From the Memorial Garden in front, one looks down upon the harbor. The two old Turkish cannon standing here are survivals of a fort that once guarded the town.

High up on the mountainside stands the most arresting object in Haifa, the Bahai Shrine, with its gleaming golden dome. The whole slope below it, right down to the German Colony, is a terraced Persian garden through which runs a stairway lined by cypress trees. The garden is being continued upward behind the Shrine so that the whole effect will be that of a Persian carpet spread down the mountainside from top to bottom. To one side of the domed building is another one modeled on the Greek Parthenon, to house their museum and archives.

The Bahai faith, founded in Persia in 1844, upholds the unity of God and takes its inspirations from the Old and New Testaments as well as the Koran. It has no priesthood but attempts to adapt basic religious truths to modern needs. Haifa is the world center of the religion, which now has several million adherents scattered over many countries.

The Panorama road intersects the Bahai Garden above the Shrine and winds up to the top of the Carmel, with a more breathtaking vista opening up at each dizzy curve. Looking down from this vantage point, one gets a clear idea of the planned development of the bayshore area between Haifa and Acre, to the north. It now contains a number of Israel's major industrial plants, surrounded by housing projects, set in green belts, for workers and immigrants. The plain was known as the Valley of Zebulun, after the seafaring tribe of Israel that settled in this part of the country in the period of the Judges. (Their emblem was a galley with a square sail and banks of oars.) The silted mouths of two small rivers, the Kishon and the Na'aman, had turned the area into a malarial swamp, until it was drained and reclaimed by Jewish settlers more than forty years ago.

The most conspicuous plant in this bay industrial area is the oil refinery, with its giant concrete cooling vats, fretwork metal superstructure and shining tanks. Other large enterprises concentrated in the industrial zone produce chemicals and fertilizers, textiles, steel, glass, cement, and soap. There are also automobile assembly plants which use a growing number of components manufactured locally.

MOUNT CARMEL

There can be few more attractive residential districts anywhere than Har ha-Carmel (Mount Carmel), the top of the Carmel Range. It is an area of ridges and woody ravines, sunlit boulders and pine trees, summer breezes and glorious views of the Mediterranean and the Galilee highlands, with the white cap of distant Mount Hermon floating over the eastern horizon on a clear day. The heavy dew keeps this a verdant oasis even in the dry, hot summer, and the very name Carmel (which means Vineyard of the Lord) suggests the blend of fertility and holiness which belongs to the mountain. From earliest times, mystery shrouded the habitation of Carmel. Its high places held the altars of strange gods, and its hidden places, the sanctuaries of fugitives and hermits.

> And though they hide themselves in the top of Carmel,
> I will search and take them out thence; . . .
> —Amos 9:3

Above all, there broods over it the memory of that fierce old man of God, Elijah, and his war against idolatry.

The Bible tells us, in the First Book of Kings, that after a three-year drought which God had sent to punish King Ahab and the Israelites for their pagan cult, the Prophet Elijah gathered together on Mount Carmel 450 priests of Baal and proved by a miracle that their gods did not exist. Elijah built an altar for sacrifice, as did the other priests; but Baal did not come to the altar dedicated to him, whereas God sent a fire which burnt up the sacrifice offered by Elijah. As a result of this miracle the people turned to the true God and all the idolatrous priests were put to death. Then, in answer to Elijah's prayer, came rain in abundance. The place where this miracle was performed is traditionally identified with Muhraka or El Muhraka (Place of Burning), seventeen miles from Haifa by the mountain road to the southeast. The spot where the pagan priests were then put to death is by tradition identified with Tel el-Kuassis (Mount of the Priest), at a bend in the River Kishon.

There are several religious institutions on the Carmel which are associated with Elijah; among them the Carmelite monastery on the French Carmel; another small Carmelite monastery at El Muhraka; and a big cavern at the foot of the promontory, overlooking Haifa, where the prophet took refuge.

The main built-up area of Har ha-Carmel radiates out from the Merkaz (center), with its bus station and its neat shops and cafés. On a bright morning it is pleasant to ramble on foot through the public parks or past the villas and summer boarding houses, framed in flowering shrubs. The Merkaz, and nearby garden suburbs like Ahuza and Neve Sha'anan, have a well-ordered and relaxed feeling, and one is grateful that this beautiful setting of hill and sea has not been ruined by unplanned jerry-building.

A fifteen-minute drive southward along a winding mountain road brings one to Technion City, the campus of the Haifa Institute of Technology of Israel, set in 750 acres of pine forest. It has impressive functional buildings for its lecture halls and laboratories, a beautiful auditorium named for Sir Winston Churchill by its English donors, and students' hostels with split-level bedroom-studies ingeniously adapted to the slope.

The Technion has an enrolment of 5,000 full-time students, of whom 7 percent are women—a high percentage for a technological university. There are two groups of thirty-two students from twelve African and Asian countries taking courses (in English) leading to a Bachelor of Agricultural Engineering degree. The Technion also runs part-time refresher courses in a number of cities. It turns out 600 graduates a year in general science, engineering in various branches—civil, electric, chemical, mechanical, hydraulic and aeronautical—and architecture. On the campus is the Junior Technical College for training building technicians; it awards a technicians' diploma after three and a half years of work. There is also the Technical High School, with more than 1,000 pupils, offering four-year courses in eleven technical fields.

Also on Mount Carmel are the first buildings on the campus of the Haifa University College, opened in 1967 as an affiliate of the Hebrew University in Jerusalem. It has been designed by the world-famous architect Oscar Niemeyer, creator of Brazilia. The college now offers liberal-arts and social-studies courses to more than 2,000 students.

The Carmelite Monastery, on top of the jutting promontory of the Western (or French) Carmel, has behind it nearly eight centuries of history. The order to which it belongs was founded here, and obtained its official charter in 1212. Elijah is its patron saint. The monastery was twice destroyed and the monks put to the sword; first by the Arabs after the fall of Crusader-held Acre, and again by the Turks after Napoleon's unsuccessful siege of Acre. It is not surprising that the present monastery was constructed like a fortress and located at a spot chosen with an eye to defense. Across the road from the monastery is the old lighthouse building, appropriately called Stella Maris (Star of the Sea), which now houses Israel's naval headquarters.

Not far away, dominating the ridge, is the Dan Carmel hotel, with every bedroom window framing the glorious view. All the same, Haifa people regret that the skyline of the mountain has been broken in this way by a building.

From the suburb of Ahuza on Mount Carmel, it is a wonderful drive southeastward through the pine woods on the top of the range to the kibbutz of Beit Oren. From here the road descends through a rugged defile to the coastal highway, passing the forest of Ya'arot ha-Carmel. The many caves which pit the rock-faces along the road have held strange tenants in their time, from Stone Age men to Byzantine hermits.

Just before Beit Oren is reached, a narrow side road turns off to the two big Druse villages of Isfiya and Daliyat el-Carmel. The handsome and dignified Druses from the Carmel move easily around Haifa city and frequent its Oriental coffee shops, the men distinguished by their big cavalry mustaches. Isfiya, which is populated by both Druses and Christian Arabs, stands on the site of the ancient Jewish village of Huseifa. A piece of a mosaic synagogue floor has been dug up here and it depicts a pretty garland of yellow flowers surrounding the Hebrew inscription *Shalom al Yisrael* (Peace be unto Israel); it is now in the Israel Museum in Jerusalem, and is reproduced in the design of the Israel one-pound note. At the end of the main street in Daliyat el-Carmel is the house occupied in the eighties of the last century by Laurence Oliphant, an early English supporter of the Zionist cause. The tomb of Mrs. Oliphant is in the village. Visitors to these clean and picturesque Druse villages can enjoy a friendly cup of Turkish coffee while they buy the gay basketware for which the Druse women are noted.

Nowhere else in the world can there be the same curious human mixture as upon the Carmel: Jewish suburbanites, kibbutzniks, Carmelite monks, Druses, Christian Arabs, Moslems, and Bahais—all living side by side among the lingering echoes of primitive cavemen, pagan altars, hermits and Crusaders.

Haifa has one exquisite moment which every visitor should capture if he can. It is the sight from the top of the Carmel of a huge orange-red sun sinking into the sea while a spangled veil of lights is flung along the ancient coast from the Ladder of Tyre to Caesarea.

CHAPTER 12

The Galilee

WESTERN GALILEE

Acre

Running out along the northern tip of the bay eight miles from Haifa, Acre (Akko) forms a romantic frieze of bubble domes, minarets, crenellated sea walls and palm trees etched against sky and water.

No other place in Israel except Jerusalem has had a more stirring history. Acre was a strategic prize from ancient times as a sheltered harbor astride the coastal route to Phoenicia over the Ladder of Tyre (Rosh ha-Nikra) a day's march to the north. History has recorded seventeen sieges of the city. As a Canaanite town it resisted capture by the Hebrews in the time of Joshua: "Neither did Asher drive out the inhabitants of Accho"—Judges 1:31; and more than a thousand years later, Simon the Maccabee also failed to take it.

THE GALILEE

In the Hellenistic period it was renamed Ptolemais; it is referred to by that name in the account of St. Paul's journey to Jerusalem (Acts 21:7). But the most spectacular chapter in Acre's history was written by the Crusaders.

In 1104, after the First Crusade had secured Jerusalem, Baldwin I carried Acre by a combined land and sea assault with the aid of the Genoese fleet. Its commercial importance revived and it became known as St. Jean d'Acre in honor of the Order of the Hospital of St. John of Jerusalem (the Knights Hospitalers). The city fell to Saladin, the Saracen leader, after he had wiped out the Crusader army at the Horns of Hattin near Tiberias. Richard the Lion-Heart of England retook it, and after the fall of Jerusalem it remained the Crusader capital for a century, when its loss marked the end of the Latin Kingdom in the Holy Land.

In 1799, Napoleon's advance from Egypt round the eastern edge of the Mediterranean was blocked at Acre. After two months of unsuccessful siege he withdrew, abandoned his whole Near Eastern campaign and returned to Europe. His defeat was primarily due to British naval power, for Admiral Nelson destroyed his fleet in the Battle of the Nile and Admiral Sir Sydney Smith captured his siege guns on their way to Acre by sea.

In 1948, in the War of Independence, Acre surrendered to the Israelis after a daring amphibious landing just north of the city.

The Turkish style dominates the architecture of the Old City. At the end of the eighteenth century the Ottoman governor, Ahmed Jezzar Pasha (known as Ahmed the Butcher), tried to restore Acre's commercial importance and to make of it a "little Constantinople." He built the splendid Mosque of El Jezzar, using for the arcades marble

NORTHERN ISRAEL

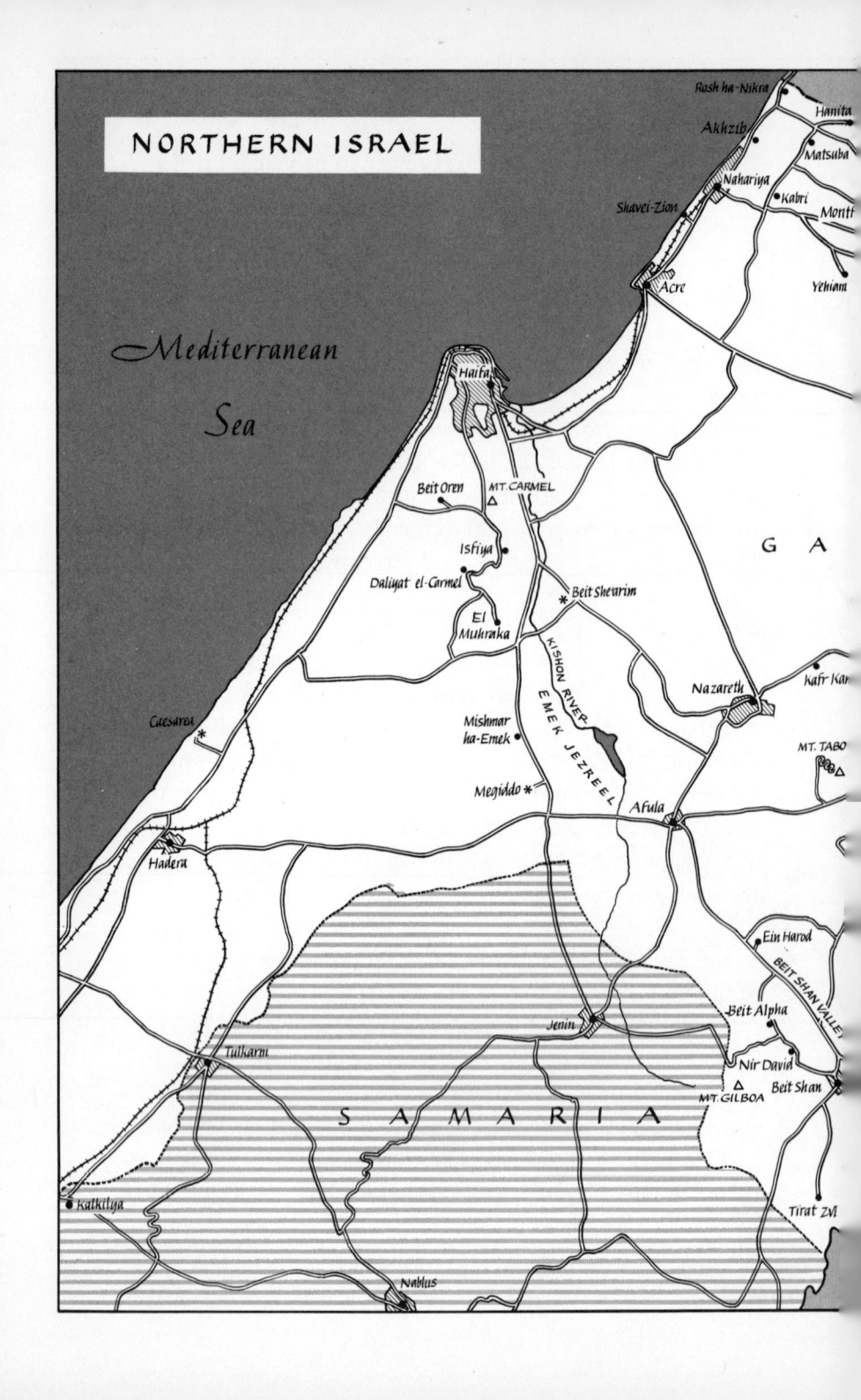

MAP 1.6

columns brought from the Roman ruins of Caesarea farther down the coast. These arcades enclose three sides of a large, sunny courtyard; behind them are small domed cells for the scholarly. The courtyard is paved with worn flagstones, and trees and flowering shrubs spring up in the corners. The sundial gives it charm, and the fountains gaiety. The mosque closes off the fourth side of the square. The Ministry of Religions has painted it and restored the ancient inscriptions. The visitor who slips off his shoes and enters will find the proportions good, but the effect one of emptiness.

At the bottom of the stairs leading to the square is Ahmed Jezzar's fountain, and next door are luxurious eighteenth-century steam baths modeled on those in Cairo but used today as a municipal museum. Here the Turkish tiling forms an attractive background for the collection of medieval ceramics and archaeological fragments through which the tumultuous history of the city can be traced, and also for a series of tableaux showing Arab and Druse village life and costumes.

Most of the buildings in the Old City of Acre are squeezed together and threaded by narrow alleys in which a rich assortment of communities amicably rub shoulders. The population includes nearly 5,000 Christian and Moslem Arabs and 20,000 Jewish immigrants from a score of different countries. New immigrant quarters have spread to the east, across the highway.

The chief meeting place is the winding bazaar which crosses the Old City. Here Arab pottery jars jostle plastic cups and saucers, while in the metalworkers' street European tinsmiths hammer out zinc buckets next door to Arab coppersmiths making traditional coffee urns. Little donkeys share with trucks the deliveries of fresh fruit and vege-

THE GALILEE

tables, and prices are settled in a dozen different tongues. Travelers to Palestine in the eighteenth and nineteenth centuries talked of the grain trade carried on in Acre, where two to three thousand camels arrived daily in the season from the Hauran in Syria. The grain caravans have disappeared, and the trucks piled high with produce from the fertile Galilee have taken their place.

The most important Crusader monument in Acre is known as the Crypt of St. John. The entrance can be reached from a lane off the bazaar. This magnificent vaulted stone hall under the Turkish Citadel has been excavated and is now believed to have been the refectory of the Hospitalers. A secret tunnel has been found and cleared at the base of one of the big columns that support the Gothic arched roof. It leads right through the city to the water's edge and was almost certainly designed as a secret passageway which in times of emergency offered the knights direct access to their vessels from the central hall.

In the course of the clearance work, other openings were found in the walls of this tunnel. These lead to what appears to be a considerable network of wider tunnels marking the streets of the old Crusader city beneath the present street levels. When all this is cleared, which may take years, it will perhaps prove one of the most exciting Crusader sites in the world. There is also the possibility that beneath the Crusader city is the city of Roman times, for remains of that period have already come to light.

The Citadel, whose stone walls rise sheer above the lane leading to the so-called Crypt of St. John, was built by the Turks in the eighteenth century and rests on Crusader foundations. During the Mandate the Citadel was used as the central prison of Palestine. In its dungeons were locked captured members of the Jewish underground resistance movement; and tablets in the execution chamber, which now serves as a small museum, record the names of those who were hanged. The novel and film *Exodus* recall the 1947 jailbreak of resistance fighters from the Acre prison. Here too are the cells where the Bahai apostles were imprisoned by the Turks more than half a century ago. The Citadel today, looking less grim after being repainted a soft pink color, serves as a government psychiatric hospital. As new institutions are built the patients will be moved out, and there are plans afoot to clear the moat and restore the Crusader citadel.

On top of the walls is a restaurant and night club called Chumot Acco (Walls of Acre). It can be approached through a secret tunnel.

The road down to the old port passes a number of Jezzar's cannon, mounted on the sea wall, and some captured French pieces that Sir Sydney Smith presented to him after the defeat of Napoleon. The road ends at the port, now sanded up and shallow with small fishing boats riding at anchor in the lee of a crumbling medieval tower.

Between Acre and the Lebanese border stretch twelve miles of fertile coastal plain.

An avenue of eucalyptus trees just beyond the city limits of Acre marks the entrance to the Government Experimental Station, where a former Turkish *khan* (caravan inn) with a spacious cobbled courtyard now houses Israel's most important stud farm for horses and mules.

A mile to the north is the house and tomb of the prophet and founder of the Bahai sect, Baha-Ullah (Glory of God), set in a beautiful flower garden. This is where he lived when

THE GALILEE

he was released in 1892 after twenty-four years of imprisonment in the Acre jail. The house is preserved exactly as it was and its furnishings are an odd blend of Victorian and Persian.

The dramatic stone aqueduct that runs parallel to the main road was built by Jezzar atop the remains of an ancient Roman one to bring fresh water to Acre from the Springs of Kabri. Each of the aqueduct's hundreds of arches is a separate picture frame enclosing a vista of farms and hills, orange groves and cypress trees, surmounted by a curved slice of blue sky.

On a small plateau next to the aqueduct stands a square museum exhibiting scenes of the Nazi period. It was established by the nearby kibbutz Lohamei ha-Ghettaot, which is composed of ghetto fighters.

Nahariya (River) gets its name from a small stream that runs down the center of the main street of this town. With its fine beach, its gardens and its clean, pleasant pensions (boarding houses) and cafés, it has become a popular summer resort. At the beginning, Nahariya remained a stronghold of the German Jews and the German language; there is an apocryphal story that when the Royal Commission of 1936 recommended a partition plan by which their town would fall within the proposed Arab state, the angry inhabitants cabled Dr. Weizmann that, come what may, "Nahariya bleibt immer Deutsch" (Nahariya remains forever German).

The faintly scandalous archaeological pride of this very respectable town is the remains of a Canaanite temple that was discovered while the foundation of a house was being dug near the beach. A little figure of 1500 B.C. was found at the site; it seems to be that of Astarte, the Goddess of Fertility of the Canaanites. It may be pure coincidence that Nahariya is a well-known honeymoon resort.

Farther up the coast, the Club Méditerranée of France has a summer camp on a sandy cove. The living quarters are little huts of woven matting. The young men spend their time skin diving, while the girls in bikinis concentrate on their tans.

Where the highway crosses the frontier, high up the cliff, there are Israel and Lebanese police posts just round a bend from each other. Hundreds of feet below, the restless water worries at the stark black rock, hollowing out the caves which give this cape its name of Rosh ha-Nikra (Headland of the Grotto). Its ancient name was the Ladder of Tyre, after the great Phoenician seaport a little farther up the coast. Above the sheer cliff the armies of the ancient Pharaohs, the Assyrians, Alexander the Great and many others threaded their way. The rusting ends of the severed railway line above the rocks are a mute symbol of the suspended relations between Israel and Lebanon.

A little bright red or yellow cable car now takes visitors down the hundred or so yards of sheer cliff to the grottos below. Rather like Capri, the wind and waves have hollowed out the rock and created picturesque caves into which the sea rushes with a tremendous noise. Narrow tunnels, walks, steps and platforms have been cut into the rock, and electric light makes it possible to watch the sea thundering in and out down below. The walk with a guide through the grottos takes about fifteen minutes and costs about 75 cents. A cafeteria has been built at the top, hanging over the sea.

On the border ridge running inland from Rosh ha-Nikra there is a triangle of kibbutzim—Hanita, Matsuba and

THE GALILEE

Eilon—established in 1938 during the Arab rebellion, in circumstances of great danger and isolation. In the last years of the Mandate these settlements played a risky role in the smuggling into Palestine of Jewish children from Syria and Lebanon, who came across the mountain trails on foot.

From Eilon a huge ruined castle can be reached by hiking across two miles of intervening hills and valleys. This is Montfort (Starkenberg), once the main base of the order of Teutonic Knights. It can also be reached by car through the kibbutz of Kabri, near the old Roman wellhouses that fed water into the aqueduct of Acre. The road winds along the side of a stream up one of the most beautiful glens in the country, with thickly wooded sides. Suddenly, the jagged outline of the castle ruins perched on the top of a commanding hill are seen etched against the sky like something out of a medieval fairy tale. The broken walls contain blocks of stone so massive that one wonders how they were dragged to the top.

The great northern wall, curving with the contours of the hill, seems indestructible, and the view from the towers of the inner wall, rising ninety feet above the summit, is breathtaking. The lack of a good access road has helped to preserve the character of this remote and lovely spot.

Some miles away, at the kibbutz of Yehiam, is another Crusader ruin, the Castle of Judin. It too passed into the hands of the Teutonic Knights and was destroyed by the Sultan Baibars in 1265.

THE GALILEE HIGHLANDS

The Galilee hills would easily head a national poll as Israel's most beautiful landscape, especially in the spring. At that season their slopes and valleys are brilliant with scarlet, yellow and mauve wild flowers, their thickets are noisy with bird song, the groves of ancient olive trees turn a soft gray haze in the distance, and the Arab villages and Jewish settlements seem to stretch themselves in the flood of warm sunshine after the winter rains.

Among the rural Arabs of the Galilee hills the slow rhythms of Biblical life still seem to remain undisturbed. The appearance is misleading, because the Arab villages have been caught up in Israel's progress and their conditions are changing rapidly. Yet, to the outward eye, this could still be the Galilee of Jesus' time as one drives along the winding mountain roads and sees primitive ploughs being drawn by bullocks, villagers busy on the hill terraces with their fruit trees and tobacco patches, the chaff being winnowed from the wheat, comely women walking from the wells with water jars on their heads, camels swaying along the roads beneath huge burdens of hay or firewood, resigned-looking little donkeys staggering under the rumps of their masters, ubiquitous black goats, and a roadside café full of cheerful hubbub and as exclusively male as an old London club.

In the War of Independence the struggle for mastery of the Galilee hills and for their inclusion in the State of Israel was settled only at a late stage, in October, 1948. When Israel was proclaimed on May 14, 1948, Nazareth, as the main Arab center in the Galilee, was the headquarters of an

THE GALILEE

"Arab Liberation Army" of several thousand irregulars recruited in the surrounding Arab states and supplemented by Palestinian Arab irregulars. It was led by a celebrated guerrilla commander, Fawzi el Kaukji. In April, before the end of the Mandate, he tried to break into the coastal plain through the Wadi Ara defile, but was blocked by the settlement of Mishmar ha-Emek, close to Megiddo. In July, in the ten days of fighting between the truces, Nazareth was taken by a Jewish column advancing through the hills from Haifa. When the war was resumed in October, a renewed Israel offensive swept Kaukji's forces in three days out of the whole of the Galilee, which was thereby saved for the new State.

The best way to see the Galilee is to drive from Acre to Safad along the highway dividing the rugged terrain of Upper Galilee. The road runs through a sea of olive trees, for which this district was famous even in Biblical times, when it was the territory of the Tribe of Asher. (When Moses blessed the Children of Israel before his death, he said of Asher, "Let him dip his foot in oil"—Deuteronomy 33:24.)

A detour road round the mountain reaches the lovely little village of Peki'in, occupied by Christian Arabs, Druses and a few Jewish families. It is claimed that a Jewish community has lived here uninterruptedly from ancient times. The small synagogue has been restored.

From the crossroads at Sasa, an American kibbutz, the highway going northeast to the Lebanese frontier leads, within a few miles, to Kfar Baram, where there are the remains of a fine second-century synagogue, a drawing of which appears on the half-pound banknote of Israel. Legend has it that Queen Esther was buried at Kfar Baram, and

Jews used to gather here to read the Scroll of Esther during the Festival of Purim.

From Sasa a new road climbs up the thickly wooded slope to the top of Mount Meiron (Jarmukh in Arabic), from which visitors can enjoy a panoramic view over the whole of northern Israel.

Meiron, five miles from Safad, is a sacred place for Orthodox Jews, for here is the tomb of Rabbi Simon ben Yohai, a fierce and devout sage who lived in the second century. He was so outspoken against the Roman conquerors that he and his son Eleazar had to flee around the mountain and live in a cave at Peki'in. Tradition has it that while in the cave he compiled the *Zohar* (Book of Splendor), the fountainhead of the mystical Jewish studies known as the Cabala. Once a year, at Lag B'Omer, a festival thirty-three days after the beginning of Passover, thousands of Orthodox Jews make the pilgrimage to Meiron, where they light bonfires and a myriad of candles and spend the night singing and dancing in praise of Rabbi Simon.

Safad

Safad (Observation Point), with its flat-roofed houses set into the terraced slopes around a hill summit, is the loftiest and most picturesque town in Israel. The air of serene reserve, the narrow cobbled alleys and hidden patios, the bearded Orthodox Jews who can be heard chanting their prayers, recall Safad's heyday in the sixteenth and seventeenth centuries, when it was one of the four Jewish Holy cities of Palestine and the capital of Cabalist mysticism.

At the time of the expulsion of the Jews from Spain in 1492, the Safad community was small and obscure. Emi-

THE GALILEE

nent rabbis and sages from Spain came to settle here and made the town famous. A century later it boasted twenty-one synagogues and eighteen Talmudic colleges.

This was a period when Jews tended to believe that the coming of the Messiah was at hand. The tragedies that had befallen Jewish life—expulsion from Spain, forced conversion in Portugal, crude anti-Semitic persecution in Germany, the introduction of the ghetto in Italy—were seen as the darkness before the dawn. In such an atmosphere, Judaism turned inwards.

> Safad became what has been described as a revivalist camp in perpetual being. The traditional Jewish life was lived with an intensity rarely equalled, coupled with a mystical fervour which was all its own. . . . It was the most vital movement in Judaism which had come forth from Palestine since the days of the Second Temple.
> —Cecil Roth, *History of the Jewish People*

The central figure in this revival was Rabbi Isaac Luria. He was a man of remarkable intellect and personality, and the learned disciples who gathered round him spread his fame and teachings throughout the Jewish world. He is still referred to in Jewish writings simply as Ha-Ari (the Lion). The two oldest and best-known synagogues in Safad today were identified with Rabbi Isaac Luria, and are called Ha-Ari of the Sephardim and Ha-Ari of the Ashkenazim.

The Ari himself wrote nothing for publication, and his influence rests on the notes of his discourses, kept by his disciples. However, one member of Rabbi Luria's Cabalist circle, Joseph Caro, devoted his immense erudition to producing the *Shulchan Aruch* (The Laid Table). It has remained up to the present day the accepted guide to daily living for Orthodox Jewish congregations all over the world.

This work was published in Italy in 1563, but a few years later the Safad Jews set up their own Hebrew printing press —the first introduction of the new art of printing to the Middle East. Of the many new synagogue prayers and hymns composed in Safad during this period, the most famous is the one which starts, "Lecha Dodi, Likrat Kala" ("Go forth my beloved to meet the Bride"). It soon became part of the synagogue service ushering in the Sabbath.

By 1948 Safad was one of the "mixed towns" of Palestine, its population including 10,000 Arabs and 2,200 Jews, the latter occupying a separate quarter on the western side of the hill. From December, 1947 onward, the Jewish quarter was practically cut off and besieged. When the British left Safad in April, 1948, the Arabs, reinforced by 600 Iraqi irregulars, took possession of the two police forts which, together with the fortified crest in the Arab quarter, dominated the town. On the night of May 9, in fierce house-to-house fighting, the Haganah penetrated the Arab positions, and by the following night the hilltop and the police stations were in Jewish hands. The bulk of the Arab population fled when the fighting started, the collapse of their morale hastened by the reverberating thunder in the hills caused by the "Davidka," the homemade Jewish mortar, combined with a sudden unseasonable rainstorm. As happened in Jaffa and elsewhere, the abandoned Arab part of the town in due course filled up with immigrants.

One area on the southwestern slope, just below the main street, was set aside as an artists' colony where many leading Israel painters, sculptors and ceramicists have their summer homes and studios. In this attractive quarter, with its painted walls, gates and steps, its little patios and its profusion of flowers and shrubs, the visitor can wander at will, inspecting the works displayed for sale or simply enjoying the view.

Safad's crisp mountain air, its rustic quiet and simplicity, its lovely scenery and its background of medieval mysticism make it a popular summer resort for Israelis and a refreshing oasis for tourists in the hot season. On Mount Canaan, looking down on Safad from the north, there are several first-class hotels and a sanatorium.

Nazareth

> This is the Prophet Jesus, from Nazareth in Galilee.
> —Matthew 21:11

The first known references to Nazareth are in the Gospels, but they tell us nothing about the town itself. The period of Jesus' boyhood is a blank, to be filled in by the imagination as one wanders through present-day Nazareth. The moment the boy climbed to the southern edge of the hill basin in which Nazareth rests, He could see a map of Old Testament history spread out for thirty miles. Along the valley road below passed the pilgrim bands bound for Jerusalem through the hills of Samaria and the merchant caravans coming up from the fords of Jordan; the Roman legions swinging by or noblemen's litters on their way to the cities of the Decapolis.

The Nazareth of Jesus' time was, therefore, not cut off from the world but was equally close to the epic past and the busy present. However, it could have been no more than a modest hamlet of storekeepers and artisans, with a single spring of water (now Mary's Well) and a small synagogue, its life intimately bound up with the life of the peasants who brought their produce to market, purchased their simple needs, and exchanged leisurely gossip in the inn about the crops and the exactions of the tax gatherers. (It may be noted that although it is suggested in the Gospels [Mark 6:3] that Jesus also became a carpenter, the imagery of His teachings and parables is redolent of the life of the soil and without any allusions to the carpenter's craft.)

To recapture the feel of Nazareth at that time, one must shut one's eyes to the twenty-three fine churches and the many monasteries and convents that now adorn the town, to the new residential quarters and asphalt roads and to the bustle of automobiles and tourists. Instead, one should linger in the old Arab market, with its open stalls along a narrow cobbled street bisected by a trough. The little donkeys plod down it, their panniers crammed with fruit and vegetables over which the ritual haggling over prices takes place; and the carpenters, smiths, tailors and potters deftly wield their primitive tools in cavern-like workshops, much as Joseph must have done.

The most important Christian shrines today are:

The new Basilica of the Annunciation, the largest church in the Middle East. In the surrounding compound, excavations have revealed the remains of Byzantine and Crusader churches and the foundations of ancient houses.

St. Joseph's Church, built over the site of Joseph's workshop and a rock cave believed to have been the home of Joseph and Mary.

The Greek Orthodox Church of St. Gabriel.

The Greek Catholic Synagogue Church, so called because it is said to be on the site of the synagogue frequented by Jesus (Luke 4,16).

The Church of the Infant Jesus, belonging to the French Salesian Order, is on the hill overlooking the town.

Nazareth had a population of about 30,000 in 1967. Of the Arab residents nearly half are Moslems, with a large mosque in the center of the town. (Owing to the inability of the Christian communities to agree among themselves, the mayor of Nazareth has so far always been a Moslem.) The population has more than trebled since the end of the Mandate, and the Israel authorities have done much to improve the city, including the provision of municipal water and electricity. Several new hotels have been built and new restaurants opened. On the high ridge to the north, just above one of the biggest textile plants in the Middle East, is the new Jewish quarter. It is called Natzrat Elite (Upper Nazareth). It also boasts a fascinating factory which makes tapestries with designs from the leading artists in the country.

Four miles from Nazareth along the hill road to Tiberias is the Arab village of Kafr Kanna, which is sacred to Christians because this may have been the Cana of the New Testament, where Jesus performed His first miracle, turning water into wine at a marriage feast. The Greek Orthodox Church, with a pretty red dome, contains two stone basins claimed to have been among the six water pots of the miracle. The village itself, with its arbors of grapevine and clusters of pomegranate trees, has kept its rustic charm intact since the country wedding which Jesus' friendly miracle helped to enliven twenty centuries ago.

THE EMEK

The Emek Jezreel (Greek: Esdraelon), dividing the Galilee hills and those of Samaria, is Israel's largest and most fertile valley and in Israel is known simply as "the Emek."

Today it is a level checkerboard of green, golden and chocolate-brown fields, dotted with thriving white settlements that glint in the rays of the sun or form a chain of lights in the dark. But that is not how it looked half a century ago, when the Emek was called by the Arabs "the gateway to Hell." Its waters had dammed up into pestilential marshes, and the scattering of Arab peasants in the valley were stricken with malaria. In 1921, at the beginning of the British Mandate, the Jewish National Fund bought this tract, and Israel's first big reclamation project was launched. It coincided with the Third Aliyah, a new influx of *chalutzim* (pioneers) from Poland. (Russia was already cut off by the Bolshevik Revolution.) Of the groups of men and women who plunged into the marshes to cut drainage ditches, two-thirds burned and shivered with malaria and some died—but within a few years the swamps were gone, the mosquitoes had been stamped out and one settlement succeeded another in the now smiling valley.

The Yishuv (Palestine Jewish community) of the nineteen twenties was still a small and intimate community compared to the Israel of today. Each new settlement in the Emek was an event, and the press and public followed its progress with a strong sense of family pride. Everyone knew about Ein Harod, Merhavia, Nahalal and Ginegar. The tots in the city kindergartens sang songs about them, the teenagers visited them on *tiyulim* (excursions) and the long-suffering tourist was dragged through their cowsheds and chicken runs. Between the two World Wars, the Emek was what the Negev is to the Israel of today—the symbol of pioneering. Moreover, it became a proving ground for the different types of cooperative agri-

THE GALILEE

cultural villages—the *kibbutz*, the *moshav*, and the more recent *meshek shitufi*, a cross between the two.

Looking down today on this broad and placid farm belt, it is hard to imagine that it has been the classic battleground in the history of the country. The reason lies in geography. The Emek separates the northern and the central highlands and gives an easy passage across the country from the coastal region to the Jordan Valley and the lands beyond. It was, therefore, a vital segment of the Via Maris, the great ancient highway between the Nile and Euphrates river basins. Tilting down at its eastern end to the fords of the Jordan, it also was a point of entry for the hungry nomad tribes surging out of the desert.

Physically, the Emek is like a stage set for battle scenes, with openings carefully arranged for the soldiers to make their entrances and their exits. At the western end is the defile through which the little Kishon River breaks through hills to enter the sea in Haifa Bay. Halfway down the southern side, Megiddo guards the Wadi Ara pass from the coast. At the southeastern corner, Mount Gilboa curves out like a scimitar. At the northeastern corner stands the high hump of Mount Tabor, with the immemorial road to Damascus skirting round it to climb out of the valley.

After Joshua's conquest, the Emek was in the area allotted to the Tribe of Issachar. In the blessing of Jacob to his sons, there is a nomad's rather sarcastic view of the relatively soft life of the plainsman:

> Issachar is a large-limbed ass,
> Stretching himself between the sheepfolds:
> For he saw a resting place that it was good,
> And the land that it was pleasant.

> So he bowed his shoulder to bear
> And became a servant under task-work.
> —Genesis 49:14–15

As the last two lines foretell, the price for this "pleasant land" was a loss of the martial spirit and subjection by the Canaanites—in this case by Jabin, King of Canaan, whose capital city was Hazor. This domination of the Emek affected not only Issachar; it also cut off the Israelite tribes in the Galilee hills to the north from their brethren to the south. This was a danger to the whole people, and Deborah the Prophetess rallied several tribes to form an army under the single command of Barak. They mustered on the slopes of Mount Tabor, and when the Canaanites advanced along the floor of the valley with their 900 chariots, the Israelite highlanders charged upon them downhill. The chariots would normally have been the enemy's decisive weapon—like tanks against infantry—but they stuck in the treacherous ground, turned into a bog by the flooding of the Kishon. The Canaanites were routed and their general Sisera was afterwards rather unpleasantly killed by Jael, the Kenite woman who drove a tent peg through his head while he slept exhausted. Deborah cried in her song of triumph:

> They fought from heaven; the stars in their courses fought against Sisera.
> The river of Kishon swept them away, that ancient river, the river of Kishon. O my soul, thou hast trodden down strength.
> —Judges 5:20, 21

In the next Biblical battle in the Emek, a generation later, the Israelite forces were led by Gideon against the Midianites, a Bedouin people out of the desert who had been harassing them for seven years. This battle took place at

THE GALILEE

Ein Harod (Spring of Harod) near the foot of Mount Gilboa, the Midianites having come across the Jordan River and up the Beit Shan Valley. Gideon had been provided with an army of 10,000 men, but like his Haganah descendants 3,000 years later, he believed less in weight of numbers than in the use of psychological warfare and surprise attack by picked men under cover of darkness. When the thirsty Israelites rushed to drink at the spring, only 300 did not fling themselves down on their knees and put their faces in the water, but scooped it up with their hands. (This aptitude test presumably showed which of the soldiers were wary and alert in the face of the enemy.) These 300 were then chosen for the attack, divided into three commando groups, and provided with special equipment.

> He put a trumpet in every man's hand, with empty pitchers, and lamps within the pitchers. . . .
> And the three companies blew the trumpets, and brake the pitchers, and held the lamps in their left hands, and the trumpets in their right hands to blow withal: and they cried, The sword of the Lord, and of Gideon.
> . . . and all the host ran, and cried, and fled.
> —Judges 7:16, 20, 21

One hundred and fifty years later, Mount Gilboa was the site of a national disaster for the Israelites, when King Saul was defeated there by the Philistines. His three sons (one of whom was David's close friend, Jonathan) were slain, and the huge, moody Saul took his own life by falling upon his sword. The young David, who succeeded him as king, wrote that deathless lament which is without equal in all literature:

> The beauty of Israel is slain upon thy high places:
> How are the mighty fallen! . . .

> Ye mountains of Gilboa, let there be no dew, neither let there be rain . . .
> For there the shield of the mighty is vilely cast away, the shield of Saul . . .
> Saul and Jonathan were lovely and pleasant in their lives,
> And in their death they were not divided:
> They were swifter than eagles, they were stronger than lions . . .
> Ye daughters of Israel, weep over Saul . . .
> —II Samuel 1:19–24

Another painful Israelite defeat was suffered a few miles to the west of Mount Gilboa, at Megiddo, where Josiah, the young reformer King of Judah, rashly attacked an Egyptian force and was slain: "And his servants carried him in a chariot dead from Megiddo, and brought him to Jerusalem."—II Kings 23:30.

Down the centuries to follow, many warriors of many nations were to pass back and forth upon the stage of Esdraelon, as is vividly summed up by that erudite Scottish divine, George Adam Smith, in his classic *Historical Geography of the Holy Land*, first published in 1894:

> The elephants and engines of Antiochus, the litters of Cleopatra and her ladies, the Romans who come and plant their camps and stamp their mighty names forever on the soil. . . . Pompey, Mark Antony, Vespasian and Titus, pass at the head of their legions, and the men of Galilee sally forth upon them from the same nooks in the hills of Naphtali from which their forefathers broke with Barak upon the chariots of Canaan . . . Three centuries, and then through their old channel the desert swarms sweep back, now united by a common faith . . . then the ensigns of Christendom return. Crusading castles rise . . . once more by Bethshan the

THE GALILEE

Arabs break the line of the Christian defence and Saladin spreads his camp where Israel saw those of the Midian and the Philistine . . . Esdraelon is closed to the arms of the West till in 1799 Napoleon with his monstrous ambition of an Empire on the Euphrates, breaks into it by Megiddo, and in three months again, from the same fatal stage, falls back upon the first great retreat of his career.

It was through Megiddo Pass that General Allenby's Australian cavalry came thundering into the Emek in 1918 to break the back of the Turkish line. (When he was elevated to the peerage, the General took as his title Lord Allenby of Megiddo.) Near Megiddo, too, the settlement of Mishmar ha-Emek blocked the path of the Arab forces heading for the coastal plain in 1948.

Over and over again, through thousands of years, blood has flowed in battle for the possession of this strategic point of Megiddo. It is small wonder that in the New Testament Book of Revelation it is Megiddo that is chosen as the site of the last great battle of the world:

> And he gathered them together into a place called in the Hebrew tongue Armageddon.
> —Revelation 16:16

(Armageddon stands for Har Megiddon, "O the Hill of Megiddo.")

When the Megiddo *tel* was excavated between 1925 and 1939, the results were spectacular. The spade laid bare the ruins of twenty distinct periods lying one upon the other, dating from 4000 B.C. to 400 B.C. The structures now visible belong chiefly to the city of the ninth century B.C., to Solomon's city of the tenth century B.C., and to the early Ca-

• 287

naanite settlements of the third millennium B.C. The roadway approaching the city from the north was built by King David, and to the left are the remains of heavy gates installed by King Solomon. The gate plan is similar to that of his two other "chariot cities"—Hazor and Gezer—with flanking towers and six guardrooms, three on either side. The same architect must have designed the eastern gates of the Temple in Jerusalem, described by the Prophet Ezekiel (40:6–16).

To the west of the mount can be seen a remarkable example of engineering skill dating from the ninth century B.C. At the bottom of a shaft is a 215-foot tunnel bored through the solid rock to springs outside the city wall, thus ensuring a supply of fresh water even during a siege. The most ancient relics found in the *tel* belong to three Canaanite temples which stood at the eastern edge of the city some thirty-five centuries ago, their altars facing the sun as it rose over Mount Tabor and the Jordan Valley. Among the objects found here are the famous carved ivories dating back to the thirteenth and twelfth centuries B.C.

Eleven miles out of Haifa, just off the road to Nazareth that skirts the northern edge of the Emek, lies that strange underground city of the dead, Beit She'arim (House of Gates). It dates from the time after the Romans had destroyed Jerusalem, when the Galilee became the center of Jewish life. The traditional burial ground on the Mount of Olives had been lost, and a new national cemetery was fashioned by tunneling into the limestone of the Beit She'arim hill. It was a quiet place, off the main Roman thoroughfares, and here the bodies of the Galilean rabbis and sages could rest in peace, as could those of the wealthy and pious Jews brought from as far away as the Himyar (Yemen).

The town was destroyed about A.D. 350, and the entrances to the burial chambers were until recently covered over by landslides and vegetation.

The whole mountainside has now been cleared and terraced and grass and trees have been planted. The visitor strolls from sunlit lawns into the still, cool chambers. Each group of catacombs (there are more than twenty) leads off from an open platform sliced out of the hillside, with stone doors which still swing silently on their stone hinges. Inside, the electric light gleams on bas-reliefs of strange lions and eagles on the sides of the sarcophagi. On the walls are inscriptions in Hebrew, Aramaic and Greek; Jewish religious symbols (such as candelabra and rams' horns); and Biblical scenes (for example Noah's Ark and Daniel in the lions' den) in rather primitive style. Some of the sarcophagi weigh four tons.

Mount Tabor (1,843 feet above sea level) is a prominent rounded cone crowned by a group of buildings, visible against the skyline from the plain below. In former days, access to the top was by thousands of steps cut into the steep slope, but there is now a narrow road mounting in a series of sharp hairpin bends.

Mount Tabor was of strategic and religious importance in the Old Testament period. This was the place where Deborah and Barak rallied the northern tribes of Israel for the battle against the Canaanites. In the Jewish revolt of A.D. 66, Josephus held the top of Tabor as a stronghold before he defected to the Romans, and he reconstructed an ancient stone defense wall that can still be seen around the summit.

The chief religious interest of Mount Tabor is that it is believed to be the site of the Transfiguration of Jesus:

> And after six days Jesus taketh Peter, James, and John his brother, and bringeth them up into a high mountain apart.
> And was transfigured before them: and his face did shine as the sun, and his raiment was white as the light.
> And, behold, there appeared unto them Moses and Elias talking with him.
> Then answered Peter, and said unto Jesus, Lord, it is good for us to be here.
>
> —Matthew 17:1–4

On the summit are the Franciscan Basilica of the Transfiguration, with an adjoining pilgrim hostel; and the Greek Church of St. Elias.

From Mount Tabor the view in every direction is superb, especially from the ramparts of the Crusader-Saracen castle on the highest point. As the crow flies, it is five miles across to Nazareth.

It was in the disturbed years of the Arab Revolt (1936–39) that the frontier of Jewish settlement in the Emek was pushed eastward from Ein Harod down the Beit She'an Valley to the Jordan River. This involved the customary problems of the area—draining the swamps, fighting malaria, enduring the stifling summer heat well below sea level and facing the very real hazard of Arab attack. The isolated settlements planted here had to be ready to fight for their survival, and the first of them, Nir David, was set up during a single night with a prefabricated stockade and watchtower—a technique adopted after that for all new settlements in dangerous border areas.

The most exposed section of the frontier was the strip between Mount Gilboa and the Jordan, down to Tirat Zvi.

THE GALILEE

At the end of 1967 and in early 1968 these villages were again the target of raids by terrorist groups slipping at night across the river from Jordanian territory.

The heights to the north of the road are dominated by Belvoir, a Crusader fortress. It was built in 1168 for the Knights Hospitalers with huge halls, a chapel, stables, kitchen quarters and two great underground water cisterns, and was protected by thick stone walls and a dry moat. It probably housed about fifty knights and their retinues. Belvoir was the last Crusader stronghold to hold out against Saladin and his Arab forces, and its flag flew for eighteen months after the fall of the nearby town of Beit Shan. It was systematically destroyed 30 years later, in 1227, by order of the Caliph of Damascus, who heard rumors that another wave of Crusaders was planning to come back to the Holy Land. But the great outer walls resisted the demolition, as did the firm foundations. The castle has been partly excavated and restored by the National Parks Authority.

East of the large kibbutz of Ein Harod, a side road turns off towards two settlements right at the foot of Mount Gilboa, Hefzibah and Beit Alpha. At Hefzibah the digging of an irrigation ditch in 1928 brought to light the best-preserved colored mosaic synagogue floor in Israel, dating from the sixth century A.D. It depicts emblems of the Jewish ritual, the signs of the Zodiac and the story of Abraham and his son Isaac.

Just beyond the kibbutz is Breichat Amal or El Sachne (Arabic: Warm Water), a natural rock swimming pool surrounded by green lawns and trees. This refreshing oasis is

• 291

the picnic spot for the surrounding area. There is another bathing pool and picnic place where the spring of Harod comes bubbling out of a mossy cave.

Beit Shan, situated 400 feet below sea level where the terrain slopes down to the Jordan valley, is a small and struggling immigrant town with an antique pedigree. Its earliest records appear in the Egyptian Execration Texts of the nineteenth century B.C., and it figures in several later Egyptian records.

The First Book of Samuel (eleventh century B.C.) recounts that after Saul died on nearby Mount Gilboa, the Philistines fastened the bodies of Saul and his three sons to the wall of Beit Shan, and the men of Mount Gilead came at night to remove them (I Samuel 31:12). In the Hellenistic period Beit Shan became Scythopolis (City of the Scythians), one of the ten Greek cities around the Sea of Galilee known collectively as the Decapolis. A few hundred yards from the present town a steep scramble takes one to the high *tel* of the ancient city, which has been partially excavated.

The most recent dig at Beit Shan has revealed a large Roman theater hollowed out of the side of the hill. Its fifteen lower tiers of white limestone are in good condition, but the upper tiers of black basalt have crumbled into the hillside. The nine exit tunnels through the upper gallery remain intact. The auditorium, which could seat about 1,500, forms a semicircle facing the huge colonnaded stage, beyond which the massive *tel* of the ancient city rises abruptly from the plain. Though much restoration remains to be done to the stage area, this theater, built about A.D. 200, is the best preserved and most impressive Roman structure in Israel.

THE SEA OF GALILEE

> Jehovah hath created seven seas but the Sea of Galilee is His delight.
> —Saying of the old Jewish sages

There is no fairer sight in Israel than the view of the Sea of Galilee from the heights above, preferably towards evening, when the water turns a brilliant sapphire blue and the bleak escarpment of the mountains of Golan behind it glows pink in the dusk. The ancients called it the Sea of Kinneret because it was shaped like a *kinnor* (harp), and this is still its Hebrew name; but in English it is usually known as Lake Tiberias or the Sea of Galilee. It is but a little "sea"—thirteen miles long and six miles wide—but it was famous in antiquity for its beauty, the lush fertility of its shores, the teeming lake fish in its waters and its subtropical winter climate, which it owes to its location 700 feet below sea level. In the first century A.D., Josephus, who had been the Jewish governor of the Galilee, wrote about the "happy contention of the seasons" at this place, where:

> Nature forces those plants that are natural enemies to one another to agree together . . . it supplies men with grapes and figs continually during ten months of the year, and the rest of the fruits as they ripen together through the whole year.

At that time there were nine small towns and villages round the lake, and the Tetrarch Herod Antipas added another, Tiberias. He built it as a royal spa near the hot sulphur springs and named it in honor of his patron, the Emperor Tiberius.

The sentiment of mankind focuses on the lake chiefly as

the lovely setting for the ministry of Jesus nearly two thousand years ago, as set out in the Gospels. When one looks down upon it today and sees the fishermen going out in their little boats or drying their nets on the shore, they might be those same humble folk who became His disciples. It was while Jesus was "walking by the Sea of Galilee" that He

> saw two brethren, Simon called Peter, and Andrew his brother, casting a net into the sea: for they were fishers.
> And he saith unto them, Follow me, and I will make you fishers of men.
> —Matthew 4:18–19

On the northern shore of the Lake is Capernaum, where Jesus came to dwell when He left Nazareth as a grown man:

> And they went into Capernaum; and straightway on the sabbath day he entered into the synagogue, and taught.
> —Mark 1:21

At Capernaum today there is a Franciscan monastery on the shore, in the grounds of which are the white marble ruins of a fine second-century synagogue with broken columns, flooring, walls and benches all in the richly carved Roman style. These remains include the traditional symbols of Judaism cut into the marble, such as the seven-branched candelabrum, the six-pointed Star of David, palm branches and a *shofar*, or ram's horn. The large rectangular prayer hall was divided by columns. The synagogue was a two-story building, with the Ark of the Law facing Jerusalem. The wall and colonnade of the lower story have been restored.

THE GALILEE

Slightly south of Capernaum, also along the shore, is Tabgha, where the story of the miracle of the loaves and the fishes is charmingly told in the well-preserved fourth-century mosaic floor of the Byzantine Church of the Multiplication of the Loaves. The original church is gone, but a new one has been built over the mosaic, which shows a basket of bread set between two fish. To the left of the altar a rather more sophisticated mosaic of the next century has examples of birds and plants that are still indigenous to this lake area.

Above Tabgha, on the Mount of Beatitudes, site of the Sermon on the Mount, there is a round Italian-style church, monastery and convent belonging to the Franciscans.

Two miles north of the lake and half a mile east of the Rosh Pina–Tiberias highway is the site of Korazim (Chorazin), a small town of Jesus' time noted for His many visits and the excellence of its wheat. He prayed there but to no avail, as we know from Matthew 11:21: "Woe unto thee, Chorazin!"

Recent archaeological excavations show that this was a site of settlement from early times. The most interesting ruins are of a third-century synagogue built of the local black basalt stone. Beyond, on the high ground overlooking the delta where the Jordan flows into the lake, the rock is being stripped away and the boulders, some of them weighing more than a ton, are being bulldozed aside to create arable fields for three new kibbutzim. This development, in an area which has been desolate for centuries, is one of the boldest projects of hill reclamation in the country. At the turn-off, on the right side of the Korazim road, a group of stables, a restaurant and some attractive small bungalows have been built. This is Vered Hagalil (Rose of Galilee), an enterprise of an American from Chicago who rents out horses for a day's trip through the Galilee hills and round the lake. The rose gardens supply the local markets at a time when these flowers are scarce on the plains.

Round the curve of the lake, near Tabgha, is the gorge of Wadi Amud, where in 1925 a Paleolithic skull was found in one of the caves. It is known popularly as the "Galilee Man," and was the oldest found locally until 1959, when a much older one was found south of the lake, at Ubeidiye. In 1961, a Japanese expedition from Tokyo University started a season of excavation. Their most important find was a fairly complete skeleton of an adult male with a Neanderthal cranium.

A little to the south, the kibbutz of Ginosar has opened a comfortable air-conditioned guesthouse, with a restaurant looking over the lake and bedrooms with a view of the fertile banana and orange groves that cover the lush valley floor.

Closer to Tiberias is the ruined shore village of Migdale (Magdala), the birthplace of Mary Magdalene, who became a follower of Jesus after the "seven devils" had been driven from her body (Luke 8:2).

Poised dramatically on the edge of a cliff is the ancient site of Arbel. Here, under Judas Maccabaeus, the Jews put up a terrific fight against the Syrians in the middle of the second century B.C. A hundred years later their descendants fought bravely against Herod, making a heroic suicidal stand in caves below the city which was movingly described by Josephus (*Wars of the Jews*, Book I, Chapter 16). The ruins of the city include wells, a large cistern and a third-century synagogue.

THE GALILEE

The strangely shaped ridge southwest of Arbel is called the Horns of Hattin (Hittim). It was at the foot of this hill, shaped like two animal horns, that the Crusaders suffered their decisive defeat at the hands of Saladin in 1187.

There is a road turning right at the foot of the mountains which bypasses Tiberias and goes up to Nazareth. From this road the traveler gets a fine view of the national aqueduct as it comes through the Galilee hills in its open-trench stage until it disappears into the second pumping station, and from there underground to Rosh ha-Ayin. On this road there are prosperous Arab villages, some of which are Christian, with fine new churches dominating the huddles of stone houses, many of which carry television antennae that serve mainly to pick up the programs from the neighboring Arab countries.

Tiberias (Hebrew: Tveriah)

It is ironical that the new pagan town of Tiberias built in the first century A.D. near the hot springs soon became the center of Jewish life. Here, in the first few centuries of the Christian era, the flame of Jewish learning was kept burning brightly. With the Temple gone, the Jewish instinct for survival required that the ancestral faith be reduced to a written, portable code which could hold together a people in dispersion. About the year 200, the Mishnah was completed at Tiberias under the erudite direction of Rabbi Yehuda ha-Nasi (Judah the Prince), recognized by the Roman authorities as the Patriarch of the Palestine Jews. The Mishnah is a systematic compilation of the Oral Law covering the whole range of religious festivals, family life, farming regulations, civil and criminal law, dietetic rules and the laws of ritual purity. The scholars continued to discuss and amplify each paragraph, and the Gemarah, as this commentary is called, was in due course codified, together with the Mishnah, to form the Talmud. The Palestinian Talmud was completed at Tiberias about A.D. 400, but was rather overshadowed by the Babylonian Talmud completed a century later in the illustrious academies in Mesopotamia, where the community-in-exile was then enjoying a freedom and prosperity that had disappeared from Palestine under bigoted Byzantine rule. The whole compilation is so gigantic that the rabbis talk of the Talmud as a sea in which a student can swim all his life without reaching the other shore.

In Tiberias there are the tombs of three illustrious sages of that age—Rabbi Johanan ben Zakkai, who founded the great academy at Yavne in the first century A.D.; Rabbi Meir, whose name means Giver of Light and who is also known as Baal ha-Ness (Master of the Miracle); and Rabbi Akiba, who was tortured to death by the Romans in A.D. 135 after the revolt led by his protégé, Bar Kochba, had been crushed. In Tiberias, too, there is buried the intellectual giant of medieval Jewry, Maimonides (the Rambam), who died in Egypt in 1204.

After the Roman Empire officially went Christian in the fourth century, the luster of Jewish life in Tiberias faded. In the sixteenth century, when Tiberias was a ruined and moldering town set in a neglected landscape, it was given fresh life by the influx of scholars expelled from Spain in 1492. There was a striking attempt to create in Tiberias what might have been a pilot plant for the future State of Israel. Don Josef Nasi, scion of a distinguished family of Portuguese Jewish exiles, had become one of the most pow-

THE GALILEE

erful figures at the court of the Turkish Sultan in Constantinople. Having obtained from his royal patron the grant of Tiberias and the surrounding area, he rebuilt the town and its fortifications and tried to develop it as a textile center, planting mulberry trees for feeding silkworms and importing merino wool. But after his death in 1579 the imaginative experiment petered out.

In the twentieth century the Tiberias district revived under the impact of Zionist colonization. Today Tiberias has a population of about 24,000, and is developing as one of Israel's leading winter resorts, being able to provide swimming, sunbathing, boating, fishing, water skiing, hot sulphur baths, scenic beauty, wonderful excursions and unique historical associations. One of the pleasant things to do is to eat grilled lake fish at the outdoor tables near the black basalt forts and seawall constructed nine centuries ago when that intrepid and romantic Crusader figure, Tancred, was master of the town and before the Crusader army was smashed by the Saracens.

Among the interesting archaeological digs on the lake shore are those concerned with the Biblical Hebrew city of Hammath and the Canaanite town of Beit Yerach (House of the Moon).

In the belt of farmland on Israel's portion of the Jordan Valley to the south of Lake Tiberias, the most historic settlement is Degania, the "mother of the kibbutzim," founded in 1909 during Turkish times. There is a graphic description of its early struggles in a recent book, *Pioneers in Israel*, by Shmuel Dayan (father of General Moshe Dayan), who was one of the group which left Degania in 1921 to form the first *moshav*, Nahalal, in the Emek. Degania now has a third generation among its members and wears a settled and stable look, with its big old trees and massive barns. Other large and well-established kibbutzim nearby are Kinneret, Degania Beth, Afikim and Ashdot Ya'akov.

A Syrian tank, destroyed by a settler with a homemade Molotov cocktail, still stands in Degania as a relic of the fighting in 1948, when the Syrian forces were beaten back by these villages.

Down the river from the Degania area is the Rutenberg Dam, a pioneering hydroelectric project. Partially demolished by the Arab Legion in 1948, it has since rusted in idleness. Just above it can be seen the Jordanian canal that siphons off water from the Yarmuk River, the main tributary of the Jordan River.

On the water's edge across the lake from Tiberias is the kibbutz of Ein Gev. It is a green and pleasant place, with fishing boats, groves of bananas and dates, a fish restaurant and a big modern auditorium constructed for the annual music festival. Ein Gev can be reached by excursion boat or by road round the southern end of the lake. One way to get to it is to take part in the annual swimming race across the five miles of water from Tiberias, but this is not on the recommended list for tourists.

THE HULEH VALLEY

There is an old Jewish legend that when the Lord gave Israel the Law on Mount Sinai, the other mountains complained bitterly at being overlooked for this honor. Among them was a modest hill named Hermon, which appeared before the Lord and burst into tears. To console Hermon, God made it the tallest mountain in the land, crowned with

THE GALILEE

a cap of snow, and the envy of all the other mountains; and the tears it had shed became the sources of the Jordan.

Mount Hermon rises up at the northeast corner of Israel and gazes down into the beautiful green Huleh Valley, twenty-five miles long and five miles wide, enclosed by the heights of Naphtali on the west and the mountains of Golan and Bashan on the east. Two small tributaries, the Banias and the Dan, start from the foothills of Hermon and combine with the Hasbani from Lebanon to form the Jordan River, which flows down the Huleh Valley near its eastern edge. Until recently, the river flowed through Lake Huleh, to the north of which was a great expanse of marsh.

In ancient times this area was constantly being buffeted between contending foreign rulers, since it was astride important international routes. The road to Damascus from Egypt (the Via Maris) crossed the Jordan at the B'not Ya'akov Bridge (Daughters of Jacob) south of the marshes. The road from the Phoenician seaports of Tyre and Sidon on the Mediterranean (now the Lebanese coast) went round the top of the valley and connected with the Via Maris near Damascus. When Joshua and the Children of Israel entered the land, the most powerful local Canaanite ruler in the north of the country was the King of Hazor, the city which commanded the bridge:

> And Joshua at that time turned back, and took Hazor, and smote the king thereof with the sword: for Hazor . . . was the head of all those kingdoms
> . . . and he burnt Hazor with fire.
> —Joshua 11:10–11

Later, when the Tribe of Dan was ousted by the Philistines from its earlier location in the coastal plain, the tribe trekked to this northern corner and established itself

• 301

at the head of the Huleh Valley. At the time of Jesus the Huleh was part of the domain of King Herod, and Josephus describes it as "a region of swamps and small lakes." In spite of this excess of water, it was always regarded as a fertile area; in early medieval times it grew rice and produced paper, mats and rope from the papyrus reeds.

Modern Jewish settlement in this eastern part of Upper Galilee started as far back as the eighties of the last century.

Rosh Pina was founded in 1882, followed by the villages of Yesud Hama'ala, Mishmar ha-Yarden and Mahanayim. These early settlers had a hard time, living in tumbledown hovels or ruined Arab houses, suffering from overwork, starvation, malaria and Bedouin marauders. They survived with the assistance of Baron Edmond de Rothschild, who built the village of Metulla on top of the mountain ridge at the northern end of the valley. This group of villages passed under the direct control of PICA, the land company which was founded by the Baron but which failed to make much progress.

A fresh impetus to the Jewish settlement of this area came only towards the end of World War I. Groups of ardent young pioneers obtained grants of land from PICA and set up the kibbutzim of Kfar Giladi and Tel Hai in the northwest corner of the valley and Ayelet ha-Shachar (Hind of the Dawn) on the level ground near Rosh Pina. In 1920, Tel Hai was overrun by an insurgent Arab band after a heroic last-ditch stand. Eight of the Jewish pioneers were killed—six men and two women—among them Joseph Trumpeldor, a remarkable Zionist leader. He had been an officer in the Czarist army and had in 1917 returned to Russia to organize Jewish settlement groups for Palestine, thereby launching the Hechalutz (Pioneer) Movement.

THE GALILEE

The grave of Trumpeldor and the other defenders of Tel Hai, surmounted by a monument of a lion with its head defiantly flung upward, has remained a symbol of Jewish self-defense.

The Huleh was included in the British mandated territory of Palestine. In the dozen years from 1937 onward, the Jewish presence in the valley was rapidly expanded by the establishment of twenty-four more villages, all except five of them kibbutzim. More have been added in the period since statehood, as has the new immigrant town of Kiryat Shmona (or Town of the Eight), strung along the foot of the western slope, with about 12,000 inhabitants. It was named after the eight settlers killed at Tel Hai, just to the north.

This drive to settle and secure the Huleh has been inspired by its vulnerable strategic position and by the all-important water sources it contains. It is the sources of water which explain why the frontier jutted northward in this corner and enclosed a narrow finger of Israel territory. After World War I there was disagreement about where the border should be fixed between Palestine, under British mandate, and Syria and Lebanon, under French mandate. The French insisted on drawing the line further south, and the dispute reached the highest level at the Versailles Peace Conference in 1919, where it was discussed between Lloyd George and Clemenceau. Lloyd George relates in his memoirs that Great Britain would not accept the mandate for a Palestine

> which should merely include the barren rocks of Judea, that might at any moment be rendered a desert through the cutting-off of the waters flowing through the same . . . The waters of Palestine were essential to its exist-

ence. Without those waters, Palestine would be a wilderness . . . On the other hand, those same waters were of no use to anyone holding Syria. They could in effect only be used for the purpose of bargaining or for the purpose of obtaining concessions from Palestine.

The French gave way, and by the Franco-British Treaty of 1923 the international frontier placed the Huleh inside Palestine. The frontier was in places a few hundred meters to the east of the Jordan and ten meters from the water's edge round the northeast shore of Lake Tiberias.

Plans now took shape for the draining of the marshy area, with the triple objective of reclaiming more land, releasing more water for irrigation and stamping out the malaria which infested the valley. The area involved (10,000 acres) included Lake Huleh and the adjacent swamps. But it was not until after the establishment of the State in 1948 that the main project could be developed.

The marsh at that time was a watery expanse covered by a jungle of papyrus reeds (bulrushes similar to those on the Nile in which Pharoah's daughter found the infant Moses) and acres of beautiful white and yellow water lilies. The water buffalo of the Arab villages and wild boar from the mountains of Golan wallowed in its margins. But it was for its water birds that the Huleh swamp was famous—some of them permanent residents, others spring or autumn migrants between northern Europe and tropical Africa. They included many different species of crested grebes, herons, pelicans, cormorants, gulls and wild duck. Happily, one part of Lake Huleh and the swamp has been set aside and preserved as a nature sanctuary, with facilities for visitors. A little north of the lake is Churshat Tal, a favorite picnic

THE GALILEE

place, with pools filled by natural springs and shaded by ancient oak trees.

The first phase of the reclamation was the widening and deepening of the river channel to the south of Lake Huleh. Two large canals were cut through the marshes and Lake Huleh itself, converging to form a V at the point where the river issued from the lake. When a temporary dam at this point was removed, the effect was like pulling out the plug in a basin. Within a short period the accumulated water discharged itself down the river, and most of the lake bottom and marshland emerged as extremely fertile soil.

Connected with the drainage and reclamation of the Huleh is the use in the arid south of water from the Jordan River system. In accordance with the original plan, a canal was constructed to divert water at the B'not Ya'akov Bridge. But the Syrians launched armed attacks to stop the project, leading to Security Council debates.

The following year, President Eisenhower sent a personal envoy, Eric Johnston, to try to negotiate a regional water plan to be partly financed by the United States. During the next two years a proposal was worked out that was acceptable in principle to the riparian states, the two mainly concerned being Israel and Jordan. The plan included within its scope the Jordan and the Yarmuk, a tributary flowing into the Jordan from the east just below Tiberias. Then the Arab League vetoed the Johnston Plan for purely political reasons. Since then Jordan has, with United States assistance, proceeded with the diversion of the Yarmuk, while Israel has carried on with the development of its own national aqueduct, pumping water directly out of Lake Tiberias.

The water is brought by a canal to Beit Netufa, the large natural basin in Lower Galilee behind the Nazareth hills, and from there carried through the central conduit, a great 108-inch pipeline burrowing underneath two hill ranges through five miles of tunnels and then running down the coastal plain. This main pipeline threads together local water supplies and links up with the irrigation network feeding the northern Negev.

When the hostilities started in May, 1948, it was an obvious strategy for the Arab forces to attempt to lop off the Huleh "finger" by attacking it on both sides. Indeed, the valley was not easy to defend. On the east the frontier ran along the lower slope of the escarpment, leaving all the high ground in Syrian hands, and their dug-in positions looked straight down on the border settlements. On the Lebanese (western) side, the frontier is just behind the top of the crest. In 1948 the Syrians pushed into the valley with strong forces, overran Mishmar ha-Yarden, and established a bridgehead across the river. Their advance was halted only by desperate counterattacks. On the western flank Kaukji's Liberation Army tried unsuccessfully to take Manara, on top of the ridge.

In October the Arab forces were chased out of the Galilee and pursued into Lebanon, thus freeing the Huleh from pressure. In the armistice agreement of 1949, fifteen Israel-occupied Lebanese villages were handed back, while the Syrians withdrew again behind the international frontier.

In the Six-Day War in 1967, the Golan Heights, the plateau to the east of the Huleh Valley and Lake Tiberias, was occupied by Israel forces and has remained under Israel military government. The constant harassment of the

THE GALILEE

Huleh villages and the threat to the sources of the Jordan had been rolled back for the first time in Israel's history.

In the Huleh, the most conspicuous reminder of ancient struggles for this fertile valley is the *tel* of the Biblical city of Hazor, next to the kibbutz of Ayelet ha-Shachar, to the west of the B'not Ya'akov Bridge. That this had been a place of strategic importance for many centuries before Joshua's conquest is shown by the references to Hazor in Egyptian and Mesopotamian documents, some dated as far back as the nineteenth century B.C.

After Joshua had defeated Jabin, King of Hazor, this area was allocated to the Tribe of Naphtali. But the tribe could not have occupied it very effectively, because it was against the forces of another Jabin, "King of Canaan, who reigned in Hazor," that Deborah and Barak fought in the Emek of Jezreel. King Solomon rebuilt Hazor and made it, like Megiddo, a fortified garrison city for his chariot troops (I Kings 9:15). In 732 B.C. it was captured and finally destroyed by the Assyrian invaders who wiped out the Northern Kingdom of Israel.

Systematic excavation of the Hazor site was started in 1955 by Professor Yigael Yadin and continued for four seasons. The *tel* itself is a mound some 25 acres in area, with sides 120 feet high. Here was found a series of fortified citadels built one on top of the other, and also the casemate wall and characteristic gate of Solomon's city. Next to the *tel* is a large rectangular plateau 175 acres in area, with the remains of a well-built Canaanite city. This was destroyed by fire in the thirteenth century B.C., as shown by the pottery and other finds. This discovery has settled one of the great controversies of Biblical scholarship, the dating of

Joshua's conquest of Canaan. During another season of excavation in 1968, Professor Yadin uncovered the water system in the upper city. It is similar to the one at Megiddo, but on a larger scale. Work is continuing on the site.

To get a bird's-eye view of the Huleh, visitors should drive up the hill to the Nebi Yusha police post, which commands the western ridge. If time permits, the drive should be continued northward along the ridge past Manara to Misgav Am, which looks straight down into Lebanon—in fact, the frontier runs along the settlement's perimeter fence.

From these heights, or from the Golan Heights on the other side, one sees the living map of the Huleh, with its new towns, white settlements, rich fields and shining carp ponds. Held between its two escarpment walls and dominated at its head by the bulk of Mount Hermon, this is today a thickly settled and thriving corner of Israel.

THE GOLAN HEIGHTS

After the Six-Day War, the most eager tourists in the country were the settlers from the Jewish villages in the Huleh Valley. In buses and trucks and on foot they swarmed up the steep side of the Golan Heights, crawled through the Syrian bunkers and trenches, and stared down at their homes and fields 2,000 feet below. For nineteen years they had lived in the shadow of these enemy positions, not knowing at what moment the sudden gunfire would make them dive behind their tractors or send their women and children dashing for underground shelters. The same front-line existence had been led by the green-bereted border police *green berets*, patrolling in jeeps and by the Israeli

THE GALILEE

fishermen in the northeastern part of Lake Tiberias, for whom it was unsafe to approach the shore.

What the settlers had not known was that the Syrian posts they could see from the valley were just the forward positions of a gigantic "Maginot line" of pillboxes, mine fields, dug-in artillery and tanks, and underground command posts, storerooms and galleries. The line was five miles deep and ran for forty miles from the foot of Mount Hermon to the Yarmuk Valley. Years of labor and millions of dollars had gone into these fortifications, built with the help of Russian advisers and technicians. It seemed beyond belief that the line should have been broken and captured in twenty-four hours, from Friday to Saturday, just at the end of the Six-Day War. The Israeli infantry had come charging straight up from the valley in a desperate frontal assault on the forward posts. Behind them the tanks had climbed up what seemed an impossibly steep ridge, since every road and defile into the mountains was covered by antitank fire. With the Israelis sweeping through the breach and fanning out beyond it, the Syrian army fell back in disorder towards Damascus. The cease-fire line came to rest behind the small garrison town of Kuneitra, nineteen miles east of the old border. The occupied plateau of Golan lay practically empty. Nearly all the sparse population, except the 6,000 Druses, had fled eastward into Syrian-held territory during the fighting.

The Golan Heights took its name from the Biblical town of Golan in Bashan, which belonged to the Tribe of Manasseh (Joshua 21:27). The most picturesque locality of the Heights is in the north, around the foot of Mount Hermon. Only 800 yards from the old Israel-Syrian armistice line, mountain springs gush from the lee of the hill and become the Banias River, one of the tributaries of the Jordan. Since the British were so concerned after World War I to include vital water sources in Palestine, it seems odd that the Banias Springs were left just outside the border. The reason doubtless was that from antiquity the route from the Phoenician coast (now Lebanon) to Damascus skirted around Mount Hermon at this spot. In recent years the Syrians tried to divert the Banias before it entered Israel, as part of the Arab design to block Israel's water supply. A stretch of the canal they had dug can be seen nearby.

The best way to see the Golan Heights is to take one of the bus tours that start in Tel Aviv or Jerusalem. You will cross the Jordan River near the kibbutz of Dan and climb to Banias (or Baniyas). The water now pours out at the foot of the hill, though it once came from a grotto a hundred yards higher. This grotto was dedicated in Greek times to Pan, the goat-footed nature god, and the place was thus called Paneas (a name the Arabs kept, pronouncing the *p* as a *b*).

Herod the Great had a temple erected in front of the grotto in honor of Augustus, and broken columns scattered in the area suggest that it had a portico of Egyptian granite. His son, Herod Philip, made Banias the capital of his tetrarchy and called it Caesarea Philippi to distinguish it from the coastal Caesarea. Jesus came here in the last year of His ministry and uttered to Simon Peter the historic words: "Thou art Peter, and upon this rock I shall build my Church"—Matthew 16:18. The Crusaders took the town in the twelfth century, and high above it you can see the remains of the massive Crusader castle of Banias or Nimrod. A very steep path leads to the castle, which controlled the

THE GALILEE

strategic road below. Its shape was adapted to the terrain—it is long and narrow, with turrets at regular intervals.

From Banias the road climbs along the side of the mountain and from the top a waterfall, caused by the melting snows of the Hermon range, roars down the gorge. The upper slopes of Mount Hermon are normally snow-covered in winter and ski facilities are being developed, including a ski lift. There are four solid-looking Druse villages in this area, the largest of them being Majdel Shams on the slope of Mount Hermon. The Druses, a stalwart and independent people whose men and women both wear snow-white headcloths, are the cultivators of the valley filled with fruit orchards.

The town of Kuneitra (El Quneitra) remains abandoned, except for army personnel and tourists, and a restaurant opened by a kibbutz. From Kuneitra the old pre-1948 main road from Damascus runs southwest till it descends to the Jordan River and crosses at the historic B'not Ya'akov Bridge, where the deserted customs house still stands.

Another road turns southward from Kuneitra and travels along the top of the plateau. This area is less rocky and more arable. Nahal groups have ploughed and sown it, turning a plateau of death into fertile land. The road reaches the top of the escarpment and twists down 2,000 feet in about six miles to the Yarmuk River at El Hamma, a spa with hot sulphur springs where the remains of Roman baths can be seen. A new road takes you back across the Jordan River as it leaves the southern end of the Sea of Galilee.

After the Six-Day War, teams of Israel archaeologists surveyed the areas of Judea, Samaria and Golan, listing and mapping some 2,500 sites from dim prehistory onwards.

• 311

The results were surprising on the Golan Heights, till now a blank on the archaeological map. The most intriguing discovery is a series of concentric circles marked out by large basalt stones, revealed by Air Force photographs south of Kuneitra. This "stonehenge" was apparently a prehistoric cult center.

The survey has confirmed that Golan was an area of Jewish settlement in earlier times, and the sites of at least ten synagogues have been located.

Here again, one glances backwards at thousands of years of human habitation, with the recurrent Hebrew theme woven through it.

CHAPTER 13

Information Please

THE CLIMATE

Israel has a temperate and healthy climate rather like that of the Riviera or Southern California. But there are considerable variations in climate from one part of the country to another and from one season to another. The prevailing wind between October and April is from the west and southwest. It precipitates its moisture when it strikes the hills, so that the winter has short periods of rainy weather, giving the country a soft green look and replenishing its precious water supply. In general the rainfall lessens from north to south. The annual average rainfall in the hilly parts of Upper Galilee is more than 40 inches, Jerusalem receives 25 inches, Tel Aviv 21 inches, Beersheba 8 inches and Eilat 1 inch.

It can get quite cold in winter in hill cities like Jerusalem and Safad, with an occasional fall of snow. The coastal area remains warmer, and even in midwinter has weeks of continuous, pleasant sunshine. Tiberias (situated well below sea level) and Eilat are winter resorts, being warm enough at that time of year for swimming and sunbathing.

Spring comes to Israel in April and the whole country is softly green and carpeted in wild flowers. The stony Judean hills are brilliant with red anemones, exuberant yellow daisies, mauve cyclamen and tiny cream-colored lupins. And then one morning the almond blossom is out and the harsh outlines of the hills are smudged with pink and white clouds. Lambs gambol on the Galilean hills in the north, and the ploughed earth is a rich chocolate color. Down south, dark-brown irises and small red lilies spring out of the dun-colored landscape, and all along the coastal plain the air is intoxicating with the smell of orange blossom. It is in the midst of this joyous freshness of a young year that the great religions born in this country celebrate their beautiful spring festivals—the Jewish Passover and the Christian Easter.

In the long summer, from May to October, the country is completely rainless, with the barometer permanently stuck at "fair." Midsummer (July–August) can be very hot, but even then the nights up in the hills are fresh and cool and there is a sea breeze on the coast. During this period of the year, the grass and wild flowers which marked the brief spring dry up, and much of the landscape becomes brown, except for the irrigated fields which are spreading over the countryside and the tens of millions of trees with which the Israelis are steadily reforesting what had become an utterly denuded landscape in the centuries of Arab and Turkish rule.

More trying than summer heat are the short spells of a

INFORMATION PLEASE

hot, dry, sirocco-like wind out of the desert to the east, known locally by the Arabic word *khamsin*, which literally means "fifty," or the Hebrew *sharav*. These winds can come in the early summer (May–June) and may last for one to three days.

MEASUREMENTS

Time: In Israel, standard time is two hours ahead of Greenwich Mean Time.

Currency: The Israel pound (written IL) is divided into 100 *agorot* (slang: *grush* or *piastres*).

£1 (British) = IL 8.4
$1.00 (U.S.) = IL 3.50

Temperatures are measured on the Centigrade scale. To convert to Fahrenheit, multiply by 9, divide by 5, and add 32 degrees.

Thus 10°C. = 50° F.
20°C. = 68° F.
30°C. = 86° F.

Normal body temperature is 37°C. or 98.6°F.

Measures: Israel uses the metric system.

1 kilometer (km) = .62 (about ⅝ths) of a mile
1 meter (m) = about 39 inches
1 centimeter (cm) = .4 of an inch
1 kilogram (kg) = 2.2 pounds
1 liter = 1.06 quarts
1 dunam = ¼ acre

Electric Current: AC 220 volts, single phase, 50 cycles.

WHERE TO STAY

There are several hundred hotels and pensions in Israel. They are in the cities and resort centers, and they have a wide range of quality and price. Since new ones are constantly being built and existing ones altered, it is best to get an up-to-date list from the Government Tourist Office or from a travel agent. The list will specify whether a particular hotel keeps a kosher table, whether it is large or small, whether it is air-conditioned and whether it has a swimming pool, a tennis court or other recreational facilities.

In addition, there are guesthouses and rest homes in a number of the agricultural villages, and good youth hostels and summer camps for children from Israel and abroad.

WHAT TO WEAR

In town or country, Israelis dress informally. You will not need a dinner jacket or evening dress. A business suit and tie for men and an afternoon dress for women will be adequate for dining out, for concerts or for the theater.

During the day, open-necked shirts and slacks are the regular wear for men, and cotton dresses for the women. The summer tourist needs neither topcoat nor raincoat. A sweater round the shoulders for women and a jacket for men might be needed in hill towns. Israel women seldom wear stockings in summer, and open sandals are the coolest footwear.

Swimsuits are essential; and a light hat or cap should be kept handy for protection against the sun.

In the winter it can get quite cold, and you will feel this

indoors more than at home, since central heating is not general outside good hotels and floors have stone tiling—wall-to-wall carpeting is unknown. You will need a good cloth coat and a pair of heavy shoes that can stand up to rain.

In the spring (March–April) you should still be prepared for occasional rainy days between spells of pleasant sunny weather. Knitted suits are ideal for women, for the jacket can be removed if the day gets hot.

LANGUAGE

How much Hebrew do you need? The answer is, None! Israel's population comes from seventy-odd countries, and is used to visitors who do not know Hebrew. English is taught in all the schools, and the inhabitants are happy to practice on tourists. You can also paddle around the country in Yiddish, French, German, Spanish (the local dialect, brought by the Sephardic Jews from Spain, is Ladino), Russian, Polish and any other European tongue.

All the same, it makes your visit more fun if you can pick up a smattering of tourist Hebrew. This is not easy for Westerners. To start with, Hebrew is not written in Latin characters but in the old Biblical alphabet, which is generally familiar only to those who have learned it in their youth for religious purposes. It is a Semitic language, with hardly any links with European languages deriving from Greek and Latin. It is written from right to left. There are twenty-two letters in the Hebrew alphabet and the vowels, which take the form of dots and dashes under the letters, are seldom used in printed matter except in the Bible, poetry and beginners' textbooks.

But even if you cannot read Hebrew, you can easily pick up a number of conversational phrases, starting with the greeting *shalom* (peace), which is used in the morning, afternoon and evening and for both hello and good-bye. Other "naturals" are *bevakasha* (please) and *todah* (thank you). Every now and then you will find a familiar word cropping up, such as *telephone, auto-bus, cafeh, tay, taxi, manikoor* and *bar*.

SOME ISRAEL DISHES

Most of Israel's better restaurants, both in the hotels and elsewhere, serve Central European food of familiar kinds, but there are quite a few Oriental restaurants, and the visitor with a little culinary curiosity should try some of the dishes. The list below is a brief guide to the unfamiliar.

Tachina: A paste of ground sesame seeds to which oil, garlic and other ingredients are added.
Hummus: Similar to tachina salad, although its basic ingredient is ground chickpeas.
Pitta: This is unleavened bread shaped like a flat pancake. It is often called Arab bread. Both tachina and hummus are eaten not with spoon or fork, but by tearing off pieces of pitta and dipping them into the paste.
Shashlik: Pieces of lamb, broiled on a skewer over charcoal.
Kebabs: Ground meat broiled on a skewer.
Leben or Lebeniya: Forms of sour milk that are eaten with white cheese.
Machshi: Peppers stuffed with rice and ground meat, with tomato sauce.
Felafel: This snack, bought off a stand in the street, is a highly spiced combination of deep-fried balls of ground chickpeas, small peppers and pickled cucumbers, served hot between

halves of pitta. It can be ordered hot (pepper-hot) or mild.
Schwama: Slices of mutton turned on a spit, served in pitta with a hot Oriental sauce.
Sum-sum: Sweetmeats made with sesame seeds.

THE CALENDAR

The dates when the different feast days are celebrated may be perplexing to the visitor, because they relate to different calendars.

There are two Christian calendars—the Gregorian, which is the one in general use in Western countries and is observed in the Holy Land by the Roman Catholic and Protestant churches; and the older Julian calendar, which governs the year for the Eastern churches such as the Greek Orthodox, Armenian and Jacobite. Easter, Christmas and New Year's are thirteen days later on the Julian calendar than on the Gregorian.

The Jewish year is based on the lunar (moon) cycle and catches up with the solar year by adding on an extra month seven times in every nineteen years. For instance, the State of Israel was established on May 15, 1948, which was the fifth day of the month of Iyar by the Jewish calendar. Nineteen years later, in 1967, Israel's Independence Day fell again on the same day.

The Moslem year is divided into twelve lunar months, but in their calendar there is no leap year, extra month or other device to adjust the twelve-month period to the full solar year. The Moslem year is thus about fourteen days shorter than the Christian year, so each of the Moslem Holy Days slides, in time, through all the different seasons.

In short, Christians balance accounts with the solar year

every fourth year; Jews every nineteenth year; and the Moslems not at all.

Christians reckon dates from the birth of Jesus; Moslems from the Hegira (Mohammed's flight from Mecca to Medina, which was on July 1, 622 by Gregorian reckoning); but Jews start counting from the Creation. The Christian year 1968 overlaps the Jewish year 5728 and the Moslem year 1388.

The English-language daily, *The Jerusalem Post*, carries the date according to all three calendars, but this is for the visitor a matter of interest and not of practical necessity, because the ordinary "Western" date is in general use throughout Israel.

All three faiths have a seven-day week. The Hebrew and Arabic languages do not have special names for the days of the week (such as Monday, Tuesday, Wednesday, some of which are derived from names of Teutonic gods and goddesses). For Jews, the working week starts with Sunday, which is called "the first day." For Moslems the week starts on Saturday because their Sabbath is Friday. Tourists should remember that the Jewish Sabbath runs from dusk to dusk; therefore stores and public offices close early on Friday afternoon.

SOME SUGGESTED TOURS

Note: All those mentioned below are regular, organized tours with professional guides. The ones suggested can be varied—for instance the eastern Galilee and the Golan Heights can be reached from Tel Aviv by road, from Jerusalem by road through the West Bank, or by local plane from Tel Aviv or Jerusalem to Mahanaium landing-strip

INFORMATION PLEASE

near Rosh Pina. The suggestions can also be expanded for longer visits. The trips by road are in comfortable tourist buses, air-conditioned in summer, or in rented automobiles with driver-guides. Your travel agent, your hotel, or the nearest Government Tourist Office will supply details of available tours and will help you make reservations. The number of hours allotted below for local trips is approximate.

One-Week Visit

A. Three days based on Jerusalem

First Day: Tour of Old City (three hours, walking).
Trip to Jericho and Qumran (four hours by bus or car).
Second Day: Tour of sites around Old City, including Mount Scopus and Mount of Olives (three hours by bus or car).
Trip to Bethlehem and Hebron (three hours).
Third Day: Tour of West Jerusalem, including Knesset, Israel Museum, Hebrew University (three hours by bus or car).
Tour of Hadassah Medical Center (including Chagall windows); Yad va-Shem Memorial, Mount Herzl (two hours by bus or car).

B. Four days based on Tel Aviv

Fourth Day: Tour of Tel Aviv–Jaffa (two hours by bus or car).
Trip to Weizmann Institute, Rehovot, and visit to kibbutz (three hours).
Fifth and Sixth Days: Tour of Galilee and Golan Heights, returning to Tel Aviv.
Seventh Day: Shopping, meeting people, possible visits to

Tel Aviv University and Ha'aretz Museum complex. A swim in summer.

Alternative for the energetic: A one-day flight by Arkia over the Sinai Desert to Sharm-el-Sheikh, lunching at Eilat on the way back (eight hours).

Ten-Day Visit

A. *Three days based on Jerusalem*
First to Third Days: Same as in one-week visit above.

B. *Seven days based on Tel Aviv*
Fourth Day: Same as in one-week visit above.
Fifth to Seventh Days: Longer tour of Galilee, including Caesarea, Haifa, Nazareth, Safad, Eastern Galilee, Golan Heights, returning to Tel Aviv.
Eighth Day: Same as seventh day in one-week visit above.
Ninth Day: Negev trip, including Beersheba, Arad, Masada, Sdom.
Tenth Day: To be spent in and around Tel Aviv.

SUMMARY OF HISTORICAL EVENTS

Early Biblical Period
   The Patriarchs   B.C. 1800–1600
   Exodus and Joshua's conquests   1300–1200
   The Judges   1200–1020

The Kingdoms
   Saul   1020–1000
   David   1000–961
   Solomon   961–922
   Division into Israel and Judah   922

INFORMATION PLEASE

Fall of Kingdom of Israel 722
Fall of Kingdom of Judah 587

The Second Temple
   Return from Babylonian Captivity 536
   Second Temple 515
   Ezra and Nehemiah 445–424

The Hasmoneans
   Alexander the Great in Palestine 332
   Hellenistic period 320–167
   Maccabean Revolt 167–141
   Hasmonean (Maccabean) rule 141–63 *and* 40–37

The Roman Occupation 63 B.C.–A.D. 324
   Pompey occupies Palestine 63 B.C.
   Herod the Great 37–4
   Birth of Jesus 5(?)
   Crucifixion of Jesus A.D. 28(?)
   Revolt of the Jews 66–70
   Destruction of Jerusalem 70
   Fall of Masada 73
   Revolt of Bar Kochba 132–135
   Mishnah completed c. 200

Byzantine Christian Period 324–638
   Jerusalem Talmud compiled c. 500
   Persion invasion 614–627

The Arab Occupation 638–1099

FROM DAN TO EILAT

Crusader Kingdom 1099–1291
   Conquest by First Crusade 1099
   Saladin's Victory at Hattin 1187
   Fall of Acre 1291

Mameluke Period 1291–1517
   Expulsion of Jews from Spain 1492

Ottoman Turkish Rule 1517–1918
   Napoleon defeated at Acre 1799
   Allenby's army takes Palestine 1918

The Zionist Movement
   Petah Tikvah (first Jewish settlement) 1882
   The Bilu Pioneers 1888
   Founding of World Zionist Organization 1897
   Founding of Tel Aviv 1909
   Degania (first kibbutz) 1909
   Balfour Declaration 1917

The Period of the Mandate 1918–48
   Military government 1918–20
   Mandate granted to Great Britain 1920
   Arab riots 1921
   Trans-Jordan separated 1922
   Arab riots 1929
   Arab Revolt 1936–39
   Peel Commission Report 1937
   Palestine White Paper 1939
   Anglo-American Committee of Inquiry 1946

Partition Resolution at United Nations,
    November 29 — 1947
    Mandate ended, May 14 — 1948

The State of Israel
    Proclamation of Independence, May 14 — 1948
    War of Liberation — 1948–49
    Armistice agreements — 1949
    Israel admitted to United Nations, May 11 — 1949
    Sinai Campaign — 1956
    Six-Day War (June War), June 5–10 — 1967

INDEX

Abdul Hamid Jubilee Clock Tower (Jaffa), 229
Abraham, 4, 82, 105, 139, 140, 180
Absalom, Pillar of (Jerusalem), 119
Abu al-Azam, tomb of, 170
Abu Ghosh, 43, 79, 80
Accadia hotel, 237
Acre (Akko), 12, 43, 264–71
Adullam area, 171–74
Afikim, 300
Agriculture, 63, 64, 70–73
Ahmed Jezzar's fountain (Acre), 268
Ahuza (Mount Carmel), 260, 261
Ahuzat Bayit, 214
Airlines, 67, 211
Alexander River, 239
Alhambra Theater (Jaffa), 223
Aliyah, 13, 14, 18, 32, 36, 40, 62, 71, 79, 282
Allenby, Edmund H. H., General, 12, 16, 84, 160, 170, 181, 216, 230, 287
Allenby Street (Tel Aviv), 225, 226
American Colony Hotel (Jerusalem), 122
Annunciation, Basilica of the (Nazareth), 280
Aqaba, Gulf of, 7, 23, 28, 179, 197, 203
Aquabella, 81
Arabs, 16–17, 22, 23, 43–46, 51, 89, 96
Arad, 48, 183, 186–88
Arbel, 296
Ariadne restaurant (Jaffa), 231
Arid Zone Research Center (Beersheba), 182
Armed services, 57–60
Ashdod Yam, 66, 163–64
Ashdot Ya'akov, 300
Ashkelon, 164–67
Ashkenazim, 30, 31, 33
Assyria and the Assyrians, 8, 173
Atlit, 248–49; Castle of, 247
Augusta Victoria area, 92
Augusta Victoria Hospital (Jerusalem), 115
Avdat (Adbe), 176, 199, 200–1
Ayelet ha-Shachar, 302

Bab-el-Wad, 78, 80
Bahai Shrine (Haifa), 257
Baha-Ullah, house and tomb of, 270

Balfour Declaration, 15
Banias, 310
Banias River, 310
Bar-Ilan University, 234
Bar Kochba, Simon, 10, 194
Bar Kochba Inn, 193
Beatitudes, Mount of, 295
Bedouins, 43, 44, 46–48, 51, 110, 176, 180
Be'er Ora, 197, 202
Beersheba, 21, 175, 176, 180–82, 221, 313
Beit Alpha, 291
Beit Eshel, 178
Beit Guvrin, 172
Beit Haluzot (Natanya), 238
Beit Oren, 261
Beit Shan, 291, 292
Beit She'arim, 288
Beit Shemesh, 172
Beit Yerach, 299
Beitan Aharon, 239
Belvoir fortress, 291
Ben-Gurion, David, 17, 21, 83, 199, 224
Ben-Gurion Garden (Eilat), 205
Ben Yehuda Street (Jerusalem), 85
Bethabara, ford at, 145
Bethany, 117
Bethlehem, 27, 134–39
Bezalel Art Museum (Jerusalem), 128
Billy Rose Sculpture Garden, 128
Bishop Gobat's School (Jerusalem), 113
Blue Fish restaurant (Eilat), 205
B'nai Darom, 162
Bnei Brak, 35, 234
B'not Ya'akov Bridge, 305, 311
Breichat Amal, 291
British Commonwealth Military Cemetery, 115
"Burma Road," 21, 89

Cabala, 276
Caesarea, 240–44
Calendar, the, 319–20
Calvary, Hill of, 95
Cameri, 222–23
Canaan, 3, 4; Mount, 279
Canaanites, 6–7, 284
Canon, the, 162

• 327

INDEX

Capernaum, 294
Carmel, Mount, xvi, 255, 257–63
Carmel Boulevard (Haifa), 256
Carmelite Monastery, 261
Castel, 81
Chagall, Marc, 126, 133
Channukah, 10, 158
Children, 33–35
Christian Street (Jerusalem), 110
Christians and Christianity, 11, 16, 44, 81, 92, 134–39
Christmas, 134–35
Chumot Acco (Acre), 270
Church of All Nations (Jerusalem), 118
Churshat Tal, 304
Circassians, 49–50
Citadel (Acre), 269–70
Citadel (Jerusalem), 110
City Hall (Hadar ha-Carmel), 257
Climate, 313–15
Club Méditerranée of France, 272
Coast, the, 161–67, 237–39
Constantine, Emperor, 11, 83, 99, 138
Cooperative farming, 70–73. *See also* Kibbutzim; Moshavim
Crusades and Crusaders, 12, 80, 81, 99, 105, 106, 111, 165, 170, 240, 249, 265, 269, 297, 310

Dagon, temple of (Gaza), 7
Dagon grain silo (Haifa), 256
Dalia, 245
Daliyat el-Carmel, 262
Damascus Gate (Jerusalem), 108
Dan Carmel hotel, 261
Dancing, 34, 49, 245
David, King, xvi, 7, 8*n*, 80, 83, 95, 112, 136, 192, 228, 246, 288
David's Tomb (Jerusalem), 112
"David's Tower" (Jerusalem), 111
David Street (Jerusalem), 110
Dayan, Moshe, 25, 91, 158
Dead Sea, 66, 184, 186, 187
Dead Sea Works, 184, 187
Deborah the Prophetess, 7, 284
Decapolis, 292
Degania, 21, 70, 299–300
Degania Beth, 300
Deir el Ballah, 169
Der Judenstaat (Herzl), 13, 131
Desert Inn (Beersheba), 182
Dimona, 183
Dizengoff, Meir, 213, 216, 226
Dizengoff Street (Tel Aviv), 224
Dolphin restaurant (Eilat), 205

Dome of the Chain, 106
Dome of the Rock (Jerusalem), 96, 103–6
Dominus Flevit (Jerusalem), 118
Dor, 246
Dormition Monastery (Jerusalem), 113
Dress, 316–17
Druses, 43, 48–49, 51, 262, 311

East European Jews, 30, 31, 34, 36, 93
Economic growth, 63–68
Egypt and the Egyptians, 22, 25, 27, 88, 90, 168, 179
Eilat, 7, 24, 65, 197, 203–7, 313–14
Eilon, 273
Eilot, 197
Ein Bokek, 193
Ein Gedi, 192–93
Ein Gev, 21, 300
Ein Harod, 282, 285
Ein Hashofet, 245
Ein Hussub, 195
Ein Karem (Jerusalem), 133
Ein Yahav, 195
Ein Zohar, 193
El Aksa Mosque (Jerusalem), 96, 105, 106–7
El Arish, 14, 51, 169, 208
El Fatah, 24
El Hamma, 311
El Jezzar, Mosque of (Acre), 265
Elijah the Prophet, xvi, 158, 261
Elisha the Prophet, 142
Emek, the, 281–92
Emek Jezreel, 281
End of the World Club (Eilat), 205
Ephraim, Hills of, 245
Eshkol, Levi, 25, 54
Essenes, 144–45, 191, 194
Et Tur, 115
European Jews, 30, 32. *See also* East European Jews
Evil Counsel, Hill of, 90

Flagellation, Church of the, 104
Foods, 34, 49, 318–19
Foreign Service, 60–61
Fureidis, 43

Galei Zohar sulphur baths, 193
Galilee, 43, 44, 48, 49, 264–312; Sea of, 11, 293
Gaza, 7, 27, 168, 169
Gaza Strip, 23, 25, 50, 168–70
Gedera, 159

328 •

INDEX

Gemarah, 298
George Street (Jerusalem), 85
Gerizim, Mount, 148
German Jews, 30, 88. *See also* Ashkenazim
Gethsemane, Garden of, 118–19
Gezer, 153, 288
Gihon, Spring of (Jerusalem), 119
Gilboa, Mount, 283, 285
Ginegar, 282
Ginosar, 296
Givat Brenner, 161
Givat Hamivtar, 94
Golan Heights, 26, 27, 51, 306, 308–12
Goldmunz Art Museum (Natanya), 238
Government, the, 53–62
Government Experimental Station (near Acre), 270
Government Hospital (Haifa), 256
Government House (Jerusalem), 90, 91
Great Britain, 16, 19, 27, 42, 85, 101, 106, 170, 216–18, 251
Great Mosque (Jaffa), 229
Great Mosque (Ramla), 156
Great Rift Valley, 184
Great Synagogue (Tel Aviv), 226
Greeks, 84, 88
Gush Etzion, 139
Gvulot, 178

Ha'aretz Museum (Tel Aviv), 228
Ha-Ari of the Ashkenazim (Safad), 277
Ha-Ari of the Sephardim (Safad), 277
Habimah, 220, 222
Hadar ha-Carmel, 255, 257–58
Hadassah–Hebrew University Medical Center (Jerusalem), 132–33
Hadassah Hospital (Jerusalem), 90, 114, 115
Hadassim, 237
Hadera, 234, 239–40
Haganah, 14, 18–20
Haifa, 43, 65, 66, 250–63
Haifa Institute of Technology of Israel, 260
Haifa Technion, 45
Haifa University College, 261
Hamaktesh Hagadol and Hakatan, 196
Hanita, 272
Haram-esh-Sharif (Jerusalem), 95–96, 104–7
Har ha-Carmel, 255
Hartuv Highway, 154–58

Havatzelet, 239
Hebrew language, 34
Hebrew University (Jerusalem), 45, 90, 114, 115, 127–28
Hebrew University–Hadassah Medical School (Jerusalem), 132–33
Hebron, 27, 31, 139–41
Hechal Shlomo (Jerusalem), 124
Hefzibah, 291
Helena Rubinstein Art Center, (Tel Aviv), 220
Herbert Samuel Esplanade (Tel Aviv), 219
Hermon, Mount, 300–1, 311
Herod the Great, King, 83, 111, 136, 150, 165, 166, 188, 236, 240, 296, 310
Herodium, 135
Herod's Family Tomb (Jerusalem), 122–23
Herzl, Theodor, 13–14, 131, 158, 214, 250
Herzl, Mount (Jerusalem), 131, 158
Herzliya, 219, 234, 237
Herzliya Pituah, 237
Herzl Street (Hadar ha-Carmel), 257
Hinnom, Valley of, 83, 120
Hisham's Palace (Jericho), 143–44
Histadrut House (Eilat), 205
Historical events, table of 322–25
Holy Sepulcher, Church of (Jerusalem), 95, 99–102
Horns of Hattin, 297
Huleh Valley, 300–8

Immigration, 16, 29–32, 35–52, 236, 252
Industry, 63, 65–67, 223–24
Infant Jesus, Church of the (Nazareth), 280
Ingathering, the, 29–52
Intercontinental Hotel (Jerusalem), 117
International Cultural Center for Youth (Jerusalem), 125
Iraq, 4, 25, 38–39
Irgun Zvai Leumi, 18
Isaac, 4, 105, 140
Isaiah the Prophet, 4, 8
Isfiya, 262
Israel, Gulf of, 23
Israel Museum (Jerusalem), 128–30, 243, 262
Israel National Opera, 224
Isarel Philharmonic Orchestra, 220–21

• 329

INDEX

Jabaliya, 168
Jacob's Well (Nablus), 148
Jaffa, 43, 216–18, 223, 229–32
Jaffa Gate (Jerusalem), 95, 110, 113
Jaffa Road (Jerusalem), 85
Jeannette's restaurant (Jaffa), 231
Jebel Catherina, 209, 210
Jebel Musa, 209
Jehosaphat, Tomb of (Jerusalem), 119
Jenin (Janin), 151
Jericho, 6, 27, 142–45
Jerusalem, xvi, 7–9, 19, 20, 31, 35, 40, 77–133, 140, 189, 313 (*see also* Old City); Crusader invasion of, 111; history of, 78–94; rule of, 16, 84, 85; Six-Day War and, 26, 51; War of Independence and, 21, 88, 221
Jerusalem Boulevard (Jaffa), 229
Jesus of Nazareth, 11, 112, 114, 116–18, 130, 134, 138, 279–81, 289, 294, 295, 310
Jewish National Home, 16, 17
Jewish Temple Mount, 96, 103, 104
Jezreel, Valley of, 6–7
Job, Well of (Jerusalem), 120
John the Baptist, 115, 133, 145
Jordan and the Jordanians, 25, 90, 91
Jordan River, 6, 24, 64, 301, 305
Jordanian Arab Legion, 21, 84, 88, 140
Joseph, 4, 6, 139–41
Josephus, Flavius, 122, 189, 190, 240, 296
Joshua, 4, 81, 142, 180, 264, 301, 307
Judea, 50, 134–51
Judin, Castle of, 273

Kafr Kanna, 49, 281
Kantara (El Qantara), 169
Kassit (Tel Aviv), 224
Kenites, 187
Kerem Yavne, 162
Kfar Baram, 275
Kfar Etzion, 140
Kfar Giladi, 302
Kfar Saba, 236
Kfar Shmaryahu, 219
Kfar Vitkin, 239
Khan, the (Jerusalem), 124
Khan Yunis, 169
Kibbutzim, 14, 70–73, 283
Kidron, Valley of, 119–20
Kinneret, 300
Kiriat Ye'arim (Kirjath-Jearim), Hill of, 80
Kiryat Gat, 170

Kiryat Shmona, 303
Kiryat Zans, 238
Kishon River, 283
Knesset, 53–55, 126
Korazim (Chorazin), 295
Kuneitra (El Quneitra), 26, 309, 311
Kurnub, 183

Lachish (Lakhish), 170–74
Lahav, 186
Language, 317–18
Latin Americans, 42
Latrun, 89, 153–54
Latrun Monastery, 153
League of Nations, 15, 61
Lebanon, 22
Legal system, 33, 46, 55–56
Le Toron des Chevaliers, 153
Little Triangle area, 44
Lod (Lydda), 21, 43, 156–58
Lohamei ha-Ghettaot, 271

Ma'aleh ha Hamisha, 91
Maccabees, 10, 111, 158, 162, 230, 264, 296
Machpelah, cave of, 141
Magen David Square (Tel Aviv), 225
Mahanayim, 302
Mahne Yehuda, 84, 93
Majdel Shams, 311
Maktesh Ramon, 196
Mamphis, 183
Manara, 306
Mandelbaum Gate (Jerusalem), 27, 90
Mann Auditorium (Tel Aviv), 220
Mar Elias (Elijah), monastery of, 135
Mareshah, 172
Maritime Museum (Eilat), 205
Marriage, 33, 46
Mary (mother of Jesus), 80, 107, 113, 138
Mary's Well (Nazareth), 279
Masada, 10, 188–91
Matsuba, 272
Mea Shearim, 35, 84, 93
Megiddo, 283
Meir, Golda, 54, 55
Meir Shefeya, 245
Merhavia, 282
Merion, Mount, 276
Meshed, 39
Meshek shitufi, 283
Mevaseret Yerushalayim, 81
Michmoret, 239
Migdale (Magdala), 296
Mikveh Israel school, 158

330 •

INDEX

Milk Grotto (Bethlehem), 138
Miramar hotel (Michmoret), 239
Misgav Am, 308
Mishmar ha-Emek, 275, 287
Mishmar ha-Yarden, 302, 306
Mishnah, the, 162, 297
Mitla Pass, 208
Moriah, Mount, 95, 104
Moses, 4, 6, 208, 275
Moshavim, 71–72, 283, 299
Moslems, 44, 46, 49, 81, 92, 141, 201
Mossad Ruppin, 239
Mount of Corruption, 120
Mount of Olives, 90, 92, 99, 115–17
Muhraka, 259
Multiplication of the Loaves, Church of the (Tabgha), 295

Nabataeans, 176, 197–200, 203
Nablus, 27, 145–49
Nahalal, 282, 299
Nahariya, 271–72
Nahsholim, 246
Napoleon I, Emperor of the French, 156, 170, 230, 265
Natanya, 238
Nativity, Church of (Bethlehem), 99, 138
Natzrat Elite, 281
Nazareth, 11, 21, 43, 274, 279–81
Nebi Da'ud, Mosque of (Jerusalem), 113
Nebi Samuel, Mosque of, 81
Nebi Yusha police post, 308
Nebuchadnezzar, King, 4, 8, 126, 173
Negev, the, 43, 44, 46, 175–80
Negev University (Beersheba), 182
Neot ha-Kikar, 186
Nes Harim highway, 171
Nesher brewery, 159
Ness Ziona (Nes Tsiyona), 159
Neve ha-Midbar, 194
Nir David, 290
North Africa, 40–41

Oak of Mamre, 140
Old City (Jerusalem), 83, 85, 86, 92, 94–112, 122
Omar Khayam (Jaffa), 231
Opera, 224
Ophel, Mount, 95
Oriental Jews, 29, 32–34, 46
Orthodox Jews, 35, 93
Our Lady of the Covenant, convent of (Jerusalem), 80

Palestine, 11, 13, 15–19
Palestine Conciliation Commission, 22
Palestine Mandate, 15, 16, 20, 61, 88
Panorama road (Haifa), 258
Paran, Brook of, 196
Passover, 6
Paternoster, Church of the (Jerusalem), 116
Peki'in, 275, 276
Persia, 39, 84
Petah Tikvah, 13, 70, 234
Phasael tower (Jerusalem), 111
Philip Murray Cultural Center (Eilat), 205
Philistines, 7, 165, 228
Pilate, Pontius, 11, 114, 148, 242
Police, 60
Population, 31, 63, 213, 223
Pross' restaurant (Haifa), 256
Purim, 226–27

Qumran, 144–45, 191, 194

Rachel, Tomb of (Bethlehem), 136
Rafah, 169
Ramallah, 146
Ramat Gan Sports Stadium (Tel Aviv), 227
Ramat Hashofet, 245
Ramat Rachel, 88, 125–26
Ramla, 21, 43, 154, 156, 157
Ramon, Mount, 196
Ras-en-Nakeb, 206
Raziel Street (Jaffa), 229
Reading Power Station (Tel Aviv), 227
Redeemer, Church of the (Jerusalem), 110
Rehovot area, 159–61
Religion, 35–36, 56, 57
Remembrance, Hill of, 131
Revivim, 178
Rihaniya, 49
Ring Apollonia hotel, 237
Rishon-le-Zion, 13, 70, 159, 245
Robinson's Arch (Jerusalem), 98
Rockefeller Museum, 121, 144, 149
Rome and the Romans, 10–11, 80, 81, 176
Rosh ha-Ayin, 236
Rosh ha-Nikva, 272
Rosh Pina, 302
Rosh Zohar, 187
Rothschild, Baron Edmond de, 13, 15, 159, 236, 244, 245, 302
Rothschild Boulevard (Tel Aviv), 220

• 331

INDEX

Russia, 14, 23
Rutenberg Dam, 300

Safad, 31, 35, 140, 276–79, 313
St. Anne, Church of, 107
St. Catherine, Church of (Bethlehem), 138
St. Catherine, Monastery of (Sinai Desert), 209
St. Constantine's Monastery (Jerusalem), 122
St. Elias, Church of (Mount Tabor), 290
St. Gabriel, Church of (Nazareth), 280
St. Helena, Pool of, 156
St. James, Grotto of (Jerusalem), 119
St. John, Cathedral of (Sebastia), 150
St. John, crypt of (Acre), 269
St. Joseph's Church (Nazareth), 280
St. Mary Magdalene, Church of (Jerusalem), 118
St. Peter, Church of (Gallicantu), 113
St. Stephen's Gate (Jerusalem), 92
Samaria, 50, 134–51
Samuel Bronfman Biblical and Archaeological Museum (Jerusalem), 128
Sanhedrin, Tombs of the (Jerusalem), 123
San Martin Hostel (Rehovot), 160
Sasa, 275
Saul, King, 7, 165, 192, 285, 292
Savyon, 219
Schools, 45, 47, 58, 127–28, 227–28, 234, 260, 261
Scopus, Mount, 90–92, 114–15
Sde Boker, 199–200
Sde Boker Institute of Negev Studies, 199
Sdom, 66, 184–86
Sdot Yam, 245
Sebastia, 149–51
Seilum ruins, 146
Sephardim, 30, 31
Sha'ar Hagai, 78. See also Bab-el-Wad
Sharm-el-Sheikh, 28, 203, 210
Sharon hotel, 237
Sharon Plain, 233–49
Shefelah, 153–74
Shfaram (Shefar'am), 48
Shikmona tel, 251
Shivta (Subeita), 176, 197–99
Shrine of the Book (Jerusalem), 128
Sidna Ali, Mosque of, 237
Siloam, Pool of (Mount Zion), 95, 114
Silwan, 119

Sinai, Mount, 6, 208
Sinai campaign, 168, 203, 208
Sinai Desert, 25, 27, 51, 65, 207–11
Sisters of Sion, Convent of the, 104
Six-Day War, 50–52, 90–92, 203, 306; Egypt and, 90, 179; in Gaza Strip, 168, 207, 208; in Golan Heights, 309
Solomon, King, 7, 83, 95, 120, 187, 202, 204, 246, 288, 307
Solomon, Pillars of, 202
Solomon, Pools of, 139
Songs, 34, 38
Spanish Jews, 30, 31
Spring, Castle of the, 80
Springs, sulphur, 193
Starkenberg (Montfort), 247, 273
Stations of the Cross, 102–3
Stella Maris, 261
Strato's Tower (Caesarea), 244
Suez, Gulf of, 65
Suez Canal, 23, 25
Suleiman the Magnificent, Sultan, 83, 94, 108, 111, 154, 156
Synagogue Church (Nazareth), 280
Syria, 22, 24, 25

Tabgha, 295
Tabor, Mount, 283, 289
Talmud, 296
Tantura, 246
Technion City, 260
Tel Aviv, 14, 212–28, 313
Tel Aviv Country Club, 228
Tel Aviv University, 227–28
Tel Aviv Zoo, 228
Tel el-Kuassis, 259
Tel Hai, 302, 303
Tel Kassile archaeological dig, 228
Temple Mount, 96, 103, 104
Temptation, Monastery of, 144
Theater, 222–23
Tiberias, 31, 140, 293, 297–300, 314; Lake, 293, 306
Timna, 197, 202
Tiran, Straits of, 24, 210
Tombs of the Kings (Jerusalem), 121–22
Tours, 320–22
Transfiguration, Franciscan Basilica of (Mount Tabor), 290
Tribes of Israel, 4, 6, 8, 133, 180, 275, 301, 307, 309
Truman Peace Center (Jerusalem), 115
Turkey and the Turks, 16, 80, 84, 170

332 •

INDEX

United Nations, 8, 19, 22–27, 168, 178
Uriel, 161

Vale of Ayalon, 153
Vered Hagalil, 296
Via Dolorosa, 102

Wadi Araba, 185, 197
"Wailing Wall." *See* Western Wall
War of Independence, 20–22, 48, 81, 84, 125, 156, 158, 252, 254, 306; in Acre, 265; Egypt and, 88, 168, 179; in Galilee hills, 274; in Gaza Strip, 168–70; in Jerusalem, 88, 89, 221
Weizmann, Chaim, 15, 16, 19, 67, 160
Weizmann Institute (Rehovot), 67, 68, 160, 161
Western Wall (Jerusalem), 90, 93, 96–98
White Paper, 17, 36, 56
Wilson's Arch (Jerusalem), 98
Wingate Institute, 238
Wizo Baby Home and Child Care Centre (Jerusalem), 130

Ya'arot ha-Carmel, forest of, 262
Yad Chaim Weizmann, 161
Yadin, Yigael, 129–30, 190, 191, 307, 308
Yarkon River, 64, 227
Yavne, 161
Yavne Yam, 162
Yehiam, 273
Yemen, 36–38, 84, 236
Yemin Moshe (Jerusalem), 83–84
Yemin Orde, 238
Yercham (Yerucham), 183
Yesud Hama'ala, 302
Yiddish, 30, 31
Yotvata, 197, 201–2

Zaletimo pastry shop (Jerusalem), 109
Zealots, 189, 191
Zebulun, Valley of, 258
Zechariah, Tomb of the Prophet, 119
Zichron Ya'akov, 13, 245
Zin, Wilderness of, 195
Zion, Mount, 84, 112–14
Zionist movement, 14, 19, 30, 31

• 333

ABOUT THE AUTHOR

Joan Comay was born in Johannesburg, South Africa, where she attended school and graduated from Capetown University. She is married to Michael Comay, former Israel Ambassador and Permanent Delegate to the United Nations, and they have lived in Jerusalem with their children since the end of World War II.

Mrs. Comay is an architect, journalist and lecturer and is the author of *The U.N. in Action* and *Introducing Israel*. Her original book *Israel* was for years the standard guide to that country; at present she is the editor of the new *Encyclopaedia Judaica*.

ISRAEL
AND HER NEIGHBORS

Areas occupied in June, 1967 after the Six-Day War
0   Miles   200